DATE			

DISCARD

THE POLITICAL ECONOMY

OF FRANCE

THE POLITICAL ECONOMY
OF FRANCE

From Pompidou to Mitterrand

Volkmar Lauber

PRAEGER SPECIAL STUDIES • PRAEGER SCIENTIFIC

Library of Congress Cataloging in Publication Data

Lauber, Volkmar.
  The political economy of France.

  Bibliography: p.
  Includes index.
    1. France—Economic policy—1945– . 2. France—
Politics and government—1969–   3. Political
parties—France. I. Title.
HC276.2.L319   1983   338.944   83-13982
ISBN 0-03-063691-4

Published in 1983 by Praeger Publishers
CBS Educational and Professional Publishing
a Division of CBS Inc.
521 Fifth Avenue, New York, NY 10175 USA

©1983 Praeger Publishers

3456789 052 987654321

Printed in the United States of America
on acid-free paper

ACKNOWLEDGMENTS

Several people contributed to this book in important ways. Marie Mendras helped with an important part of the research. Stanley Hoffmann provided valuable encouragement for someone living in a beautiful yet isolated part of the world. Lewis Bowman reviewed a partial draft and gave many suggestions for better formulation. West Virginia Wesleyan College and the Mellon Foundation supported research for and preparation of the manuscript, which Betty Davidson typed with remarkable precision, and for which Jackie Colson handled many odd requests for interlibrary assistance. Hugh and Bethene Hull helped in the most general way and thus facilitated the carrying out of a major project, while Alexander showed as much tolerance as could be reasonably expected. At Praeger, the manuscript was handled by Betsy Brown, and by production editors Raymond Kanarr and Susan Goodman. To all I would like to express my thanks.

TABLE OF CONTENTS

LIST OF TABLES

LIST OF GRAPHS

LIST OF ABBREVIATIONS

ACADI   Association des cadres dirigeants de l'industrie pour le progrès social et économique. An association of progressive employers.

C.D.S. Centre des démocrates sociaux. One of the elements of the U.D.F.

C.E.R.E.S. Centre d'études, de recherches et d'education socialistes. One of the subgroups of the Socialist party; often close to the Communists.

C.F.D.T. Confédération francaise démocratique du travail. Second largest labor union, close to the Socialist Party.

C.G.P.M.E. Confédération générale des petites et moyennes entreprises. Federation of small and medium-sized business.

C.G.T. Confédération générale du travail. Largest labor union, under the hegemony of the Communist party.

C.N.P.F. Conseil national du patronat francais. The French Employers' Association.

E.M.S. European Monetary System.

E.T.H.I.C. Entreprises à taille humaine dans l'industrie et le commerce. An association of progressive employers, founded by Yvon Gattaz.

F.O.   Force ouvrière. Reformist labor union.

I.F.O.P. Institut francais de l'opinion publique. Public opinion research institute.

M.R.G. Mouvement des radicaux de gauche. Left-wing radicals, allies of the Socialist party.

O.E.C.D. Organization for Economic Cooperation and Development.

P.C.(F.) Parti Communiste (Francais).

P.S.   Parti Socialiste.

P.S.U. Parti Socialiste Unifié. A leftist splinter party, led by Rocard until 1974.

R.P.R. Rassemblement pour la République. The Gaullist party as renamed by Chirac.

SICAV   Societe d'investissement à capital variable. Investment funds set up under a 1978 law to popularize ownership in stock.

SMIC   Salaire minimum interprofessionel de croissance. French minimum wage.

S.N.C.F. Société nationale des chemins de fer francais. French National Railroads.

SOFRES	<u>Société française d'enquêtes par sondage.</u> Survey research firm.
T.V.A.	<u>Taxe sur la valeur ajoutee.</u> French sales tax.
U.D.F.	<u>Union pour la démocratie francaise.</u> The party which organized the supporters of Giscard (Parti Republicain, C.D.S., and Radicaux).
U.D.R.	<u>Union des démocrates pour la République.</u> Name of the Gaullist movement during the first half of the 1970s.
U.N.M.	<u>Union pour la nouvelle majorité.</u> Electoral coalition of UDF and R.P.R. set up in May 1981.

INTRODUCTION

This book proposes to study the politics of the French economy since de Gaulle's resignation in 1969. It is not just a study of the political business cycle; in fact, it shows that political leaders attempt to influence the economy over a wide range, and the business cycle may not even occupy a position of prominence in that context. Perhaps this is so because in France there is less of a consensus on what the state's role in the economic process should be, and on the direction that economic policy should take; many lines of political conflict exist over these issues. In the 1970s, the four major political parties took up quite different positions in this regard, despite the fact that two of them jointly supported the government, while the other two had subscribed to a Common Program; in both cases the unity turned out to be fictitious in the face of sufficiently severe tests.

In order to understand French economic policy, it is important to understand the assumptions that the different actors make about economics, the internal logic that in their view explains the developments that are taking place at home and abroad. The purpose of this book, then, is not only to describe the positions and programs of the major actors with regard to economic policy, but also their assumptions, their logic and perhaps their philosophy. The actors described are the major political parties, business, and labor unions; their description relies on a great variety of previously published material, ranging from articles and interviews to books and memoirs, and spanning a period of over a decade. The positions of the major actors are also contrasted with the expectations, aspirations and judgments of the French, as expressed in a series of public opinion surveys.

The three parts of this book correspond to chronological divisions; however, the approach varies somewhat from one period to another. When the exploration takes us back to the early 1970s, the focus of the study is not the same as later on. The first part deals with the situation as it existed before the crisis of the mid-1970s began to settle in, both in economic reality and in the minds of the major actors. This corresponds roughly (though not with any degree of precision) to the time of the Pompidou presidency, a time period characterized by rapid economic and industrial growth, but also by growing conflict over the direction of economic policy and the publication of a variety of blueprints for social change coming from the major political and economic groups. With regard to this time period, the emphasis of the study is not on detailed policy measures; rather, it is on the systems of beliefs and values held by the major political actors with regard to economic and social life. For this reason, the first part should not be separated from the rest. Policy programs evolved considerably in recent years, in response to a changing economic and political situation, but the assumptions of the actors, their philosophy in the economic and social areas, showed considerable stability. An understanding of this philosophy provides a valuable perspective on later years, and on the policy measures as practiced, advocated, or criticized in the early 1980s.

The second part of the book analyzes the years of the Giscard presidency. In economic terms, this was a much more difficult time, for France as for most other Western countries. Energy, currency and trade problems combined to impose a new set of restraints, particularly on those industrial economies which participated most heavily in international exchanges. In France, prescriptions on how to deal with the resulting problems diverged not only between Left and Right, but also between Gaullists and Giscardiens, between Socialists and Communists. The second part of the book describes the political responses of the different actors in some detail, against the background of the policy carried out by President Giscard and his two prime ministers, Jacques Chirac and, particularly, Ramond Barre. A considerable amount of statistics is furnished in order to illustrate and bring out the background against which these responses took shape, though little of it is very technical in nature. Again, public opinion surveys help to provide yet another perspective; these surveys show that there is in France a particular civic — or perhaps political-economic — culture, in any case a set of attitudes and expectations regarding the state's role in the economic sphere, which may put important constraints on the kind of policy that any government can put into practice.

The third and last part of this book describes the French political economy during the beginning of the Mitterrand presidency, especially the attempts by the Socialist government to loosen the grip of external constraints while at the same time enacting a program of controversial social reforms. Here, the emphasis is clearly on the concrete, on the specific policy measures taken by the government. Other parties and actors are considered primarily in relation to the Socialists' ability to carry out their program successfully. This is so in part because the adversaries of the Socialists simply did not have much of a program during their first year in opposition. For a brief time they seemed like the <u>émigrés</u> who came back after the French Revolution, and of whom it was said that they had not learned anything — nor forgotten anything either. Their criticisms of Socialist policy were quite predictable; their future program was not. But they will need programs, and probably compatible ones, if they are to return to a position of prominence on the national level.

Thus the book moves from relatively high levels of generality and abstraction, in its first part, to very concrete policy measures in the third part. Again, the different parts should not be read in isolation. Together, it is hoped, they will shed light on the goals that successive governments, and most recently the Socialist government, tried to achieve, and on the methods and approaches that they used in the process. Actual policy results reflect these goals and efforts only imperfectly, a testimony to a difficult world. Economic power and national independence are clearly the most important goal for all the major parties that held office during the last decade. The disagreements are primarily over means, and also over the distribution of efforts and rewards. Rare are those political leaders who question the prevailing pattern of development.

It is not clear that the French population shares the ambitions extolled by its political leaders, despite the continuous exhortations from various directions. This should not surprise. The race for economic success is absurd at one level; it is eminently meaningful, though, for a nation-state in an international environment marked by relentless competition. The structure of this environment may be tragic, but to change it is beyond the power of most countries.

PART I
BEFORE THE CRISIS:
THE ECONOMIC AND
SOCIAL PHILOSOPHIES
OF THE MAJOR
POLITICAL GROUPS

1
GAULLISM

Until 1974, the Gaullists had near-exclusive control over national policy in the Fifth Republic, so they quite naturally occupy a special place. Although they were usually allied with other political formations, they unquestionably dominated the political scene during those years and made few concessions to their allies, particularly as long as de Gaulle himself was in power. However, they were far from representing a homogenous group, especially at the lower ranks. This is not surprising; after all, the Gaullists for a long time were France's most successful catchall party, at least until the 1970s when the Socialists began to take on this role.[1] They had support among nearly all groups of French society.

What is at the core of Gaullism is not a specific policy, least of all a specific domestic policy. Rather, it is the emphasis on certain key goals to orient all policy, as well as a basic attitude towards the political institutions of the Fifth Republic, which represent the essence of Gaullism. As to the actual course of policy and the means used to put it into practice, Gaullism is very pragmatic. Even so, there was a definite continuity during the General's years in office. But in 1968 the political consensus which had supported de Gaulle and his policy became brittle, and finally minoritarian in 1969; this led to the resignation of de Gaulle and the emergence of another, quite different policy under his successor Georges Pompidou. Because of the continued importance of de Gaulle for the Gaullist movement in the 1970s (and probably the 1980s as well), his ideas shall be discussed here even though they precede the time period under consideration.

THE FIRST DECADE

Elaborate programmatic statements on detailed matters were never characteristic of the Gaullists' style, at least not as long as they occupied the centers of power.[2] Society and its organization in accordance with particular schemes is not as important to the Gaullists as to most other political parties. It is the <u>nation,</u> and its place in the world, which represent the starting point of their thinking about politics. Only a Gaullist could write, with a clear sense of outrage, that Giscard and the Left "place their views of society above their view of France," and that to both "to save a certain type of society (or to set up the opposite type) seems more important than the permanence of France as a nation."[3] In this respect — in the primacy they accord to foreign policy — they resemble other major historical figures. An obvious parallel is Bismarck whose main concern was to build a strong and cohesive Germany that would have a secure place in the world but who had "no preconceived opinion" on how people should live in it.[4]

The supreme goal of the Gaullists is very straightforward: to ensure the strength, vitality, permanence and <u>grandeur</u> of the French nation. If this required painful change, even the disappearance of a certain civilization, then it had to be accepted; to act otherwise would have seemed irresponsible to them and nostalgic, even destructive. The economy played a key role in achieving these goals. In order to fulfill its function, it had to be efficient and productive, resistant to outside manipulation, innovative with regard to technical progress, and sufficiently productive to secure the loyalty and adhesion of the citizenry, putting an end thereby to ruinous class conflict. To de Gaulle, "the aim of the struggle for prosperity was not so much to make life more comfortable for such and such a category of Frenchman as to build up the wealth, the power and the greatness of France as a whole."[5] Thus the Gaullist idea of economic growth as a duty, the result of effort, discipline and sacrifice (key references in the Gaullist vocabulary); thus also the idea of the Plan as a "burning obligation."

The measures taken during the first year in office illustrate this thinking. The Treaty of Rome had been signed under the Fourth Republic, but in May 1958, in the face of overwhelming economic problems, the French government had to ask for a suspension of its provisions. A conference on the future of the Common Market was held in December. The French delegation alone insisted then on the application of the Treaty; this led to humiliating remarks on the part of the British delegate, whereupon the French delegate threatened to break off talks altogether. The new French confidence was based on a plan which the other delegates ignored, a plan (drawn up by Rueff and

Baumgartner) that was to restore the French economy to a place of competitiveness at a very high cost to some of its individual sectors. Only the political authority of de Gaulle made this plan possible; despite intense protests the government did not yield, and the viability of the French economy was restored.6

After the stabilization of 1958 rapid growth started again in 1959. But after 1963 the new stabilization by Giscard d'Estaing (then finance minister) was put into practice; by 1965 it produced its full effect. A period of "controlled" growth set in,7 characterized by relative austerity, particularly for those earning the minimum wage. For them, growth brought almost no

GRAPH 1.1

Evolution of Minimum Wage and of Hourly
Wages in Real Terms, 1958-1969
(Index basis: 100 on January 1, 1958)

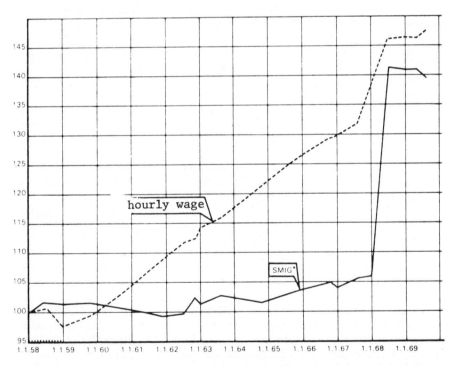

*SMIG stands for salaire minimum interprofessionel garanti (the minimum wage before the introduction of the SMIC).

Source: Maurice Parodi, L'économie et la société française depuis 1945 (Paris: Armand Colin, 1981), p. 255.

material improvements during the first ten years of the Fifth Republic. In addition, economic growth and modernization meant acute hardships for those employed in the lagging sectors of the French economy, primarily the small peasants who seemed to be condemned to extinction. To the Gaullists, their suffering was part of a painful yet necessary adaptation, justified by the fact that the nation needed to be strong, and there could be no strength without efficiency.

> In order to be prosperous, to be masters of ourselves and to be powerful, we French have done a great deal. Much remains for us to do. For progress demands effort. Independence is not free. Security is costly. That is of course why the State, whose role and raison d'être is to serve the general interest, has no right to let things go.[8]

Thus the primary purpose of growth was to enhance the role of the French nation on the international scene. Michel Debré, one of the most outspoken members of the Gaullist old guard and de Gaulle's first prime minister, stated expressly that for middle-sized powers such as France, all economic policy is necessarily inspired by the will to achieve greater political influence in the world. In these countries, he argued, foreign policy comes first; it is in accordance with foreign policy aspirations that economic modernization is carried out and attempts are made to solve domestic social problems. In his view, a nation, even its culture and independence of thought, can only thrive if backed up by economic strength and industrial growth. In his words,

> If France wants to pursue a politics of independence and international cooperation, if it wants to stand up in the world in political and economic terms, it must equip itself with certain industries and modernize certain others. This also has a psychological aspect. It is of utmost importance to provide a country with goals . . . of conquest. As soon as we no longer conquer either territories or populations, what we need is . . . a capacity for influence, which rests on a certain economy.[9]

Affluence was one of the possible results of growth, but as already stated, this was not what the early Gaullists emphasized most. In fact, they were concerned that the excessive development of private consumption, along the lines of the "affluent society" in the United States, would not only reduce the investment effort but also lead to other problems in the future.[10] It was somewhat ironic that one of the slogans of the May movement criticized the société de consommation as if the latter had been a goal of governmental policy. At least before 1968, many Gaullists were explicitly opposed to it.[11]

In order to grow and to improve its productivity, French society needed to be reorganized on the basis of efficiency; this was the axiom of the technocrats. But while the technocrats typically looked upon such a reorganization with great optimism, de Gaulle saw other things as well; his view was partly tragic. Not that he questioned modernization; that France had to modernize was "simply a matter of common sense. The country could only thrive internally and carry weight abroad if its activity was in tune with the age. In an industrial era, it must be industrial . . . it must undergo a profound transformation."[12] But he also saw the reverse side of the medal. He was moved by the passing away of rural society, "the world of changeless villages"; he was sensitive to the uniformization and mechanization of life in the industrial age, so contrary to French culture. If this had to be accepted, it was because it was "due to the force of circumstances, but I knew that it weighed more heavily on our people, by reason of their nature and antecedents, than on any other, and felt that some sudden additional provocation might well precipitate them one day into some irrational crisis."[13] Thus he shrank back from "brutally dismantling" the existing structures; such "terrible surgery" was indicated only if a catastrophe threatened France, which was not the case. Accordingly he felt it appropriate to proceed more gradually, "healing" and "binding up" the wounds that economic transformation inflicted.[14] This was not done out of respect for particular interests; for those, de Gaulle had only contempt. But there had to be a place in the national community for the economically obsolete; they could not be simply cast out, the way some technocrats might have preferred.[15]

The passages quoted above make clear de Gaulle's sympathy for the peasantry. He also felt that a great injustice had been done to the French working class, which was denied its appropriate place in French society. Furthermore, de Gaulle was not a friend of business.[16] Under these circumstances, the way in which economic policy was formulated during the de Gaulle years is all the more surprising. The models were the Plan and the économie concertée. De Gaulle would have liked to see them both organized on a corporatist basis, with all the large groups of the nation participating under the guidance and control of the state, which would set the general goals and thus orient and direct the economy (diriger l'économie, as de Gaulle would have put it).[17] This idea can be found as early as 1943, in de Gaulle's wartime program,[18] and as late as 1969, in the proposals for the referendum which proved to be de Gaulle's undoing. But corporatist practice never went very far. Limited steps were taken to secure union cooperation, and an effort was made to end the isolation in which the cold war had placed the C.G.T., the Communist-dominated labor union. However, the C.G.T. remained strongly opposed to Gaullist corporatism, and the cooperation of other unions was limited at best.19 Under these circumstances, économie concertée came to mean the close cooperation between big business and the state — an arrangement that seemed to facilitate modernization, for broader participation, one observer noted, would have brought in "peasant and shopkeeper groups, nostalgic for an irrational past; trade unions nostalgic for an irrational future; and politicians all too eager to serve those groups."20

Although union cooperation could not be secured for de Gaulle's economic policies, the General still hoped to involve the French workers in the economic life and progress of the nation in another, more direct way. Thanks to participation, they would share in reinvested profits and thus have a stake in the national economy, similar to the stake that the middle classes had through property. However, participation remained a distant goal, removed from actual policy measures. Pompidou in his days as prime minister failed to take any steps to implement it; to his entourage he confessed that he did not understand what participation could possibly mean. Only after the explosion of 1968 did de Gaulle intervene directly, by imposing a participation scheme on Pompidou's successor, Prime Minister Couve de Murville, under whom a limited participation law was passed in 1969.21

By that time however, the events of May 1968 had already marked the end of an era — an era of political stability as well as continuity in policy (see Table 7.1). They had also brought out the differences and disagreements between de Gaulle and Pompidou in an unprecedented manner. Many of the policies which had characterized de Gaulle's first ten years in office were now modified or abandoned, partly during the settlement (the accords de Grenelle) that followed the May riots and strikes. The General tried to regain some of the lost ground during the subsequent year (thus the participation law, and the refusal to devalue the franc). But he was no longer able to govern against an unruly majority which was already looking to Pompidou as a viable alternative. When he tried to take on the politicians and reestablish his legitimacy in the 1969 referendum, the French electorate failed him as well.22 De Gaulle's Gaullism was replaced by another version — pompidolisme.

GAULLISM UNDER POMPIDOU

Where de Gaulle, in his addresses, had spoken of grandeur, independence, and effort, Pompidou now spoke of growth, industrialization, and prosperity. Nor was the change merely rhetorical. Economic growth now became the main criterion of governmental performance.23 The means to achieve it: rapid industrialization and modernization of all the sectors of the French economy. The purpose: prosperity, a prosperity "which will increase every day, and which is a source of honor and greatness to the country."24 The target: a "living, free and dynamic, truly competitive economy, domestically for the benefit of the consumer, internationally in order to increase the national wealth."25 There is little mention of grandeur in Pompidou's speeches, and the appeals to sacrifice are dropped altogether. If May 1968 had seen the critique of the société de consommation by leftist intellectuals, Pompidou rejected such a critique as arch-reactionary. In his view, the 1968 events were not the result of some metaphysical "crisis of civilization," but simply the result of over-extended austerity policies. He was persuaded that the great majority of the French wanted above all an increase in material goods, and a rapid and significant increase at that, and that other "goods" (including cultural ones) could and should wait.26 Prosperity was the appropriate remedy, then; in addition, it would frustrate the attempts of the Communists (whom Pompidou thought to be the only serious alternative to Gaullism) to mobilize the working class for their cause. Communism would remain unsuccessful "as long as economic prosperity allowed a steady improvement in the workers' standard of living."27

The Pompidou years were in fact characterized by very rapid industrialization, all the more remarkable since many other OECD countries experienced difficulties during the same time period, caused in part by American economic and monetary policies. The immense number of work days lost to strikes in 1968, and the large wage increases granted afterwards, were expected to lead to major difficulties for French business. De Gaulle refused to devalue the franc (a sign that he was determined to reimpose economic discipline). But Pompidou carried out a devaluation in the summer of 1969 and gave generous aid to the private sector — so much so that the years 1969-70 were unusually good ones for French business (see Table 7.1). High profits were viewed as necessary if France was to plunge into the headlong drive for industrialization. "Pompidou, the Sixth Plan he inspired, the majority of the ministers whom he directs, all have for industry the kind of fetishism of a Napoleon III," wrote Roger Priouret, one of France's leading economic journalists.28 Most observers made the same point.29

Industrialization was to create a competitive economy, a competitive industry that would lead to the development of exports, itself a further condition of long-term industrial growth.30 This industrial growth in turn would sustain France in her new role. Priouret wrote that in the President's view, industrialization alone

>gives power. The President never believed much in
>Europe. He no longer believes in it at all. So France
>will have to go it alone. And she will stand a better
>chance if she is the world's fourth industrial power, more
>or less on a par with Germany.31

Weighed against this objective, even the concern over inflation
became secondary. Industrial production, Pompidou declared in
1970, had to double over a span of ten years.32 The goal was
to eventually surpass Germany as an industrial power.

The Sixth Plan (1971-75) incarnated Pompidou's "industrial
imperative." During its operation, the target rate for the annual
growth of the GDP was 5.8 to 6 percent, and 7.5 percent for
the growth of industrial production.33 A report by the Hudson
Institute Europe, commissioned by the French government before
the 1973 elections, projected these figures into the future and
came up with surprising results which were widely quoted in the
French press at the time. Assuming that the target growth
rates of the French government would be achieved in the 1970s,
and calculating the performance of other countries by extrapo-
lation from the past, the report concluded that France would in
fact surpass Germany quite soon. In terms of per capita GNP,
France was — so the report said — destined to surpass all
European countries (even Sweden and Switzerland), and by 1985
perhaps even the United States.34 Things have of course turned
differently; but the Hudson Institute's report gave a measure of
what governmental ambitions were at the time.35

Pompidou was much more favorably disposed towards business
than de Gaulle had ever been. At the same time, he also
(particularly in his first years as president) wanted to bring
about changes that would more closely integrate the workers
into French society. In Pompidou's view, growth policies should
bring strong improvements for the workers, both in absolute and
in relative terms, that is, by raising their net income and by
reducing the gap that separated them from the rest of the population. Such changes, Pompidou hoped, would also alter the
social climate in France and make the unions resemble more
closely their less militant counterparts in Germany or Sweden.
In an interview he stated his

>motivating idea: the transformation of social relations in
>France. It is unreasonable that in 1969 the relationship
>between patrons and wage earners should be one of end-
>less conflict. We must establish new habits, built on the
>spirit of, and respect for, contracts.36

Eventually, he hoped, France would become another Sweden
(though "with more sun").37

Improvements in the situation of the workers would not come primarily from political changes. "Unions have to make their members understand that their true interests depend on the prosperity of the economy," Pompidou wrote.[38] Growth would be the most important factor that would allow redistribution. "The real solution therefore lies in economic growth and the rapid augmentation of the national income."[39] This would also allow an effective social policy, which would reduce "the distance between the rich and the poor, in other words . . . raise the living standards both absolutely speaking and . . . transfer part of the income of the wealthy."[40]

The first three years of Pompidou's term as president saw in fact many important steps in this direction. An attempt was made to introduce more cooperative labor relations; unions were given greater recognition (it was hoped that in exchange they would show greater "responsibility" by not striking), and certain laws gave workers a status close to that of employees.[41] It was hoped that negotiation would become the prime mode of interaction between "social partners," rather than high-handedness or paternalism on the part of employers, mirrored by "revolutionary" (and in any case "non-cooperative") unions.[42] At the same time, rapid expansion changed the economic climate. Unemployment receded slightly, and with full employment expectations, real wages rose rapidly, 5 percent on the average but a full 14 percent (annually) for the minimum wage. At least for wage-earners, rapid growth had clear material benefits.[43]

While the government encouraged generous wage settlements, for which it showed the way in the public sector,[44] it held back in other areas. Participation was shelved, and was not rediscovered by Gaullists until nearly a decade later (it is true that labor had never shown much interest in it anyhow). Public services and investments were cut back drastically from the levels set out in the Sixth Plan, victims of "productivism": while the immediately productive investments (autoroutes, telephones) were singled out for privileged treatment, expenditures on hospitals, public transportation, day care and the like had to wait. Likewise, the structure of power in business enterprises, often criticized for being excessively authoritarian and autocratic, remained unchanged. A Common Market proposal which would have allowed direct incorporation of business firms under European law was rejected by the French government essentially because it provided for a measure of workers' representation on the corporation's board; this was unacceptable to the hard-liners in French business, and Pompidou counted on this group to lead the growth of the French economy. In these situations, growth effectively stood in the way of reform.[45]

On the whole, Pompidou's overtures to labor did not achieve the desired effect. The unions were not converted to labor peace and reformism, and Pompidou did not win back the political support that de Gaulle had once had among French workers.46 At the same time, the politics of growth and industrialization hurt other population groups in the economically declining sectors, and these groups contained large numbers of Gaullist voters. Conservative Gaullists, led by Pierre Juillet, Pompidou's "gray eminence" and political advisor, persuaded the president that a turnaround was urgently needed. In 1972 the architects of the nouvelle société, who had set out to get the "stalled society" moving again,47 were all dropped: Prime Minister Chaban-Delmas along with his advisors Jacques Delors and Simon Nora. They were replaced by Pierre Messmer and a new approach which placed the emphasis on those groups that were negatively affected by the economic evolution, in particular the small peasants and shopkeepers, the nouveaux pauvres (newly poor) who had fallen by the wayside during the years of "rapid progress." "Aggressive Gaullism" was giving way to "defensive Gaullism."48

Somewhat paradoxically, it was one of France's most famous technocrats who showed how economic growth met with resistance among much of the French population. In his report, 1985, La France face au choc du futur,49 Paul Delouvrier pointed out that only a very small group of executives in government and industry subscribed to the values of rapid growth and modernization, whereas the majority of the population felt threatened by it, primarily in its security and stability.50 Pompidou agreed with the analysis of the Delouvrier report; however, this did not lead him to conclude that growth should be held up. He thought it would be "useless to try to slow down the rate of scientific, technical and material progress. One can only accept it and try to preserve or recreate the elementary values which everyone needs to be satisfied with his life and condition."51 He admitted that it was more painful for France to experience these changes, since it was an "older and to a certain extent less dynamic civilization" that was more keenly aware of what was lost, and was not "carried forward by the optimism which inspires the American adventure in science and the economy."52 The appropriate answer to this was more leadership by "moral authorities" from intellectual and religious life.53

Pompidou did concede that there must be limits to the human costs of these social transformations. It was "not desirable, not even imaginable" that France would go through a mutation comparable to the industrial revolution of the last century: "No Western people — and the French less so than any other — would accept the sacrifices which were imposed on the working class in the first two thirds of the nineteenth century."54 The way out of the dilemma as to ease the pain of transition for those most immediately affected: the small farmers, the artisans and shopkeepers, the obsolete workers, and the old. Retraining, early retirement, lifetime pensions — such measures would make certain that their recipients would no longer stand in the way of economic progress. Expansion would help finance all these measures.[55] A partial exception to this pattern is the Royer law, which was passed towards the end of Pompidou's presidency; it provided protection for small shopkeepers against the large-surface hypermarchés.[56] But Pompidou never accepted the idea that it might be desirable to slow economic growth altogether.[57]

In the early 1970s, in France as in other countries, industrialization often came into conflict with new aspirations and concerns regarding the environment. In France, a Ministry for the Protection of Nature and the Environment was created in 1971. From the outset, it suffered from very modest funds and a narrow definition of its role. Robert Poujade, the first minister to fill this position, relates how Pompidou was quite surprised to hear that Poujade planned to expand his responsibilities to deal with problems of urban and industrial pollution.[58] (One of Pompidou's pet projects was in fact to open up Paris for more automobile traffic.) To the president, environmental problems meant litter on the beaches or in forests; in Priouret's words, "he had already absolved industry in his heart."[59] Most of the Gaullists probably felt the same way. To Pompidou the ecologists were arch-reactionaries in the same way as the "gauchistes" of May 1968 utopian in their nostalgia for a world which belonged to the past.

Most Gaullists did not take seriously the controversy over economic growth which erupted in the early 1970s.[60] One of the few to discuss the problem was Jacques Chirac, then viewed as one of Pompidou's rising men. Growth, Chirac wrote in 1972, must not be a purely quantitative and mechanical phenomenon, otherwise it would become "a source of ecological and social pollution." Instead, it must be organized to assure the "development of social groups and the flowering of individuals," to secure greater social justice and to give priority to social, intellectual and cultural progress. And that, the article concluded, was exactly what de Gaulle and Pompidou had been seeking all along.[61]

In sum, the great achievement of the Gaullists was to realize, with a remarkable single-mindedness, many of the aspirations for national renewal which were common at the time of the Liberation, but which were occasionally neglected as the Fourth Republic was side-tracked by colonial wars or domestic resistance. In some respects, the Gaullists may have depleted themselves by achieving the task which they set out to achieve, a task which required great energy and determination.[62] In some respects though, their realizations fell short of their goals. The greater integration of French society (for example, by corporatism), the breakup of old hierarchies and inequalities, remained largely a distant goal. Perhaps to keep the eyes trained on the nation was more important; in any case, thinking about society remained atrophied and was often out of touch with social reality. The Gaullists, like the Communists, seemed to have particular trouble relating to the new "social movements" of the 1970s, movements which often protested "not against the failure of state and society to provide economic growth and material prosperity, but against their all-too considerable success in having done so, and against the price of this success."63 If Gaullism lost so much of its electoral strength in the 1970s, this may be due not only to the disappearance of its founder, but also to the difficulty in formulating a response to the new situation in France. Such a response would have had to take into account those problems which Gaullism never resolved; those which resulted from the transformation it helped initiate; and those resulting from an international crisis over which France had little control. The Gaullists largely failed to come up with such a response. In this they were probably not alone, but no other party had had the chance to show what it could do until Gaullist rule ended in 1974.

NOTES

1. Jean Charlot, Le phénomène gaulliste (Paris: Fayard, 1970).
2. William R. Schoenfeld, "The RPR: From a Rassemblement to the Gaullist Movement," in William G. Andrews and Stanley Hoffmann, The Fifth Republic at Twenty (Albany: State University of New York Press, 1981), p. 104.
3. Philippe de Saint-Robert, Les septennats interrompus (Paris: Laffont, 1977), p. 208.
4. Ralf Dahrendorf, Society and Democracy in Germany (Garden City: Doubleday, 1969), p. 56.
5. Charles de Gaulle, Memoirs of Hope (New York: Simon and Schuster, 1971), p. 160.
6. Ibid., pp. 137-47; and Alain Peyrefitte, Le mal francais (Paris: Plon, 1976), pp. 94-99.
7. Maurice Parodi, L'économie et la société francaise depuis 1945 (Paris: Armond Colin, 1981), p. 49.
8. Speech by General de Gaulle, 19 April 1963.
9. Michel Debré, Une certaine idée de la France (Paris: Fayard, 1972), p. 93. See also pp. 218 and 280.
10. Ibid., pp. 225-26; and Pierre Massé, La crise du développement (Paris: Gallimard, 1973), pp. 38-41.

11. Société de consommation in fact was a criticism not only of the "affluent society"; the term also connotes passivity (instead of activity and creation).

12. De Gaulle, Memoirs of Hope, p. 133.

13. Ibid., p. 341.

14. Ibid., pp. 150, 343, and 351.

15. See Louis Armand's position in John Ardagh, The New France (Harmondsworth: Penguin, 1973), p. 79.

16. Roger Priouret, Les Francais mystifiés (Paris: Grasset, 1973), pp. 104-05.

17. Massé, La crise du développement, pp. 30-31. See also next note.

18. In a BBC broadcast in 1943 de Gaulle outlined his program:

> An economic and social system in which no monopoly or grouping can weigh on the State or govern the individual; where therefore the main sources of collective wealth are either directly administered or at least controlled by the nation; . . . where the different associations of workers and technicians are organically associated with the working of the firm . . . .

Quoted in Pierre Viansson-Ponté, Des jours entre les jours (Paris: Stock, 1974), p. 56.

19. George Ross, "Gaullism and Organized Labor: Two Decades of Failure?", in Andrews and Hoffmann, Fifth Republic at Twenty, p. 332.

20. Stephen S. Cohen, Modern Capitalist Planning: The French Model (Berkeley: University of California Press, 1977), p. 130.

21. Priouret, Les Francais mystifiés, pp. 56-57. See also Michel Debré, appendix to Andrews and Hoffmann, Fifth Republic at Twenty, p. 509.

22. Peter Alexis Gouretitch, "Gaullism Abandoned, or the Costs of Success," ibid., p. 117.

23. Georges Pompidou, Le noeud gordien (Paris: Plon, 1974), pp. 103-07; Robert Poujade, Le ministère de l'impossible (Paris: Calmann-Levy,1975), p. 254.

24. Jean-Denis Bredin, La République de Monsieur Pompidou (Paris: Fayard, 1974), p. 41.; Priouret, Les Francais mystifies, p. 104.

25. Pompidou, Le noeud gordien, p. 168.

26. Ibid., pp. 121 and 177; Priouret, Les Francais mystifies, p. 105.

27. Pompidou, Le noeud gordien, p. 38.

28. Priouret, Les Francais mystifiés, p. 13.

29. Poujade, Le ministère de l'impossible, p. 27; Andre Laurens, D'une France à l'autre (Paris: Gallimard, 1974), p. 13; and Gilles Martinet, Le système Pompidou (Paris: Le Seuil, 1973), pp. 17-51.

30. VIe Plan de développement économique et social, 1971-1975. Rapport général. Les objectifs généraux et prioritaires du VIe Plan, by Christian Bourgeois and Dominique de Roux (Paris: Editions 10/18, 1971), p. 18.

31. Priouret, Les Francais mystifiés, pp. 104-05.

32. Ibid., p. 121; and Georges Valence and Albert du Roy in L'Express, 8 April 1974, p. 30.

33. VIe Plan de développement économique et social, 1971-1975, pp. 18-19.

34. Edmund O. Stillman, James Bellini, William Pfaff, Laurence Schloesing and Jonathan Story, L'envol de la France dans les annees 80 (Paris: Hachette, 1973), pp. 52, 57, 59 and 61.

35. By 1980, many European countries had surpassed the United States in terms of per capita income, calculated on the basis of current exchange rates; France however was not leading, and surpassed the United States by only a very small margin. OECD statistics cited in Le Monde, Bilan économique et social 1981 (supplément aux dossiers et documents du Monde, January 1982), p. 64.

36. Ross, "Gaullism and Organized Labor," in Andrews and Hoffmann, Fifth Republic at Twenty, p. 339.

37. L'Express, 9 June 1969, p. 21.

38. Pompidou, Le noeud gordien, p. 168.

39. Ibid., pp. 153-54.

40. Ibid., p. 149.

41. A list of these measures is given in Parodi, L'économique et la société francaise depuis 1945, pp. 224-27.

42. Ross, "Gaullism and Organized Labor."

43. Priouret, Les Francais mystifiés, pp. 122-24.

44. Ross, "Gaullism and Organized Labor," pp. 340-41.

45. Priouret, Les Francais mystifiés, pp. 80-83 and 130; also Roy Macridis, French Politics in Transition (Cambridge: Winthrop, 1975), pp. 51-55.

46. Ross, "Gaullism and Organized Labor," p. 343-45.

47. Jacques Delors, "La nouvelle société," Preuves, 1970, vol. 2. Inspiration also came from Michael Crozier, La société bloquée (Paris: Le Seuil, 1970).

48. Martinet, Le système Pompidou, pp. 94-107; Laurens, D'une France à l'autre, pp. 44-47; Jacques Delors interview in L'Expansion, September 1972, pp. 183-87. Finally, see Vincent McHale and Sandra Shaber, "From Aggressive to Defensive Gaullism: The Electoral Dynamics of a Catch-All Party," Comparative Politics, vol. 8, no. 2 (January 1976), pp. 291-306.

49. Paul Delouvrier, <u>1985. La France face au choc du futur</u> (Paris: Armand Colin, 1972).

50. Ibid., p. 164.

51. Pompidou, <u>Le noeud gordien</u>, pp. 178-79.

52. Ibid.

53. Ibid., pp. 188-89.

54. Ibid., p. 23.

55. Pompidou, <u>Le noeud gordien</u>, p. 154; also Laurent Laot, <u>La croissance économique en question</u> (Paris: Editions ouvrières, 1974), p. 124.

56. Suzanne Berger, "Lame Ducks and National Champions: Industrial Policy in the Fifth Republic," in Andrews and Hoffmann, <u>Fifth Republic at Twenty</u>, pp. 301-02.

57. Even though this was suggested by one of his appointees at the end of his term, Philippe d'Iribarne, who headed the <u>Centre pour la recherche sur le bien-être</u>.   Iribarne in 1973 had published a book, <u>La politique du bonheur</u> (Paris: Le Seuil, 1973), which argued this point.

58. Poujade, <u>Le ministère de l'impossible,</u> pp. 26-27.

59. Priouret, <u>Les Francais mystifiés,</u> pp. 70-71.

60. Suzanne Berger, "Politics and Antipolitics in Western Europe in the Seventies," <u>Daedalus,</u> 108:1 (1979).

61. Jacques Chirac, "Finalites de la croissance," <u>Preuves,</u> No. 9 (first trimester), 1972, pp. 46-52.

62. Stanley Hoffmann, "Conclusion: The Impact of the Fifth Republic on France," in Andrews and Hoffmann, <u>Fifth Republic at Twenty,</u> pp. 456 and 494.

63. Berger, "Politics and Antipolitics," p. 32.

2

GISCARD AND THE CENTRISTS

Centrism is a problematic notion in contemporary French politics. It includes a variety of parties and ideological positions which, during the 1970s, changed with surprising rapidity. In general, "centrism" has included movements from the conservative Right (Giscard's Independent Republicans) to Catholic and social democratic reformists. Much of this confusion may simply reflect the condition of the marais, that amorphous "swamp" or shapeless middle ground of French politics. Not surprisingly, most of these formations did not develop programs or ideologies that were coherent over time. However, they produced an outpouring of programmatic statements in the early and mid-1970s; this was due to the tactical shifts of the various politicians which belonged to centrist formations.1

VALERY GISCARD D'ESTAING

Even though the Center was not marked by cohesion, it nonetheless came to represent a political force that could influence policy — when it was federated (and dominated) by the personality of Giscard d'Estaing during his term as president. Thus united, the regrouped center achieved rough parity with the three other major political parties. While the center had no clear program that could have been binding on the political leadership, its constituent elements did have a common stock of ideas.

That the center would be led by Giscard is surprising in some respects. After all, many centrists were unyielding in their hostility to Gaullism, and Giscard had been closely associated with the Gaullist regime, supporting the General in 1958 and

1962, and then serving as finance minister both under de Gaulle and Pompidou. Only a small group of centrists (Giscard's Independent Republicans excepted) ever joined a Gaullist government. Also, Giscard himself came from a somewhat different background. He secured his own political basis by becoming the leader of the conservative Centre National des Indépendants et Paysans, which he transformed into the more progressive-looking Parti Républicain Indépendant. As a junior partner in an alliance overwhelmingly dominated by the Gaullists, it was not easy for him to establish a political identity of his own. As finance minister, he conducted a restrictive policy under de Gaulle, from 1963 on. This was the famous plan de stabilisation which many Gaullists criticized severely. In 1966, he was replaced as finance minister by Michel Debré, who changed to a more expansionary policy.[2] Called back to the finance ministry by president Pompidou whose election he supported in 1969, Giscard followed a different policy this time, giving priority to rapid industrialization and putting concern over inflation in the background.[3] At the same time, he waited for the opportunity to come into his own.

The presidential elections of 1969 might have offered an opportunity to do so; however, it seems that Giscard felt then that "the time had not yet come for men of his generation."[4] While holding office in a regime that he only accepted with reservations, he felt it was not possible to speak out too openly and clearly.[5] He did however express some of his thoughts during this time period, and it was obvious that, if taken seriously, they implied an economic policy quite different from that practiced by the governments of the Pompidou presidency. Many of these thoughts were restated a few years later in Giscard's book, Démocratie française.[6] Even though the work was published only in 1976, it does not really bear the marks of the intervening economic crisis. Most likely, Giscard felt that this crisis was only temporary and would soon be overcome.[7]

What is it that distinguishes Giscard from the Gaullists? Many observers stated that it was primarily a matter of style rather than content; this led them to view the clash between Giscard and Chirac, in the second half of the 1970s, as a conflict of personalities and ambitions rather than one over substantive policy issues. Such a view is incorrect. To be sure, there is a difference in style, in the political vocabulary of the two leaders in their groups. Giscard has none of the stirring rhetoric of the Gaullists, and there are none of the usual appeals to effort, will and sacrifice (but then Pompidou had already abandoned some of this). In fact, Giscard very deliberately avoided such rhetoric.[8] But beyond the differences in vocabulary, there was also a difference in outlook, regarding the very objectives that should be given priority in economic policy.

Giscard is a representative of the liberal tradition in France. Among other things, this means that he wants to see the role of the state reduced, so that society can develop more freely and more spontaneously. This contrasts strongly with the Gaullist vision of a society directed by the nation. It is true that the differences should not be exaggerated; in French Democracy, Giscard made it clear that the economic forces of the country should not be left to themselves entirely. The state has to intervene not only to ensure competition (which many would always try to escape); it also must direct development in such a way as to "place economic activity at the service of man"; society must be able to "consciously manage its own evolution."9 But at the same time the state must not try to do too much; to do so would quickly lead to inefficiencies. In order to work, complex social systems have to rely also on automatic mechanisms (such as the market); otherwise they are quickly condemned to failure. And the means of control used by the state should be indirect whenever possible, attempting to modify behavior through taxation and incentives rather than direct legislation. The state should above all try to achieve those goals which are essential for a democratic, pluralistic society, that is, full employment and the mastery of inflation.10 Beyond that, it should try to direct economic development in such a way as to meet the needs and aspirations of the French, more so than had been the case in the 25 years since 1950.

The first statement that something was wrong, or at least undesirable, about the rapid growth of the postwar decades came in 1972, when Giscard as finance minister sponsored a symposium on the topic "Economy and Human Society," in the course of which he intervened personally on several occasions.11 The tentative criticisms he made on that occasions were repeated in an article published during the same year.12 They are formulated more forcefully in the outline of the Seventh Plan (1975) and, finally, in French Democracy. In that book, he compares the rapid postwar change to "a sort of a hurricane" that struck the quiet, highly developed yet also strongly compartmentalized society of the prewar days. The main reason for this was "unprecedented economic growth," accompanied by the massive spread of education and the audio-visual media. The result was "first and foremost progress";13 on the other hand, some problems remained unsolved, and new ones were created by growth itself.

One of the problems that growth created was large-scale social disruption. This problem increased with the rate of growth. As Giscard stated in 1972,

To pass from a medium rate of growth to a higher rate, it is necessary to a certain extent to unnerve (énerver)

> society . . . through the organization of permanent dissat-
> isfaction and at the cost of an accelerated transformation
> of urban, technical and professional structures which cre-
> ate particularly . . . exhausting conditions of existence.14

It was rhetorical to ask the question whether "an extra percentage point of growth was worth the cost of an unnerved,
restless society," or whether it was not "necessary for the sake
of social peace to moderate growth."15   Only slower growth
could lead to a satisfactory insertion of French society into an
acceptable physical and natural environment.16

These conclusions were translated into policy — or rather,
into a policy project which soon fell by the wayside under the
impact of the economic crisis — with the formulation of the
Seventh Plan. One of the Plan's four orientations stated that

> It is indicated to pay greater respect to the needs of
> security and stability. Growth over the last thirty years
> has meant many an uprooting; while these were costly for
> the national community and a heavy burden for the work-
> ers and their families, perhaps not all of them were indis-
> pensable from an economic point of view. While it is im-
> possible to put an end to all the displacements imposed
> [by growth], an effort should at least be made to reduce
> their scope. . . .17

French Democracy takes up the same ideas, and calls for a new
growth that is to be "civilized" and "gentle";

> It has recourse to massive investment and massed concrete
> buildings only when no other solution is available; it is
> sparing of its resources and keeps human tensions to a
> minimum; it respects balances such as the balance of
> generations and social groups in towns, of activities in a
> region, of plant and human ecology.
>
> A democratic state ought to promote gentle growth by
> providing information, recommending certain courses, and
> setting an example.18

In this context Giscard justifies some of the measures he took
immediately after coming to office: stopping the auto route
that would have run through the historical center of Paris, past
the Notre Dame cathedral; creating a park where les Halles
used to be, and limiting the spread of the "dark, anonymous"
high-rise towers — all things which were directly in conflict
with Pompidou's vision of a modern Paris. In general however,
Giscard believed in change through fiscal and budgetary incentives rather than by direct intervention.

The most important old problem that growth, in Giscard's view, had failed to solve was that of great inequalities in income and wealth; these, he thought, represented a lasting obstacle to the greater unity of French society. Such a view may seem surprising for a man coming from the Right, from a political milieu which usually wants to uphold social hierarchies, and which at best professes a faith in redistribution through growth.[19] But Giscard did not accept an analysis of French society in which classes played a key role. In his view, the divisions of French society were largely artificial, "more ideological than sociological, and they do not respond to class divisions."[20] He holds that both the bourgeoisie and the proletariat are progressively absorbed by a large, expanding and amorphous central group which is the sociological center of the country. The question then is to promote the integration of the marginal groups by acting directly on the evolution of incomes and wealth. For the higher income groups, this means a greater contribution to public expenditures via the income tax, for which Giscard repeatedly expressed his preference (its role in France is quite small when compared to other Common Market countries).[21] Against the traditional objection that this would reduce work incentives, Giscard argued that the objection is valid only for those who do not advance in qualifications (essentially blue collar workers). For those who are pursuing a career that allows advancement over time an important incentive to work resides in their aspiration to go up the career ladder; this affects their motivation decisively. In this way efficiency, Giscard holds, is quite compatible with justice.[22]

Even though economic growth helped to reduce the old inequalities, injustice still persists, and Giscard proposes further progress through a "new growth."[23] But the picture would not be complete without mentioning the new inequalities resulting from growth itself.[24] They demonstrate that growth alone can never solve the problem of inequalities; particularly not rapid growth, with its attendant disruption. Tensions and insecurities can be reduced only if growth becomes more moderate; to try to solve the problems created by disruption by transfer payments financed out of yet higher growth rates would be hopeless. This reasoning was developed by Lionel Stoléru,[25] one of Giscard's closest advisors on social policy.

In Giscard's view, there are other ways in which rapid growth propelled itself forward in an undesirable pattern, fueling its own tensions as it went along. Disruptive growth, by creating excessive inequalities and by ruining the quality of life (something that in turn led to demands for financial compensation), was also a contributing factor to inflation.

An excess of inequalities engenders covetousness and resentment, and is therefore a powerful force behind inflation. The struggle against inequalities is one of the conditions of anti-inflationist policy.

Moreover, there is often an inhuman side to modern industrial and urban life, and this inevitably encourages the struggle for compensation, even if only apparent, by way of excessive wage raises. The steady improvement of the quality of life, the rebalancing of our human geography so that rural zones and small towns are developed, the increase in essential public services with the consequent improvement in the quality of life — all these are also long-term weapons against inflation.[26]

The correct answer to these problems was not to put an end to growth (although a certain slowdown could prove beneficial) but to reorient it along different lines. In fact, for the time being at least, material growth was still necessary to meet real needs, though as wealth increased and was better distributed, such growth would become progressively less important. But the key task was to reduce the distance between economic growth and the progress of well-being.[27] At a more distant horizon — a decade or two in the future, Giscard wrote in 1972 — growth might no longer be a central concern. Once poverty was ended, social justice achieved, and France's position as a first-rate power secured, new and nonmaterial dimensions of life would progressively become more important.[28] Giscard made no claim that he knew what new civilization would then emerge; but he was confident that the current model would become obsolete. French Democracy concludes with the following words:

After our efforts have opened new paths and liberated and humanized society, we must wait for some individual, or more likely a movement by collective consciousness, to emit the beam of light needed to illuminate the world, the light of a new civilization that takes a spiritual view of man's liberation and the future course of the human race.
As yet, we do not know what that course will be.[29]

In looking back on the record of Giscard's years in the presidency, it becomes clear that much of this thinking was never translated into actual policy. To be sure, some important changes occurred. Particularly in the early years, minimum wages were raised and an effort was made to "rehabilitate" manual labor. A modest capital gains tax was introduced. Some initiatives were taken in the environmental area. But with the advent of the Barre government in the fall of 1976, these mildly progressive policies came to an end.[30] In part this may be due to the nature of Giscard's political support, which was further to the Right than he liked to admit. In part he may have failed to come to grips with the relationship between economic growth and national power. He clearly had ambitions to make France one of the strongest industrial countries in the world; specifically, he thought that with regard to industrial production, France should be roughly on a par with Germany by 1985.[31] But could this be achieved without the industrialization policy of his predecessor — and everything that such a choice implied?

The main problem that undercut the implementation of many of his ideas was the economic crisis. Giscard's ideas might have been capable of adaptation to the new scarcity; however, this is not what happened. In 1974, he was faced with a very high rate of inflation inherited from the last months of Pompidou's term in office, when no one was really in charge while the president was dying and the first oil crisis was having its impact. He reacted with strong and rapid deflation, which for the first time in postwar history led to a contraction of the French GDP (see also Graph 6.1). This was followed in 1975–76 by a brief reflation, conducted by Prime Minister Chirac, who in turn was replaced by Raymond Barre's austerity policies. In this context, social reform quickly took a back seat.

In a way, Giscard came to power at the wrong time for his ideas to be put into practice. His prescriptions for social and economic development "beyond rapid growth" were relevant for a time when growth came easily, when the key goals of full employment and an acceptable rate of inflation were at least within reach. Giscard well knew the limits of his thinking. In 1972 he stated that the whole discussion concerning the purpose of growth would quickly be swept away if an economic downturn would lead to renewed unemployment.[32] Thus, when the economic crisis had settled in by the mid-1970s, a good part of the president's thinking had become irrelevant, at least for the duration of the economic crisis. But then the crisis never went away during Giscard's term in office.

OTHER CENTRISTS

Giscard was not alone with his open reservations about the course that economic development had taken during the postwar decades, and with his feelings that the cost imposed on French society was excessive. Similar critiques came from other centrists, in particular from the Centre Démocrate (led by Jean Lecanuet) and the Radicaux (led at the time by Jean-Jacques Servan-Schreiber). In an effort to create a viable centrist alternative, those two parties federated in late 1971 to prepare the 1973 elections to the National Assembly.[33] They also worked out a common platform, Le projet réformateur.[34] Both parties had always been very critical of Gaullism; both supported Giscard in the 1974 elections, though Servan-Schreiber did so only at the last moment. After Giscard's victory, both parties joined the "presidential majority" of Giscard, and later on the U.D.F., as will be shown below.

Of the two groups, the Radicals (thanks in part to the prolific — if not always consistent — writings of Servan-Schreiber) were by far more active in formulating political programs and platforms. In 1970, Servan-Schreiber and Michel Albert coauthored Ciel et terre, subtitled Manifeste radical (Radical manifesto).[35] Many of the ideas formulated there were incorporated later on in the Projet réformateur.

In 1967, Servan-Schreiber had already attracted wide attention with his book The American Challenge,[36] which was a hymn to growth and to "thinking big" (in industry, science, technology), an appeal to Europe to catch up with the United States in all these areas. The main critique the book addressed to the Gaullists was that they were not thinking big enough, since they thought in national French rather than in European (Common Market) terms, and also that they disturbed the market mechanism and thus raised obstacles to economic efficiency.[37] As to the social consequences of growth, Servan-Schreiber did not give it much thought at the time; ". . . there can be no progress without surrendering acquired privileges, without discarding outdated machinery, ideas, and skills."[38] What mattered was not that growth might bring a happier society, but that it would bring a society which would "form the avant-garde of human history."[39] The whole book was marked by an optimism which often seems naive in retrospect.

By the time he co-authored the Radical Manifesto, Servan-Schreiber had changed his mind on many points. Whereas the earlier book expressed a fascination with all growth and "progress," the manifesto now stressed the importance of defining the social purpose of growth. It should not simply be power or private affluence.[40] Rather, growth (and in particular a better handling of it) should emancipate people from the harsh laws of profitability and allow the institution of a truly human society which would be able to choose its own goals — goals which would no longer be economically determined.

In light of these (somewhat vague) criteria for orienting growth, several developments of the past are viewed very critically. Private consumption, the authors concluded, had been given excessive emphasis, particularly when contrasted with the decline (in relative terms) of public services and investment. Both authors of the manifesto make this point elsewhere as well. In a report to the Common Market conference in 1972, Michel Albert, then a well-known technocrat with the French government, even voiced concern whether there was not,

. . . within the Community, or, to be more exact, because of the way the Common Market operates at present, a tendency towards a type of society where private prosperity, or even opulence, would contrast with relative poverty in public services and resources."41

He concluded that the search for high growth rates in the pursuit of national power politics was self-defeating in the long run; "the more perspicacious began to understand that the future of Western society would depend not only on economic growth but also on the quality of life which developed in that society."42 Like Giscard, the Radicals are critical of the social disruption which resulted from growth. They reject the view according to which these "hundreds of thousands of routed farmers, isolated shopkeepers, scorned artisans, insufficiently qualified workers" and so on must be "uprooted, tortured by the forward march of the economy."43 Such an approach is not only unethical, it is also economically inefficient. The Radical Manifesto claims that the time for purely quantitative growth, characterized by large firms and mass production, is now gone anyhow, since the new demand emerging in advanced industrial countries is for high-quality products which call for a greater input in creative intelligence, better individual adaptation, and so forth. For an economy geared to such productions, France, with its many surviving artisans and small, nonindustrial farmers, would have a natural advantage. Rather than trying to ruin these sectors, an intelligent economic policy ought to develop them as a source of strength.44 These professions would still have to modernize; but the style and organization of work could largely remain intact. Invention and creativity, the manifesto holds, are more likely to result from small, high-knowledge firms than from large corporations.

The critique of the Centre Démocrate resembles in many points that of the Radicals. Before the 1973 election, its leaders attacked Pompidou's policy of "forced" or "accelerated industrialization"; they equally rejected the alternative proposed by the Left, that is, the "industrialized dictatorship" of the Common Program with its record growth rates.45 Growth, Lecanuet wrote, had become a fetish, "an idol to which everything has been sacrificed; social needs, public investments, nature and the beauty of the landscape, the quality of life, happiness and the personal growth of human beings."46 France had been forced to develop in the direction of a productivist society. To the industrialized imperative of the Gaullists, the Democratic Centrists oppose the "social imperative"; they propose growth measured out for human beings.47

The single-minded pursuit of economic efficiency has led to hardships, the decline of "backward" regions, industrial and urban concentration, the neglect of public services and investments, and tensions at every level of French society.48   The <u>Projet reformateur</u>, published in 1973 marks the numerous points of agreement between the two parties.   It also cites a specific quantitative target: a growth rate of 4-5 percent.49   What is remarkable about this figure is that it was lower than the rate prevailing in France at that time.

The <u>Mouvement réformateur</u> was essentially a failure at the polls in 1973; however, only a little more than a year later, the major political leaders of the two parties that formed it were included in Giscard's first government.   Among the later writings of the centrists, there is one which is particularly interesting because it shows the evolution in the thinking of Michel Albert, co-author of the <u>Radical Manifesto</u> and later planning commissioner under Giscard.   In 1975 he co-authored another book on the subject of growth, entitled <u>Les vaches maigres</u>.50   It discusses policy for the "lean years" that he saw on the horizon as a result of the various crises of the early 1970s.

A key point in that book is that France needs an entirely new approach to economic growth and development, both to meet the aspirations of her population and the constraints of the economic and physical world.   These aspirations and constraints both point in the same direction: a search for a greater quality of life, achieved by a different pattern of development.

Big cities, big factories, big housing complexes and big technology have resulted in discontent, violence, and inefficiency, the book argues.51   For the resulting dissatisfaction the system has only one compensation, and that is higher financial rewards. As dissatisfaction increases, more and more has to be spent to "buy" the loyalty of its members.   This (and not a desire for increased material consumption) is viewed as the main force behind steadily increasing wage demands.52   The emerging constraints on the system (high costs of energy and other raw materials, environmental limits, inefficiencies of all kinds linked with excessive size) make it impossible to continue on the old path.   The way to deal with both the dissatisfaction and the new constraints is to create a new model of civilization.   Quantitative growth is still important to meet some needs, but most growth should be "qualitative," that is, being an improvement in the quality of life.   This can be done by a deliberate break away from the model of urban-industrial concentration and the creation (or revitalization) of a decentralized economy, with an artisanal style of production that would be modern in its methods and tools.   Such a development would allow wage-earners to participate more closely in the organization of their work.   Not only are human aspirations better met;   economic and technical efficiency are also achieved, especially since such a course would make better use of the French heritage (smaller units, smaller energy consumption, tradition of craftsmanship and repair, lesser professional mobility).53   Overall, the proposed changes are held to reduce tensions in French society, a goal so dear to Giscard.   It is not surprising that many of these ideas can be found again in <u>French Democracy</u>.

Quite generally, the parallels between Giscard's ideas and those of the Radicals and Democratic Centrists are quite evident if one looks at their respective writings in the mid-1970s.   A federation of these parties — which occurred in 1976, leading to the setting up of the U.D.F. — was more than just an alliance of opportunists;   they did have much in common.   They all were critical of the hardships wrought by growth, particularly on the "backward" sectors of economy and society;   they all undertook an ideological rehabilitation of these sectors.   They also agreed on rejecting the extensive state role in economic life as practiced by Gaullism in the form of a close cooperation of the ruling groups in politics and the economy.   The Democratic Centrists called this <u>national-affairisme;</u>   the Radicals spoke of the <u>Etat U.D.R.;</u>   Giscard called for greater reliance on the market.   They all put great emphasis on the social purpose of growth, on domestic priorities rather than national ones.   Finally, they rejected the Left-Right division, as well as the capital-labor division, for contemporary French society.   Such divisions, in their view, were based on obsolete ideologies.

However, in the second half of the 1970s, these parties failed to maintain themselves on the territory which they wanted to occupy, that is, the center of the French political scene.   As the Giscard presidency went on, it became increasingly clear that the actual policy of the "center" was where Leftist critics had put it all along — that is, on the Right.   Unlike the Gaullists in their better days, and unlike the Socialists from the mid-1970s onwards, the centrists parties, united in the U.D.F., failed in their attempt to create another catch-all party that would appeal to broad categories of French voters.

NOTES

1.   William Safran, "Centrism in the Fifth Republic: An Attitude in Search of an Instrument," in Andrews and Hoffmann, <u>The Fifth Republic at Twenty,</u> pp. 126-35.

2.   John Ardagh, <u>The New French Revolution</u> (New York: Harper & Row, 1969), p. 17;   André Pautard, <u>Valéry Giscard d'Estaing</u> (Paris: EDIPA, 1974), pp. 62-63.

3.   Roger Priouret, <u>Les Français mystifiés,</u> p. 121, quotes Giscard as saying:

> My objective is to bring France [by 1976] up to an industrial potential about equal to that of Britain and Germany. I would prefer to reach that goal without inflation. But if I have to choose, I will opt for industrial development, and put the battle against inflation in the background.

See also L'Express, 15 April 1974, p. 33.

4. Servan-Schreiber in L'Express, 29 April 1974.

5. Michel Poniatowski, Conduire le changement (Paris: Fayard, 1975), p. 25. Poniatowski was and is one of Giscard's closest associates and friends.

6. Valéry Giscard d'Estaing, Démocratie française (Paris: Fayard, 1976). Published in English as French Democracy (Garden City, Doubleday, 1977).

7. Thus he states that "the objective of full employment is not unattainable, because it was achieved in France for twenty-five years running," and calls for a still more vigorous growth rate for the years to come (in order to secure full employment). French Democracy, pp. 79 and 85.

8. He repeatedly stressed, in French Democracy, how important it was to avoid divisiveness and dramatization; resorting to such rhetoric only played in the hands of the extremists of both the right and the left. Ibid., pp. 108-11 and passim.

9. Ibid., pp. 19, 31, 65 and 77 (quote).

10. Ibid., pp. 76-79.

11. The proceedings were published as Economie et société humaine (Paris: Denoel, 1972).

12. Valery Giscard d'Estaing, "Humaniser la croissance," Preuves, no. 10, second trimester 1972.

13. French Democracy, pp. 4 and 6.

14. Giscard, "Humaniser la croissance," p. 10.

15. Giscard in Economie et société humaine, pp. 439-40.

16. Ibid., pp. 446-47.

17. Rapport sur l'orientation preliminaire du VIIe Plan (Paris: Imprimerie des journaux officiels, June 1975), p. 14.

18. French Democracy, p. 87.

19. Pautard, Giscard d'Estaing, p. 91.

20. French Democracy, p. 27.

21. Giscard's preference for the income tax: Economie et société humaine, pp. 436-37; also L'Express, 10 June 1974, p. 16. On the modest role of the income tax in France at that time, see Towards a European Model of Development (Brussels: The European Bookshop, 1972), p. 568.

22. Economie et société humaine, pp. 434-47.

23. French Democracy, p. 85.

24. Ibid., p. 9.

25. Lionel Stoléru, Vaincre la pauvreté dans les pays riches (Paris: Flammarion, 1974).

26. French Democracy, p. 83.
27. The Rapport sur l'orientation préliminaire du VIIe Plan, pp. 26-27, states that "it cannot be ruled out a priori that the will to preserve the environment, or the desire to assure workers a more satisfactory professional life, will have a negative impact on . . . the growth rate in the future."
28. French Democracy, p. 41; and Giscard, "Humaniser la croissance."
29. Ibid., pp. 125-26.
30. The policy is discussed later on in this volume.
31. French Democracy, p. 85; see also Giscard, cited in Le Monde, weekly edition, 15 June and 12 October 1978.
32. Economie et société humaine, p. 162:

Let us imagine that in the next few years . . . we should have a crisis of high unemployment. Would then the whole discussion on the usefulness of growth not be swept away in a few instants, and would the problem of the rate of economic activity and employment not immediately appear as the most immediate social and human exigency?

33. Safran, "Centrism in the Fifth Republic," p. 127.
34. Jean-Jacques Servan-Schreiber and Jean Lecanuet, Le projet réformateur (Paris: Laffont, 1973).
35. Jean-Jacques Servan-Schreiber and Michel Albert, Ciel et terre — Manifeste radical (Paris: Denoël, 1970).
36. Jean-Jacques Servan-Schreiber, Le défi américain (Paris: Denoël, 1967); translated as The American Challenge (New York: Avon, 1969).
37. Ciel et terre, appendix I, pp. 223-38, authored by Bruce Scott of the Harvard Business School.
38. The American Challenge, p. 209.
39. Ibid., p. 65.
40. Ciel et terre, pp. 20-22 and 168-69.
41. Michel Albert, in Towards a European Model of Development, p. 545; similarly Servan-Schreiber in La lettre Mansholt (Paris: Pauvert, 1972), pp. 102-03.
42. Albert, Towards a European Model of Development, pp. 575-76.
43. Ciel et terre, p. 62.
44. Ibid., pp. 182-87 and 201-05; and appendix I, pp. 231-32.
45. Edouard Bonnefous in Démocratie moderne, 18 January 1973; Jean Lacanuet in Démocratie moderne, 1 March 1973, p. 6. (Démocratie moderne is the organ of the Democratic Centrists, with a very modest circulation.)
46. Jean Lecanuet, "Economie et politique," Nouvelle revue des deux mondes, March 1973, p. 54.

47. _Démocratie moderne_, 18 January 1973 (E. Bonnefous) and 1 February 1973 (Charles Dasville).

48. _Démocratie moderne_, 20 April 1972 (Pierre Fauchon); Servan-Schreiber and Lecanuet, _Le projet réformateur_, pp. 74-75.

49. _Le projet réformateur_, p. 86.

50. Michel Albert and Jean Ferniot, _Les vaches maigres_ (Paris: Gallimard, 1975).

51. Ibid., pp. 133-36.

52. Albert and Ferniot here adopt a view first outlined by Jean Boissonnat, "La croissance demain," _L'Expansion_, June 1972, pp. 109-24.

53. _Les vaches maigres_, pp. 251-52.

3

VARIETIES OF SOCIALISM

The early 1970s was a period of great change for the French Left. The Communist party, long known for its immobility, had begun to abandon some of its Stalinist dogmas; in the late 1960s it also developed a different outlook on the possible conquest of power, and thus formulated a governmental program of its own. At the same time it began to be accepted by the French as a party like any other, and thus was no longer relegated to the ghetto. On the other hand, if mistrust of the Communists was declining, electoral support for the party did not increase.[1] Nonetheless, when in the early 1970s the Communist party first expressed its interest in a Common Program, it was still by far the strongest party of the Left.

Also in the early 1970s, the different groups that made up French socialism consolidated to form a new (and soon very successful) party. The noncommunist Left was split into many groups in the late 1960s; moreover, it lacked clear ideas in common, and even more a clear strategy. For a long time the Socialists had cooperated with the Centrists (especially during the Fourth Republic, but some of this continued); many Socialist leaders professed a very strong anticommunism and identified socialism with humanitarianism and redistributive reforms. But when in the late 1960s the old Section française de l'internationale ouvrière (S.F.I.O.) finally collapsed, socialism also took on a new programmatic content. At its founding congress of Epinay in 1971, the new Parti Socialiste (P.S.) took a decidedly anticapitalist stand and declared that only a total break with this system of exploitation could set the working class free.[2] The new party thus placed itself further left on the political spectrum, and rejected social democracy. An alliance with the Communist party not only appeared now as the most promising avenue to electoral success, it was also more natural than it would have been during most of the preceding twenty-five years.

Such a change did not come about without conflicts. The new Socialist party contained many different elements, ranging from anticommunists and social democrats (such as Defferre and Mauroy) to the Marxist and strongly procommunist C.E.R.E.S., led by Jean-Pierre Chevènement. Mitterrand, elected to the leadership in 1971, held the different groups together in a more or less peaceful competition (which had some positive aspects of its own);[3] he also presided over the incorporation of additional elements through the first half of the 1970s. At the same time, he was a firm advocate of a strategy of cooperation with the Communists, arguing that by ending the isolation of the Communist party, the P.S. would eventually emerge as the strongest party of a united Left.[4] In 1971, this was at best an ambitious hope.[5]

In 1972, the Socialist party published its program, Changer la vie.[6] In addition to traditional socialist goals such as a more egalitarian redistribution, it also proposed selective nationalizations and steps towards autogestion (or workers' self-management). However, Mitterrand — at least privately — did not join in the militants' condemnation of social democracy. As he mentioned confidentially to a reporter in 1972,

> I am amazed by the Swedish achievements and I cannot relate them in public without shocking my own friends and a good part of the militants, not to mention the problem I would have with the Communists. And if I dared to say that the National Health Service in Great Britain is a great achievement of socialism, what an uproar this would produce with militants and voters![7]

In June 1972, the P.S. and the Communist party (P.C.F.) signed the Common Program of the Left — a list of commitments that a Leftist government (the 1973 elections were coming up) would carry out in its first five years in power. The Common Program dominated the thinking of the Left for years to come; it remained the standard reference by which each group defined its position. Thus, within the Left, one can clearly distinguish several approaches. One of them is the Common Program itself, in its nature a compromise that can be (and soon was) interpreted in different ways. Another approach is that of autogestion socialism. It is identified with those Socialist groups and movements who joined the Socialists in 1974, after the Assises du Socialisme. They came primarily from the Conféderation française démocratique du travail (C.F.D.T.) and the Parti Socialiste Unifié (P.S.U.), and they are quite critical of the Common Prográm. A third approach is that of the P.C.F., for which the Common Program is only a start and which subscribes to a very distinctive analysis of French economic life. The first two approaches shall be discussed below; that of the Communists will be taken up in the next chapter.

THE COMMON PROGRAM

Negotiated between the Socialists and the Communists in 1972, the Common Program was ratified not only by these two parties but also by the Leftist Radicals — a coalition similar to that of the Popular Front government in 1936. Even though it was abandoned before it had a chance to be put into practice, many of its provisions were incorporated in Mitterrand's platforms later on, including the one on which he was elected in 1981. At the time of its publication, the Socialists viewed the program as a first step; its implementation would represent the outline of that Socialist society that could grow from it later on.[8]

With regard to economic policy, the program contained two basic thrusts. First, it proposed a drastic redistribution of income and wealth that would benefit wage-earners and generally low-income groups, while placing a heavier burden on the affluent members of society (and on business). There is little that was revolutionary about this part; the major problem was whether its implementation was possible, and what reactions and tensions it would set off throughout the economy, society, and politics. The second thrust was in the direction of a redistribution of economic power, transferring much of it from banks, oligopolistic corporations, and business generally, to the state, its managers and finally the workers and their representatives. In this part the Common Program went substantially beyond the usual social democratic proposals. At the same time, the program stated that an important private sector would remain, that inflation would be controlled and the channels of international trade remain open except for emergencies. Since the program brought together objectives which probably could not be achieved simultaneously, one can legitimately read it in different ways, and thus arrive at different conclusions about its content.

The first thrust of the program is to redistribute income and wealth. The first paragraph in fact states that

A regular progression of the purchasing power of wage earners is indispensable to permit them a progressively better satisfaction of steadily growing needs. The development of the economy will contribute to this progression. The main elements which determine the increase of the purchasing power are the increase of direct wages and social welfare payments, price stability, and the reduction of the tax burden on small and middle taxpayers.[9]

Wages are to be increased substantially, particularly those of low-income groups; and all wages, pensions, and social welfare payments (also to be increased immediately) are to be indexed on consumer prices, so that they will be adjusted automatically with inflation. At the same time, the work week is to be shortened to 40 hours, the retirement age to be reduced (to 60 years for men, 55 for women), and vacations are to be lengthened. The minimum wage is to rise faster than the average wage.[10]

Social Security coverage is to be expanded; health care is to become, progressively, free of charge; contributions by employers and the state to the system will be increased. Public services and investments will be expanded rapidly (housing programs, public transportation, education, culture, leisure, access to nature, and so on). The tax structure is to be modified in such a way as to increase taxes on business (both private and nationalized). Traditional tax privileges of business are to be reduced or eliminated altogether; executive pay and expense account spending will be taxed as profits. A new tax on wealth is to be created, "annual, progressive and with a low tax rate," to affect corporations and the very wealthy. In general, tax advantages to investors are to be abolished. At the same time, the taxation of wage-earners is to be reduced (with regard to both income and sales tax), while high incomes are to be taxed more heavily.[11]

The second thrust of the Common Program is to reallocate economic power; in the program's own words, this will democratize economic life. This reallocation takes many different forms, ranging from very limited participation of workers in traditional management functions to an expansion of public control over investments and finally to plans for nationalizations.

In all firms, the rights of workers, works committees (comités d'entreprise), shop unions, personnel delegations, and other worker representatives are to be strengthened and expanded. Some of these representatives must be consulted before any action is taken on hiring, dismissal, classification of workers, and generally on working conditions. The arbitrary right of the employer to dismiss will be abolished; any dismissal must be submitted to the works committee, which has the right to suspend it until a decision is made by a labor tribunal. In addition, the state will guarantee that no one can be dismissed without a prior and equivalent reclassification in the labor force.[12]

The workers' representatives are generally limited to the right of being informed about the important aspects of management. They also have a right to convene the workers in the place of work, for one hour every month (during working hours, and without loss of pay), in order to discuss this information with the workers. But on the whole, they will not participate in management functions. Such a possibility is held out only for the public and nationalized sector, for which the Common Program mentions it as a possibility — provided the workers of the firm should express such a desire and provided further that the structure of the firm make this possible. In that case, the intervention of the workers in the management of the firm may take on new forms, to be decided by an agreement between the democratic government, the management of the firm concerned, and the unions. This is as far as the Common Program takes the idea of autogestion,[13] for which the Communists showed a very strong aversion, at least until 1973, when they began to reinterpret the concept.

The nationalizations are also understood as a step towards the democratization of the economy.

> In order to break the domination of big capital and to implement a new economic and social policy different from that practiced by it, the government will progressively transfer to the collectivity the most important means of production and the financial instruments which are currently in the hands of the dominant capitalist groups.[14]

From the outset, the minimum threshold of nationalizations will include the whole banking and financial sector, and those industrial firms and groups which occupy a strategic position in key sectors of the economy (public utilities, firms living on state subsidies, oligopolies, and firms which control branches that are essential for the development of the national economy). The program specifically lists the branches where all or most activities are to be nationalized. They are mining and other resource extraction, armament, aerospace, the nuclear sector, and the pharmaceutical industries. Electronics and chemicals are to be nationalized for the most part. A list of nine firms which are targets for immediate nationalization (100 percent takeover) is also included;[15] other firms are mentioned in which the government will acquire a stake, possibly going as far as a majority holding.

The Common Program states that nationalization will not mean étatisation, that is, direct management by the state. Rather, the firms will enjoy management autonomy; the control of the state will only be retrospective, a posteriori. The individual firms will choose their programs, set their own budgets, and select their own markets. These decisions will be taken by their board (conseil d'administration), which will be made up of elected representatives of workers, certain categories of customers, and representatives of the new democratic government; the latter however will not be in the majority. The board is to elect the president and to name the general managers for the firm.[16] Again, under certain conditions (as already mentioned) further steps may be taken towards workers' self-management.

As to the compensation of the current owners (of the firms that are to be nationalized), the Common Program says very little, except that an equitable solution will be worked out and that an essential distinction will be made between, on one hand, the small and medium investors who live on their savings, and the big holders of invested capital on the other.[17]

Even beyond the nationalized sector, the whole economy will be shaped decisively by governmental policy. A democratic plan, based essentially on the participation of workers and the public sector, will be drawn up. It will be binding on the public sector (notwithstanding the management autonomy of its individual firms), where it will determine the big investments.[18] There will also be substantial intervention of the state in private sector investment. A National Investment Bank will be set up which will have the task of financing a large part of all industrial investment; at the same time, internal financing of investments by the business firms themselves (from retained earnings) will be limited by taxation, price policies and other methods.[19] (Popular savings on the other hand are to be encouraged.) Combined with the proposed nationalization of the whole banking sector, the independence of private firms is thus considerably reduced. This seems at least as important as the statement, also contained in the Common Program, that an important private sector will be retained.

For agriculture, the program promises an improvement in the living and working conditions of small and medium producers. To small business it holds out the prospect of a lighter tax burden and a check on the development of the large-surface hyper-marchés. Areas of the country which have become "backward" as a result of uneven development during the process of rapid industrialization are to be revitalized, and their unemployment problems to be solved.

There is one question that hangs over the Common Program and that was much discussed in the time following its publication: How is it to be financed? The question is all the more important since Leftist governments in France, at least twice in the twentieth century, foundered on major financial problems. In January 1973, the leaders of the three formations that had endorsed the Common Program declared that the program would increase state expenditures by 15 billion; this seemed a modest estimate.[20] In addition, there would be the cost to business firms, in the form of "substantially" higher wages, reduced working hours without reduction in pay, improvement of working conditions, obligation to pay for infrastructure and pollution control costs, higher Social Security contributions, new taxes, limitation of dismissals and the like. What, it was asked, would the consequences of all these new charges be?

Assuming that the increases in wages and in public spending will indeed be substantial (the Common Program gives no figures on either), there are two theoretical possibilities on how the additional costs can be met. For one, they could be met through a high rate of industrial growth, achieved primarily by an increase in economic efficiency (the main other avenue, that is, growth in the resorption of unemployment, was limited in 1972; unemployment had not yet assumed important proportions). The program does indeed mention a "new growth," based on high productivity in industry, which would permit far-reaching change.[21] Redistribution itself can be stimulating since it will tend to increase demand. But important doubts remain, due to the fact that France in 1972 was already experiencing high growth rates. Certainly a Leftist government would not intentionally have slowed growth;[22] but how much more could be obtained through higher growth rates?

In case growth should prove insufficient to finance the extra charges on the French economy, there remains another avenue: that of inflation. The Common Program says little about inflation, except that price stability will be an essential goal of the government, and that wages and social welfare payments are to be indexed on a sliding scale.[23] A sympathetic critic of the Common Program, the French economist Serge-Christophe Kolm, concluded that recourse to inflation would most likely lead to a failure similar to that of the revolutions experienced by Chile and Portugal in the first half of the 1970s.[24] The process that he anticipated would unfold in this way: Business firms, hit by higher wage costs and higher taxes, would try to increase product prices. Because of the sliding scale, wages would keep rising with inflation. Eventually the government would resort to price control; this would lead to a dramatic fall in business profits (something the Common Program actually lists as a goal) and soon to massive business indebtedness. As a result, investment would fall, and lower product capacities would not only lead to shortages of goods but generally to a decline in the standard of living within a year or two. The shortages could lead to increased imports; but this would rapidly deplete the exchange reserves, and thus imports would come to an end. The government might of course impose import restrictions in the form of tariffs or quotas. The Common Program states that they are to be used only in an emergency;[25] but the application of the program, Kolm holds, might well create such an emergency. Again, this would lead to scarcity and a drop in the standard of living. Eventually that standard would probably reach a level lower than that prevailing before the Common Program's application. This would lead to a massive loss of political support for the Left, especially among middle-class voters, and would in turn bring about the Left's political downfall before long.[26]

In Kolm's view, the only way in which this chain of events could be avoided was by limiting wage increases and other charges on the economy. In this case the Common Program might be economically viable (and it may be that the Leftist Radicals read the program in this way).[27] But then it would not change much either. Such thoughts have led him — and other Leftists — to look for a different approach that the Left might take, should it come to power. The critics from within the Left come, to be sure, from different directions. There were those who thought the program went too far as it was, and others (especially the Communists) who argued that it did not go far enough. But there were also those critics who held that the Common Program proposed above all the wrong kind of changes. It preserved the same model of industrial society, with its large organizations in production and administration. While it enhanced the social protection and earnings of the workers, it gave them little say in actual decision making concerning their direct environment, and it did not deal with the problem raised by certain techniques (if any techniques had adverse side effects, the program always put the blame on capitalism). Its emphasis on the material standard of living, the critics argued, ruled out concern with the way people lived. Was that just going to remain the same?[28]

Indeed, many Socialists lacked a vision of a different society. Some of them simply saw socialism as a more efficient system than capitalism, with social justice added into the bargain. They admitted that capitalism was not all that bad, since it had brought considerable improvement in the provision of food, clothing, housing, appliances and the like. However, while for capitalism these things were unintended side-effects, socialism would make the achievement of such results its main task and purpose (and thus could be expected to be better at it).[29] When questioned by militants of the nascent ecology movement about the difference that the Common Program might make from their perspective, Mitterrand answered evasively: the Program was only set up for a period of five years, he said, and during that time period improving the situation of the most disadvantaged members of society would be the overriding concern. A different model of production and consumption could be prepared while the Common Program was implemented, but its actual advent would be a long-term prospect.[30] Understandably, ecology activists were very dissatisfied with the Program, which (in the eyes of one group) recognized "as the only motor, and apparently as the only goal of human society, the unlimited expansion of the economy. It is true that it wants to humanize this expansion and to reduce social injustice."[31] Similar critiques, but much more broadly phrased, come from the autogestion (self-management) Socialists.

AUTOGESTION SOCIALISM

There are many historical and intellectual precedents to the French autogestion movement. In some ways, it is a continuation of the old anarcho-syndicalist tradition. More recently, its antecedents are to be found in experiments with self-management on the firm level.[32] This is the core of autogestion socialism; however, its adherents want to see this principle extended to all spheres of social life. Many of these ideas experienced a strong revival in May 1968; the Lip conflict then popularized them more widely (cf footnote 53, below).

The strongest advocates of autogestion, in the early 1970s, were to be found in the Confédération française démocratique du travail, (C.F.D.T.) France's second largest labor union,[33] and among the adherents of the Parti Socialiste Unifié (P.S.U.), a Leftist splinter party. In a milder version, its ideas can be found in the Socialist party program of 1972 mentioned above, Changer la vie. After the presidential elections of 1974, it became one of the main themes in the renewal of the Socialist party. At a congress in 1974, leaders of the C.F.D.T. and the P.S.U. joined the Socialists of the P.S. to draft a projet de société (outline for a society) based on the principle of autogestion. This alliance and its programmatic statement were later approved by the P.S., which however did not ratify the projet formulated by the congress[34] (whereas it did ratify the Common Program). In the mid-1970s, autogestion was often presented as the long-term reform goal of the French Socialists, while the union of the Left (cooperation with the Communists) was viewed as the way to achieve that goal. However, for reasons which will soon become evident, there was a direct conflict between goal and method.

Autogestion offers a radically different model of social and economic relations, an alternative not only to capitalism but also to social democracy and Soviet-style socialism. All these models are rejected because of the centralized, hierarchical patterns which they are held inevitably to develop, and because of the deleterious consequences for man, society and nature which are perceived as flowing from such organizational patterns.

That capitalism would be criticized is not particularly surprising; but the line of criticism is crucial. It is admitted by autogestion theorists that capitalism as a form of development has produced some apparent benefits such as an increased supply of goods, but the price that was exacted for this is seen as excessively high.[35] Capitalism, these theorists argue, has to be seen as a whole complex of phenomena that are all linked together. Not only are the profit motive and the private ownership of the means of production at stake, both of which distort priorities and lead to injustice, so is a whole pattern of development:

Capitalist economic expansion does not benefit the workers; it leads simply to

- the partial development of the purchasing power of certain social strata without solving the problem of deteriorating living conditions for the workers;
- the maintenance of the residual character of collective functions;
- the aggravation of income inequalities and social segregation;
- the destruction of the environment;
- the waste of natural resources.[36]

With regard to crucial aspects, the Soviet alternative is no better than capitalism. In the words of the 1972 Manifesto of the P.S.U.,

the development of the Soviet Union is no different from that of capitalism with respect to the uncontrolled use of natural resources, pollution, and above all with respect to the fact that it gives priority to a purely acquisitive, purely quantitative model of development. Wherever up until now, socialism has come to power, it has consolidated the model of consumption of capitalist society rather than questioned it. This model itself is at stake today.[37]

The writings of the C.F.D.T. leaders have developed this critique and made it more specific. Edmond Maire and Jacques Julliard criticized the notion that socialism could be achieved by conquering political power in the bourgeois state and transferring the ownership of the means of production to the collectivity. What needs to be changed is the mode of production itself; a mere change in ownership simply has no bearing on that. This mode, however, has almost never been changed; nearly all Socialist countries (except China, and initially Cuba) followed the capitalist model of industrialization. Most of them attempted to catch up with (or surpass) the capitalist countries, with results that were the same everywhere:

Priority to heavy industry; a crushing burden imposed on the population in the name of "primary socialist accumulation"; productivist and even Taylorist technology; separation between planning and execution in work and other functions; training for specialized social roles beginning in school; the maintaining of competition between individuals, and a very wide range of salaries; the necessity of a hierarchy of command and concentration of power at the top.[38]

This concentration of power prevents people from developing their autonomy; it also makes it impossible to take such autonomy, should it ever develop, into account. Individuals as whole human beings must remain foreign to the system. Even Jean-Pierre Chevènement, the leader of the procommunist C.E.R.E.S. faction of the Socialist party, has condemned Soviet-style socialism on essentially the same grounds.[39]

After capitalism and communism, social democracy is subjected to the same critique — and found to show the same defects. Reformist socialism, the autogestion writers agree, did not come up with another form of development either; all it did was to insist on greater fairness in distribution. But by the same token it has perpetuated the capitalist form of organization and the capitalist model of development. By locking the working class into a situation in which higher wage demands become the central issue, other areas and aspects of life were neglected, or at least were subordinated to the effective pursuit of wage demands. The institutional framework of capitalism was not questioned; on the other hand, much attention was paid to the satisfaction of needs, and the fact was overlooked that it is the institutional framework which generates many of these needs. Thus, social democratic approaches not only failed to take on capitalism but in fact perpetuated its framework, which does not allow people any direct control over the most important matters which determine the evolution of a society. As Michel Rocard put it,

The Left is too much in the habit of thinking in terms of "needs," individual or collective. This logic has consequences: it leads to a battle against the inequalities, frustrations and contradictions engendered by capitalism by means of a vast apparatus of assistance. In the areas of employment, health, information and culture, the logic of the sole "satisfaction of needs" leads to the creation, above society, of a vast system of compensation which increases — whether one wants this or not — the risks of centralization and bureaucracy.[40]

Under such an approach, socialism becomes limited to redistribution — to a better sharing of the national product. By singling out the wage aspirations of the workers, wider dimensions are neglected.

Thus the social democrats [expressly mentioned are Harold Wilson, Guy Mollet, Willy Brandt, and the Swedish Socialists] have become the managers . . . of capitalism. By contrast, the hopes of the workers focus not just on an improvement of their income, but on a total change of their conditions of existence, in and outside work.[41]

Given this reasoning, it is not surprising that both the C.F.D.T. and the P.S.U. rejected the Common Program; it resembled too much those forms of socialism which had failed to bring about crucial changes in the past. They criticized in particular the program's commitment to the old logic of industrial development and a high rate of economic growth, and its disregard for the social and environmental consequences of such a policy.[42] As the P.S.U. manifesto stated, "one cannot possibly extend and even enhance the same kind of growth we have today — as in the Common Program — without regard as to what is produced, and for whom it is produced."[43]

What Soviet style, social democratic and Common Program socialism have in common with contemporary capitalism is that they deprive people (particularly people in work) of initiative; in this way they deprive them of a chance to form their own individuality. Work, housing, food, health care, transportation, entertainment . . . all these things can be provided by centralized institutions. In order to form a whole person though, an individual has to be active; he "can only constitute himself if he is given the capacity to master and unify his own life."[44] Autogestion is held to make this possible. It provides a different form of organization; more importantly, it will affect the content of what people will need and desire. The partisans of autogestion expect in particular that much of the present hunger for consumption will subside under their system.[45] Just how this is to come about is not discussed in much detail. A theoretical perspective is offered in a book by two Socialist economists, Jacques Attali and Marc Guillaume, entitled L'Anti-économique.

Attali (who was then a close advisor to Mitterrand, a position he retained after 1981) distinguishes between the two kinds of growth. One is egalitarian and collectivist, with a large measure of decentralization; as examples, he cites Norway, New Zealand, Cuba, Tanzania and China. The other is generally more rapid, relies on inequality to exacerbate those needs which can be satisfied by economic transactions, and leads to urban concentration and centralization of power. This is the principal model of development for the rest of the world, developed or not.[46] In order to explain the difference between the two models of development, Attali and Guillaume distinguish between two functions served by material goods, particularly consumer goods. Relying on the sociologist Jean Baudrillard, they distinguish a utilitarian and a symbolic function of consumption.[47] The utilitarian function is clear: food is expected to nourish, a washing machine to wash, and so on. The symbolic function consists in establishing the individual's place in society, his social integration and differentiation. (This is unlike the distinction between real versus false needs in that the needs corresponding to the symbolic function are very real, even though they are subjective; they are not to be changed by education, only by a change of the surrounding society.)

The need for social integration and differentiation is of course not new; what is new is the role played in this context by consumption. In traditional societies, personal status was established mostly through long-term personal contacts; in industrial societies such contacts, as well as individual qualities, lose much of their importance. They are replaced to a large extent by consumption. If inequalities are great, symbolic needs (for status) which now express themselves in a desire for increased consumption, know no limits; they shift and expand permanently, as some people try to catch up while others try to stay ahead. Advertising is hardly necessary to create new needs: the capitalist system need only exploit existing inequalities and the desires resulting from it. At the same time, the system is unable to provide greater overall satisfaction. In fact, it thrives on the exploitation of frustration, and satisfaction may even decrease as consumption increases. Suppose only a small group of people has access to a certain form of consumption — for example, automobiles. They may be better off; but they worsen the situation of those who do not have cars, materially (by appropriating roads for this purpose) and psychologically (frustration). In a second stage, the others will attempt to acquire cars also, often at the cost of great efforts. While for a time this may improve their sense of status, it diminishes the sense of status of the previously privileged car owners; those will now redirect their consumption towards other status symbols. In the end, the possession of automobiles no longer provides great status satisfaction to anyone, so that everyone's psychological satisfaction diminishes; at the same time, because of congestion, everyone is worse off in terms of transportation and pollution.[48]

What are the implications of all this for economic growth? While it can satisfy the utilitarian needs fairly easily (but then, those are no longer the most important ones anyhow), growth can never satisfy the symbolic needs which are by nature unlimited in a system based on inequality. If one wants an economy responsive to symbolic needs, then capitalism is a legitimate model; it is rather good at that. But the point is that capitalism not only responds to those needs; it also creates them.[49] And while it is perfectly rational from the individual's perspective to pursue a strategy of maximization of consumption, it is absurd from the perspective of society as a whole. In addition, it imposes heavy costs, as it requires a heavy organization (hierarchy and centralization in the name of productive efficiency) and produces a deleterious impact on the environment.[50]

There are essentially two ways in which such an absurd system can be curbed. One way would be to impose an upper limit on material production and consumption (for example, in the name of collective survival, should the exploitation of the natural environment reach crisis proportions). This approach, Attali and Guillaume agree, attempts to institute an artificial solidarity between the privileged and the nonprivileged (both within and between nations) by pointing out that we are all in the same boat, while at the same time perpetuating the existing situation which favors a minority.[51] But since human aspirations caused by inequality cannot be held down in this way for any length of time, the system has to become repressive sooner or later. Needs which can no longer be "satisfied" by growth must now be suppressed. Such an approach is only natural for the centralized, hierarchical industrial systems; it corresponds to their one-dimensional thinking. The other way to cope with this situation is autogestion: the creation of a new community, where the need for status, for social integration and differentiation does not find its main outlet in consumption, and where in fact the need itself is qualitatively different because the society of autogestion will be egalitarian.[52]

In the writings of the autogestion theorists, it is not always clear how much of it is near-utopian thinking relegated in its applicability to a distant future, and how much is meant as a guide to practical action. Certainly Maire and Rocard discussed the problems in very practical terms. They urged strongly that steps be taken in the right direction (such as enlarging the rights of workers, their ability to handle business questions, and so on).[53] They were also concerned that the Socialist party should take on the right targets. In particular, they argued, nationalizations plus redistribution could never by themselves bring about autogestion socialism. To give priority to those tasks was to invite failure on the greater design.

As to the leaders of the Socialist party, they did not take very clear positions with regard to autogestion during most of the 1970s (with the exception, obviously, of Rocard). To be sure, the term became part of their standard references; but its meaning was never made very clear. The idea was popular with many people on the Left, in particular with intellectuals and the "ecologists" whose ideas enjoyed increasing popularity at this time. It was also an effective slogan; but no great efforts were made to work out the practical implications of the concept. The Communist allies were certainly highly allergic to autogestion in its C.F.D.T. version.[54] Leftist leaders disagreed in their interpretation of what the Leftist "basis" wanted. The autogestion Socialists stressed the aspirations for qualitative change and greater autonomy (as well as the need for greater social justice, particularly for the poorest). As the recession deepened, they accepted the idea that wage demands could not go very far without endangering individual firms, or even the French economy as a whole. Mitterrand on the other hand, joined by many other Socialists, gave greater importance to wage increases and the nationalizations. His priorities corresponded to those of the Socialist party's main coalition partner, the P.C.F. It is true that within this agreement on principle there was place for largely divergent views. It was those divergences which dominated the internal conflicts of the Left from the mid-1970s onwards.

NOTES

1. Frank L. Wilson, "The French Left in the Fifth Republic," in Andrews and Hoffmann, The Fifth Republic at Twenty, pp. 173–80.

2. Ibid., p. 181.

3. The competition between the different groups also led to competitive membership drives; in addition, it created lively debates within the party. Ibid., p. 182.

4. George A. Codding, Jr., and William Safran, Ideology and Politics: The Socialist Party of France (Boulder: Westview Press, 1979), p. 218.

5. See graph 9.1.

6. Changer la vie. Programme de gouvernement du Parti Socialiste (Paris: Flammarion, 1972).

7. Roger Priouret, Les Francais mystifiés, p. 23.

8. Introduction to the Socialist edition of the Common Program, cited in Serge–Christophe Kolm, La transition socialiste (Paris: Editions du Cerf, 1977), p. 173.

9. Programme commun de gouvernement du Parti Communiste et du Parti Socialiste (Paris: Editions sociales, 1972), p. 53. Cited below as Programme Commun.

10. Ibid., pp. 53–58.

11. Ibid., pp. 130–32.

12. Ibid., pp. 57 and 106.

13. Ibid., pp. 105–12; also pp. 58–59.

14. Ibid., p. 113.

15. The firms that the Common Program targets for full nationalization are: Dassault, Roussel-Uclaf, Rhône-Poulenc, ITT-France, Thomson-Brandt, Honeywell-Bull, Péchiney-Ugine-Kuhlmann, Saint-Gobain-Pont-à-Mousson, and Compagnie Générale d'Electricité. Ibid., p. 116. For a comparison with the actual nationalizations of 1981/82, see the last part of this book.

16. Ibid., pp. 110–11 and 114.

17. Ibid., p. 116.

18. Ibid., pp. 117–18.

19. Ibid., pp. 137–38.

20. Priouret, Les Francais mystifiés, pp. 167–69.

21. _Programme commun_, p. 139.

22. Francois Mitterrand, "Un arret brutal de la croissance sacrifierait les plus faibles," _Le Sauvage_, April 1974. Similar Jean-Pierre Chevènement; "La gauche, hélas . . .", Ibid.

23. _Programme commun_, p. 54 and 133.

24. Kolm, _La transition socialiste_, pp. 153-54. Kolm argues that France is essentially similar to Chile and Portugal ("capitalist, Western, industrial, preponderance of wage-earners, Latin, Catholic, with strong Communist and Socialist Parties"). One may question that comparison, but then, it may not be that important for his analysis.

25. _Programme commun_, p. 135.

26. Kolm, _La transition socialiste_, pp. 153-73.

27. Annex to the Common Program; _Programme commun_, p. 188.

28. Kolm, _La transition socialiste_, pp. 177-80.

29. Michel Béaud, "Logique capitaliste et contenu de croissance," _Nouvelle revue socialiste_, May-June 1974.

30. See footnote 22 above; and La vie nouvelle, "Critiques écologiques sur le Programme commun de la gauche," Lyon, January 1975 (mimeo).

31. In discussing pollution, congestion and noise, the Common Program states that "these phenomena are not fatally linked with technical progress, industrial development or urbanization. The capitalist system is responsible for them." Solutions are to be found by modifying the production process and the products themselves rather than by attempts to curb pollution once it has been created. _Programme commun_, pp. 71-72.

32. On earlier experiences in France, see Claire Huchet Bishop, _All Things Common_ (New York: Harper, 1950). For a theoretical discussion see also Carole Pateman, _Participation and Democratic Theory_ (Cambridge; Cambridge University Press, 1970), and L. S. Stavrianos, _The Promise of the Coming Dark Age_ (San Francisco: Freeman, 1976).

33. The C.F.D.T. has its origin in the Catholic, and more conservative, C.F.T.C. It relinquished its religious orientation in 1964 and became one of France's two "revolutionary" labor unions, along with the C.G.T.

34. Jean-Francois Bizot, _Au parti des socialistes_ (Paris: Grasset, 1975), p. 486.

35. See, for example, _Pour le socialisme: Le livre des assises du socialisme_ (Paris: Stock, 1974), p. 15; _Manifeste du parti socialiste unifié_ (Paris: Tema, 1972), p. 34; Edmond Maire and Jacques Julliard, _La C.F.D.T. d'aujourd'hui_ (Paris: Le Seuil, 1975), p. 180.

36. _Manifeste du P.S.U._, p. 37.

37. Ibid., pp. 88-89.

38. Maire and Julliard, La C.F.D.T. d'aujourd'hui, pp. 164-65.

39. Chevenement quoted in Laurent Laot, La croissance économique en question (Paris: Editions ouvrières, 1974), pp. 183-84.

40. Michel Rocard and Jacques Gallus, L'inflation au coeur de la crise (Paris: Gallimard, 1975), p. 164. Gallus is also a former member of the P.S.U. At the time the book was published, both Rocard and Gallus had positions within the P.S.

41. Manifeste du P.S.U., pp. 14-15.

42. Ibid., p. 88; La C.F.D.T. d'aujourd'hui, pp. 167-68.

43. Manifeste du P.S.U., p. 37.

44. Rocard and Gallus, L'inflation au coeur, pp. 165-66.

45. Pour le socialisme, p. 91.

46. Jacques Attali and Marc Guillaume, L'anti-économique (Paris: Presses universitaires de France, 1974), pp. 121-22, citing an earlier article by Attali in La Nef.

47. Jean Baudrillard, Pour une critique de l'économie politique du signe (Paris: Gallimard, 1972), and Le miroir de la production (Paris: Casterman, 1973).

48. Similar arguments have been debated in the English and American literature; see, for example, Richard A. Easterlin, "Does money buy happiness?," The Public Interest, Winter 1973, pp. 3-10; Fred Hirsch, Social Limits to Growth (Cambridge: Harvard University Press, 1976).

49. Attali and Guillaume, L'anti-économique, p. 174.

50. Ibid., for example , pp. 196-203.

51. Ibid., pp. 118-19.

52. Ibid., pp. 205-31.

53. Rocard cited in Priouret, Les Francais mystifiés, pp. 181-82. Edmond Maire indicated that autogestion might develop out of labor conflicts. The most famous case in this context was that of Lip, a watch-maker in Eastern France who experienced serious difficulties and wanted to liquidate the business. The workers refused to accept that decision and continued production, taking over management and sales as well. Despite considerable harassment by the government, the firm had some successes. When it went bankrupt in 1976, it was questioned whether that was not the result of the government's selective refusal to extend credit. Le Nouvel Observateur, 12 April 1976, pp. 40-41.

54. In Priouret's opinion, this reflects the Soviet experience with the "Workers' Opposition" during the chaos of the Civil War in Russia. Priouret, Les Francais mystifiés, p. 229. See also Jerry F. Hough and Merle Fainsod, How the Soviet Union Is Governed (Cambridge: Harvard University Press, 1979), pp. 98-102. Later on, the communists also used the word autogestion, but gave it a meaning compatible with their own model of a centralized economy, thus voiding the term of its original content.

4

THE COMMUNIST PERSPECTIVE

As already mentioned in the introduction to the preceding chapter, the French Communist party started to move out of its isolation during the second half of the 1960s, at a time when the Socialists were themselves starting to move leftwards (though this development was not consecrated until 1971, after a brief interlude in 1969). It is generally thought — and the Communists themselves agree — that the events of May 1968 played a major role in this process for both parties. For years, the French Communists had approached politics like a party that had no chance of coming to power in the near future; as a result, it had concerned itself more with the party's orthodoxy than with practical approaches to political change. May 1968 showed how much the party was out of touch with the workers, at the same time that it exposed the relative weakness of the regime. It may well be that the Communists, like the Socialists, felt the need to take up the challenge and try to "co-opt the sprawling opposition movement by adopting its demands . . . ."[1] In any case, in December 1968 the Communist party adopted a new program, the <u>Manifeste de Champigny</u>. It drew the outlines of a Socialist society for France; many of its elements were taken over in the Common Program of the Left in 1972. The Champigny Manifesto was followed in 1971 by a program calling for a democratic government of popular union, in which the Communists offered to cooperate loyally with any group or party that was seriously committed to the democratic transformation of the country; the Communist party, the program proclaimed, would not seek hegemony over such an alliance.[2]

Thus the P.C. had clarified its goals before negotiating the Common Program — the establishment of socialism in France. To the Communists, socialism means the collective ownership of all (not just some) means of production and exchange, the exercise of political power by the working class allied with other working strata of society, the progressive satisfaction of the steadily growing material and intellectual needs of the population, and the creation of conditions conducive to the free development of the personality.[3] The Common Program seemed a step in the right direction. It would create the best conditions for winning over the majority of the people to accept the necessity of a truly socialist transformation of society, and thus represent a transition towards socialism, the "fundamental goal" that the Communists could "in no way renounce."[4]

While the Common Program thus fell short of the ultimate goals, it did meet the minimum conditions for a serious transition. In the words of the Communist leader Georges Marchais, these conditions were twofold: a minimum threshold of change that would set the country on a new path and do so from the very beginning of the new legislature, and a provision for the intervention of the masses in the implementation of the program, for the development of the struggle of the workers to consolidate the democratic orientation of the new government. At the time of the Champigny Manifesto, the Communist party still subscribed to the idea of the dictatorship of the proletariat.[5] It specified that the existing democratic parties and formations who would opt in favor of socialism would be able to participate fully in the political life of the country and enjoy all the rights and liberties guaranteed by the Constitution, but mentioned no such guarantee for the other parties and groups.[6] (The P.C. dropped the dictatorship of the proletariat concept officially in 1976; it is true that it had accepted modifications for some years before then.)[7]

The crucial role of both Communist party and the working class in bringing about political change is stressed throughout the Manifeste de Champigny; it is interesting because it reflects the Communists' understanding of their own role in politics, an understanding which is helpful in analyzing their assessment of the situation after Mitterrand's election to the presidency. The manifesto states that the party, as vanguard of the proletariat, will not try to substitute itself for the state; however, it would outline at each stage the perspectives of socialist development, propose the measures which would allow the realization of these perspectives, and finally (and most importantly) "organize the great masses for action to achieve the objectives defined."[8] René Andrieu, editor-in-chief of the communist daily L'Humanité, stated (in a book published shortly before the Champigny Manifesto) that it would be illusory to believe that a mere numerical majority in the National Assembly would be sufficient to bring about real change. For the new government to be able to carry out a mandate of change popular pressure was needed in order to neutralize the resistance of the minority to the decisions of the parliamentary majority.[9] Marchais used similar language in his preface to the Common Program. The realization of the reforms contained in that program, he wrote, would lead to a "veritable élan of participation of the workers, of the masses of the people, in the running and control of public affairs at all levels."[10]

Socialism in its Communist version remained the ultimate goal of the P.C.F.; the Common Program was an acceptable compromise because it promised a real improvement for the working class. Thus the Communists were quite clear about their ultimate objectives and the means to reach them. But what was their understanding of the French economy and its evolution, their interpretation of the problems that it was facing in the early 1970s?

The economic analysis of the Communists rests on one key notion: state monopoly capitalism. The theory was developed originally to explain the economic boom of the postwar decade; in the 1970s it was used also to explain the "environmental crisis," the economic stagnation and what was perceived as a governmental plan to impose austerity on the working class, even in Pompidou's days.[11]

State monopoly capitalism has several aspects. One of them is the domination of an increasing number of economic sectors by a few large corporations, a development which in France was sought and promoted by successive technocrats and Gaullist governments.[12] (The Communists use the term monopoly instead of oligopoly.) The rapid growth of these corporations, they claim, was possible only because it took place at the expense of other sectors of the economy. It fed on the systematic and parasitical destruction and absorption of public funds, as when the state assumed the cost of necessary infrastructure development or put at the monopolies' disposal goods and services (such as utilities or transportation) priced below their true cost.[13] In the eyes of the Communists, that is the real reason why public services and investments in such areas as schools, housing, hospitals, recreation, leisure and the like have fallen so far behind: the public funds which would be required to pay for these investments had been diverted previously and were used to finance the capital accumulation of the monopolies, at the expense of the welfare of the general population. The essence of growth under capitalism, in their view, is exclusively the growth of capital. If the population sometimes benefitted, it was only because the working class struggle was able to wring concessions from big capital.

Another essential aspect of state monopoly capitalism is that the monopolies are no longer institutions of private property and power, but are so closely linked to the state as to be in fact

inseparable from it.14 They use the state to limit public dissatisfaction, because otherwise the whole arrangement would be
endangered. They will make an attempt to please the public, not
only by maintaining the flow of commodities but also by ideological propaganda.15 But due to the exploitative character of the
monopolies, they can never in reality serve and fulfill human
needs. As a result, capitalism falls from one crisis into another,
and the so-called "environmental crisis" is just one in a series,
even though it might be more serious than some of the previous
ones. In any case, it is a crisis only of capitalism. A full
correction of the situation is possible only if the regime of
state monopoly capitalism is abolished altogether. This analysis
explains the importance attributed to the nationalizations; they
are much more important to the Communists than to the Socialists. Nationalization of the monopolies has to go hand in hand
with the conquest of political power; to separate these steps
does not make sense. Fortunately, the Communists proclaimed,
monopoly state capitalism was creating the conditions for its own
transcendence. By exploiting the whole population, it was producing a situation in which nearly everyone had an interest in
its suppression. Nearly all social groups could come together in
one great antimonopolist alliance.16

In the 1970s, state monopoly capitalism has entered a serious
crisis. Because of its tendency to waste human, technical, and
natural resources, capitalism can no longer develop the means of
production as fast as it used to in the past; also, it has pushed
the exploitation of its surroundings (workers, small business, the
state) so far that it can no longer extract monopoly profits from
it, at least not as easily as earlier on. As a result, growth, to
the extent that it is still taking place, now imposes even greater
hardships. Already in the past the monopolies modernized the
economy only at the expense of others, for example, resorting to
the depopulation of entire regions and putting great hardship on
small property owners.17

> Under the pretext of modernization, the regime has devel-
> oped an agricultural policy that aims to satisfy the de-
> mands of great capital: accelerate the exodus from the
> rural areas in order to depress the labor market; depress
> wholesale farm prices at a time when the costs of the
> farmers have gone up significantly . . . .

Monopoly state capitalism particularly exploits the small and
medium-sized firms:

> the large industrial, banking, and commercial groups im-
> pose on them their prices both when they sell to them or
> buy from them; on the other hand, they make arrange-

ments with the regime . . . to implement a fiscal, industrial and credit policy which is favorable to themselves but
which crushes the small and medium-sized firms.18

As a consequence, a whole population that lost its livelihood was
converging on the industrial centers. But nothing was prepared
for them: inadequate housing, inadequate transportation, inadequate public facilities such as schools, day care centers, hospitals and the like await them there. The necessary funds were
already appropriated by the capitalists for the construction of
the industrial infrastructure, which is financed by the capitalist
state.19

To the Communists, none of these hardships are necessary. In
part, the exodus from rural areas and collapsing small-scale firms
can be slowed down. In their view, these sectors can be modernized by the setting up of cooperatives.20 Appropriate measures
can be taken to provide more adequately for those who move to
(or live in) the cities. But all this requires a different ration-
ality, one based on human needs instead of the prevailing one
based on profits. Again, the obstacle to real improvement is
state monopoly capitalism.

As long as governmental and industrial circles had called for
high growth rates of the economy the Communists criticized this
as an effort to favor and accelerate the growth of monopoly
capital by the neglect and at the expense of popular needs.
Growth in their view was only an ideological cover — propounded
as the only way to improve the standard of living, increase employment, develop public services and investments, make work
more meaningful, and protect the environment.21 When in the
early 1970s a few people of the same bourgeoisie began to call
for a moderation of growth in the name of a more harmonious
development, environmental protection, preservation of resources
and even the abolition of poverty in the industrialized world,22
the Communists saw in this nothing but a maneuver. To them,
the real reasons for the call for moderation had to be looked
for elsewhere.

Ever since the days of Adam Smith and David Ricardo, they
argued, capitalism had taken economic growth for granted, and
viewed it as naturally good.23 If the bourgeois economists made
an about-face in the 1970s, something serious must have happened:

Fundamentally, the ideological turn, which expresses great
disorientation, results from the long crisis which state
monopoly capitalism has entered. Crisis of the system,
hence of the ideas that have supported it. If one speaks,
as Dennis Meadows does, of the "limits to growth," the
reason is that the limits of capitalism have suddenly
emerged. That is the major fact.24

Inflation and unemployment as much as pollution and reckless exploitation of resources are but symptoms and aspects of this latest crisis of capitalism.[25] Because of its logic (the maximization of profit) capitalism caused widespread poverty in the past. For the same reason, it now cannot protect the environment without creating unemployment.[26] It is not even able any longer to drown discontent in a wave of consumer goods.[27] It now runs into obstacles everywhere: popular dissatisfaction grows over the neglect of public services and investments, over the destructiveness of capitalist growth, and the deterioration of the environment. Added to this was the increase in oil prices. As a result, monopoly state capitalism is now forced to develop a new strategy: that of moderate or zero growth. Of course, that strategy solves none of the basic problems; however, it reduces their acuteness, and at the same time might create legitimacy for what would otherwise clearly appear as a repressive program of austerity, and even create support for the export of jobs to low-wage countries. The Communists want to unmask this strategy and show that the arguments put forward on its behalf are just so many mystifications.

Having become unable to give even the appearance of affluence, capitalism through its bourgeois propagandists now discovers the emptiness of the affluent society (société de consommation) and worries about the loss of true values.[28] Calls for moderate growth in the developed countries serve capitalism doubly; first by hiding its inability to come up with anything else under a mantle of virtue, and second by permitting the redirection of the investment flow to the countries of the third world where profits are still high and the old exploitative growth can still be practiced.[29] The bourgeois propaganda slogan that "we are all polluters" is designed to deflect the legitimate ire from the monopolies to "civilization in general"; it also holds the public to an impossible choice: "either the increase in material goods or the improvement of the environment."[30] Under this cover, an austerity program can be imposed and even appear legitimate; at the same time, the cost of pollution abatement can be transferred to the public.[31] Nor is this all: Extensive financing of pollution control research and technology by the state, that is, the public, creates a new and very profitable sector for the monopolies, so that instead of having to bear the cost of pollution out of their profits, the monopolies can increase those same profits by a skilled fraud.[32] The possibility of environmental catastrophe is something capitalism has caused. It now uses it to instill a false sense of solidarity, appeals to a concern for humanity as a whole conveniently sweep the class character of the present conflict under the rug. This is why every effort is made by bourgeois propagandists to demonstrate that the problems of ecology supposedly transcend class lines.[33]

According to the Communists, such an approach misstates all the important facts. Bourgeois propaganda claims that everyone is equally responsible for pollution; but in France the workers, and the salaried population in general, have no power, control neither production nor the conditions of their existence. By contrast, the bourgeois state and the monopolies control production, politics, and the media. It is they who are responsible for the degradation of nature, a consequence of their pursuit of profit. Under those circumstances, to appeal to the population in order to secure its "participation" in the battle against pollution is more than just a mystification; it is an attempt: "to integrate the workers into the system, which amounts to making them pay for the effects of capitalism and to having them accept passively — and why not actively — their exploitation within the firm as well as outside of it."[34] For all these reasons the environmental campaign is nothing but an attempt at imposing a policy of regression and reaction on the working class with the latter's help.[35] From this perspective, it becomes clear why Marchais reacted so violently against the Mansholt memorandum, during the 1972 referendum on the entry of additional countries into the Common Market.[36]

As a group, the Communists (or rather the carriers of the party orthodoxy)[37] are probably the most optimistic segment of French society when it comes to assessing the potential of modern industry, science, and technology. For them, the situation is simple: if it were not for capitalism, there would be no problem. According to their statements, the Soviet Union has no environmental problems, or none it is not coping with effectively.[38] Socialism will permit the full and rational use of technology and resources. There is no such thing as a "danger" of progress — the very idea of it shows that the bourgeoisie has lost faith in its own future.[39]

Communist economic policy would therefore encourage strong growth: growth of private consumption, but also growth of public services and investments. To them, the two go together; it is capitalist strategy to play one against the other.[40] The same thing is true for better environmental protection — its development does not mean a reduction in consumption, as bourgeois ideologists would have it. The starting point for all these measures is the Common Program and the introduction, through it, of a new logic of the economy: one which is not geared to private profit but to the satisfaction of public and private human needs. As a result, growth would no longer mean the growth of capital, but the growth of production as a means to economic and social progress.[41] This cannot happen as long as monopolies have a hold on the productive system which is in fact a stranglehold, because under their influence, "Malthusianism . . . is hampering the country and every one of its citizens."[42]

Would Communists want to see a change in production and consumption patterns? There is little to support such an idea. To be sure, Communists have expressed their aversion against advertising, or the needless variety offered with respect to certain goods. But they have done so in the name of efficiency, because these things represent waste and only make the goods more expensive. Yet on the whole, the Communists are in favor of the affluent society. As the leader of the French Communist party, Georges Marchais, has written:

> We . . . are for a society of abundance and not for austerity. We do not oppose the pleasures of life to virtue. We want everyone to have at his disposition materials goods in sufficient amounts, varied and pleasant. . . .[43]

Another author is willing to allow for the possibility that consumption patterns might change; but he warns about the dangers of too abrupt a change: That could "make very difficult the daily life of millions of people. Not only because of their habits which have to be taken into account, but also because of the existing infrastructures and the complex organization which corresponds to them."[44] Besides, the Left cannot expose itself to the accusation of ruining industry or to impose austerity. And in any case, any such fundamental change could not be decided without being preceded by a full democratic debate.[45] In practice, the Communist leaders were among the most ardent defenders of such projects as the supersonic aircraft Concorde or the French nuclear energy program, at a time when both projects came under attack in the 1970s. In this, and more generally in their enthusiasm for growth and nationalism, they had much in common with their foremost adversaries, that is, the Gaullists.

For several years, the Communists were loyal supporters of the Union of the Left, in the name of the Common Program. In 1974, they supported Mitterrand's bid for the presidency early on, despite the fact that Mitterrand downplayed the program somewhat. Things began to change as the Socialist party placed greater emphasis on autogestion, as a result of the Assises du socialisme in late 1974.[46] At the same time, the economic crisis began to leave its mark. The Communists refused to admit that anything should be changed in the Common Program, in the sense of moderating the demands and promises outlined there. When the Socialists appeared hesitant about what policy to follow (they leaned towards a more modest interpretation of the program), the Communists tried to force the issue and stepped up their demands. Eventually, this led to the spectacular breakup of the Union of the Left in the fall of 1977, and the accusation that the Socialists wanted to manage the crisis in the interest

of big capital.[47] This last line prevailed until the second round
of the presidential election of 1981.

NOTES

1. Mark Kesselman, "The French Left and the Transformation
of French Society: Sisyphus Revisited," in Andrews and Hoffmann, eds., The Fifth Republic at Twenty, p. 196; and Roger
Priouret, Les Francais mystifiés, p. 201.

2. Pour un gouvernement démocratique d'union populaire
(October 1971); cited by George Marchais in his preface to the
Common Program; Programme commun de gouvernement du Parti
Communiste et du Parti Socialiste (Paris: Editions sociales,
1972), p. 21.

3. Manifeste de Champigny, published in Cahiers du communisme, January 1969. Cited from Priouret, Les Francais mystifiés,
p. 204.

4. Georges Marchais in preface to Programme commun, p. 39.

5. René Andrieu, Les communistes et la révolution (Paris:
Fulliard, 1968), p. 231.

6. Manifeste de Champigny, cited in Priouret, Les Francais
mystifiés, pp. 207-08.

7. Frank L. Wilson, "The French Left in the Fifth Republic,"
in Andrews and Hoffmann, eds., The Fifth Republic at Twenty, pp.
174-75.

8. Manifeste de Champigny, cited in Priouret, Les Francais
mystifies, p. 212.

9. Andrieu, Les communistes et la révolution, p. 241. See
also Priouret, Les Francais mystifiés, pp. 207 and 217.

10. Marchais, preface to Programme commun, p. 33-34.

11. Mark Kesselman, "The Economic Analysis and Programme
of the French Communist Party; Consistency Underlying Change,"
in Philip G. Cerny and Martin A. Schain, French Politics and
Public Policy (New York: St. Martin's Press, 1980), p. 182.

12. Andrew Shonfield, Modern Capitalism (Oxford: Oxford
University Press, 1969), p. 148; John M. Blair, Economic
Concentration (New York: Harcourt, Brace, Jovanovitch, 1972),
pp.112-13.

13. "Les huit visages de Giscard d'Estaing," collective
article in Economie et politique, April-May 1974, p. 14.

14. Bernard Marx, "Sur la crise," Economie et politique,
January 1975, p. 14.

15. Jean-Claude Poulain, "Les questions sociales au centre
de l'affrontement idéologique," Economie et politique, September
1974, p. 11. Alsdo Jean-Claude Dufour and Patrice Grevet, "La
politique sociale démocratique," ibid., pp. 112-13.

16. Marchais in preface to Programme commun, p. 41: "The popular union is the union of all the social strata that are victims of big capital and its policy"; it is composed of the working class, the technicians and engineers, the immense mass of peasants, employees, shopkeepers, artisans, teachers, intellectuals and artists, small and medium businessmen, of youth, democrats, Christians, patriots, and so on.

17. Claude Quin and Philippe Herzog, Ce que coûte le capitalisme à la France (Paris: Editions sociales, 1973), pp. 54-59.

18. Economie et politique, April-May 1974, pp. 14-16.

19. Guy Biolat, Marxisme et environnement (Paris: Editions sociale, 1973), pp. 24-25 and 59-60, and Louis Perceval, "The Crisis of Capitalism and the Environment," World Marxist Review, November 1975, pp. 131-38.

20. See note 17; also Priouret, Les Francais mystifiés, p. 222.

21. Pierre Juquin, "Reflexions sur crise et croissance," Cahiers du communisme, January 1975, pp. 33-34.

22. Among the authors of the "bourgeoisie" are cited in particular the Club of Rome, Lionel Stoléru, Claude Gruson, and Valéry Giscard d'Estaing. See Bernard Marx, "Sur la crise," Economie et Politique, (January 1975); and Guy Pelachaud, "'Zero Growth': Ideology and Politics," World Marxist Review, June 1975, pp. 72-80.

23. This assertion is somewhat questionable for France, where "Malthusianism" had a strong influence in the 19th and early 20th centuries. However, this changed dramatically after World War II.

24. Pierre Juquin, "Réflexions sur crise et croissance," p. 32.

25. Guy Biolat, Marxisme et environnement, p. 14; and Bernard Marx, "Sur la crise," p. 34.

26. Pierre Juquin, "Réflexions sur crise et croissance," pp. 42-43.

27. Biolat, Marxisme et environnement, p. 144.

28. Jean-Claude Dufour and Patrice Grevet, "La politique sociale démocratique," pp. 19-20.

29. Juquin, "Réflexions sur crise et croissance," p. 42-43.

30. Biolat, Marxisme et environnement, p. 148.

31. Juquin, "Réflexions sur crise et croissance," p. 37.

32. Biolat, Marxisme et environnement, pp. 16-19 and 167.

33. Marx, "Sur la crise," p. 5; Juquin, "Réflexions sur crise et croissance," p. 37; and Pelachaud, "'Zero Growth,'" p. 79.

34. Biolat, Marxisme et environnement, pp. 150-52.

35. Marx, "Sur la crise," p. 4.

36. In February 1972, Sicco Mansholt, vice-president of the European Commission, deeply impressed by Donella H. Meadows, et al., The Limits to Growth (New York: New American Library, 1972), proposed several measures for study by the Commission.

They included: limitation of the birth rate (possibly by suppressing aid to large families);   priority to food production; strong reduction of per capital consumption of material goods, compensated for by an increase in the supply of nonmaterial goods (leisure, self-realization, social security);   extending the lifetime of industrial products;   fiscal advantages to "clean and recyclable" production;   and the like.   The memo was at first ignored by the press;   but it was highly publicized by the French Commuists during the referendum on the Common Market. For the text of the memo and the succeeding controversy, see La lettre Mansholt (Paris: Pauvert, 1972).

37.   In this they are in an interesting contrast with the Communist voters, who according to public opinion research are among the most pessimistic.   See Chapter Five.

38.   Biolat, Marxisme et environnement, pp. 51-52 and 66.

39.   Ibid., pp. 110 and 132-36.

40.   Marx, "Sur la crise," p. 15.

41.   Quin, Ce que coûte le capitalisme à la France, pp. 171-76.

42.   Pelachaud, "'Zero Growth,'" p. 80.

43.   George Marchais, Le défi democratique (Paris: Grasset, 1973).   Quoted in "Pour une croissance civilisée," Cahiers francais, September-October, 1973.

44.   Juquin, "Réflexions sur crise et croissance," pp. 44-45.

45.   Ibid., p. 45.

46.   See Chapter Three note 34.

47.   George Marchais, "Introduction," Programme commun de gouvernement actualisé (Paris: Editions sociales, 1978), p. 9.

5
PUBLIC OPINION

The preceding chapters described the different positions that the major political groups took toward economic policy in the early 1970s. All of these groups were favorable to growth. Some, it is true, had reservations (thus the Centrists, who were alone even to contemplate a slowdown in the rate of growth as a real possibility). Others — the Left, and in particular the Communists — questioned what they perceived as the capitalist pattern of growth while extolling growth that would follow a different "logic." This overwhelmingly favorable attitude towards growth among elites was itself a phenomenon that dates from the postwar period. Stanley Hoffmann and Charles Kindleberger have described the change from the earlier, "stalemate" society, when growth was often perceived as a threat to established situations and thus blocked at every corner. They both argued that after World War II, there was a noticeable change among French elites, who were determined to foster growth as part of their overall determination to promote the renewal of the country as a whole. But both Hoffmann and Kindleberger see the change as going deeper, extending also to the French citizenry.[1]

The early 1970s probably brought a change in this general pattern. Throughout the industrial world, growth was suddenly questioned. Its cost for society, the individual, and the environment, which had so long been neglected, suddenly became a subject of widespread concern. This was a general phenomenon in advanced industrial countries. A report to the secretary general of the OECD, published in 1970, stated that

Faith in growth has been replaced by a feeling of unease in the face of the prospects opened by it . . . far from bringing only benefits, it is accompanied by more or less traumatic effects, less and less acceptable to large sectors of public opinion.[2]

France, with its high growth rates during the 1960s and the early 1970s, was not likely to represent an exception in this regard.

The present chapter makes an attempt to describe the attitudes and expectations that the French had with regard to economic development and proposed economic policies. Most of the evidence comes from public opinion surveys that offered the respondents a choice among a limited number of answers. This is not ideal -- unstructured, open-ended interviews might have been preferable. However, we know of no such work conducted during this time period. The surveys were usually based on a sample of about 1,000 cases, and were carried out by respected public opinion research institutes. Fortunately, they offer a wide variety of choices — perhaps May 1968 helped in raising new questions and thus contributed to a lively public debate.

There is one respect in which the questions presented to the respondents are very much characteristic of the early 1970s or more generally of the long boom that was coming to an end. What is striking about them are the choices which they offer. On the whole, they offer choices between kinds of "goods" (rather than between two or more "evils"). Shall the resources created by economic progress be devoted primarily to consumer goods, to public investments, or to the third world? Whatever the choice, all answers imply that economic progress is a fact, and that it will add to the range of objectives that society can set for itself. In the second half of the 1970s, these things could no longer be assumed as easily.

Back to the questions. In general, respondents were asked to make choices that were structured for them essentially by public debates or controversies at the time. Some of the choices were implicit in the economic policies advocated by this or that particular group; others corresponded to proposals coming from alternative elites, such as intellectuals or the ecology movement. The choices can be grouped under several headings. They concern economic modernization; economic growth, technological progress and the protection of the environment; the reduction of social inequalities; the development of public services and investments and that of private consumption; the economic power of France; and finally, strategies for reform. Our purpose is to find out how these objectives were ranked by French respondents in terms of priority. It is of course important to remember that the responses have to be viewed in the context of developments prevailing at the time. When private consumption is growing rapidly, its further promotion may safely be assigned a relatively low priority; on the other hand, public services and investments will appear all the more urgent the more their development is lagging.

For the first ten years of the Fifth Republic, there was considerable continuity in terms of public policy. This was changed first by the events of May 1968, and then by Pompidou's election to the presidency and the subsequent drive for industrialization. In May 1969 a survey outlined different ways in which economic modernization could be implemented, and asked respondents to react to them. The difference consisted above all in the fact that some of the formulations stressed the social costs involved in this process, while others did not mention them. The survey results showed that economic modernization as such was widely accepted — but only as long as it did not lead to serious difficulties. Problems (such as "the closing down of non-profitable businesses and localized unemployment") would greatly divide the public. The polarization in this case followed well-established political lines, with resistance strongly increasing as one moved from right to left. Political orientation predicted reactions more effectively than occupational category. However, occupational differences were also very important. Only executives and members of the liberal professions were strongly in favor of economic modernization (in the current survey also farmers — but it must be pointed out that they were not likely to be affected by the social costs mentioned in the survey question). On the other hand, workers were strongly opposed, a phenomenon that is in line with the conclusions of Gérard Adam's book on French workers.[3] According to the Delouvrier report, one would expect small business (shopkeepers, artisans) and farmers also to be opposed.[4] Small business as a category does not show up in the survey under consideration, but there is probably a strong small-business element in the second group ("manufacturers and businessmen"), which would explain that group's ambiguous attitude. If the survey had mentioned the costs of modernization to farmers, it seems likely that their reaction would have been different as well. Laurence Wylie, who had studied "typical" villages in France during the 1950s and again during the 1960s, returned there one more time in 1973. He found that vast changes had taken place. Most of the farmers were no longer there. In one village, one of the few farmers who was left was obviously in a deep depression.

He began to talk about the problem he had fixed on as causing his depression. Bourdin finds the Government and the whole economic system is against him, and he has given up trying to fight them. . . . he has stopped going to his fields. His asparagus had not been harvested. His cherries would not be picked. His melons could rot on the vine.

TABLE 5.1

Modernization of the Economy (in percent)

According to candidate preference in the 1969 presidential elections:

	Total	Pompidou (UDR)	Poher (Centrist*)	Defferre (Socialist*)	Duclos (Communist)
Our economy has to be modernized because one cannot indefinitely assist those economic sectors made obsolete by progress.					
Agree	69	77	70	65	79
Disagree	9	7	11	21	5
If one has to choose between rapid modernization of the economy and the protection of the population categories threatened by it, it is better to choose modernization.					
Agree	47	59	49	30	39
Disagree	31	22	32	57	46
The economy has to be modernized without delay even if this means temporary difficulties such as the closing down of nonprofitable businesses and localized unemployment.					
Agree	41	51	44	29	27
Disagree	39	34	38	57	59

Undecided responses are not listed.

	Total	Executive, Liberal Professions	Manufacturer and Businessman	Employee	Blue-Collar Worker	Retired/ Unemployed	Farm

If one has to choose between rapid modernization of the economy and the protection of the population categories threatened by it, it is better to choose modernization.

	Total	Executive, Liberal Professions	Manufacturer and Businessman	Employee	Blue-Collar Worker	Retired/ Unemployed	Farm
Agree	47	54	46	49	44	46	49
Disagree	31	36	29	39	33	27	24

The economy has to be modernized without delay even if this means temporary difficulties such as the closing down of nonprofitable businesses and localized unemployment.

	Total	Executive, Liberal Professions	Manufacturer and Businessman	Employee	Blue-Collar Worker	Retired/ Unemployed	Farm
Agree	41	64	41	44	33	35	49
Disagree	39	25	39	44	47	42	27

*The equation Poher-Centrist and Defferre-Socialist is somewhat questionable; Poher attracted more than just the Centrist vote, and Defferre far less than the regular Socialist vote.

Source: Survey by IFOP, 13-15 May 1969, IFOP report No. 7.085.

TABLE 5.2
Objectives for Economic Development (in percent)*

What two goals should be given priority in the economic development of a country such as France?

	Total	UDR (Gaullists)	Rep. Indep. (Giscard)	Centrists (Lecanuet)	Noncommunist Left	Communists
Reduction of inequalities	55	45	47	54	70	65
Protection of environment	31	38	35	38	28	22
Reduce work, more leisure	25	21	17	23	29	42
Develop public investments, services	25	21	32	23	21	28
Increase French economic power	23	34	30	20	19	10
Aid to underdeveloped countries	15	21	18	25	10	7
Development of individual consumer goods (domestic appliances, cars, television sets, and so on)	12	10	14	8	11	17
No opinion	5					

What two goals should be given priority in the economic development of a country such as France?

	Total	Executive, Liberal Professions	Junior Executive	Blue-Collar Worker	Retired/ Unemployed	Farm	Shopkeeper/ Artisan
Reduction of inequalities	55	49	60	50	58	56	62
Protection of environment	31	34	35	24	38	23	35
Reduce work, more leisure	25	14	29	41	17	11	17
Develop public investments, services	25	37	29	22	22	27	23
Increase French economic power	23	44	26	17	25	16	21
Aid to underdeveloped countries	15	13	9	13	16	29	12
Development of individual consumer goods (domestic appliances, cars, television sets, and so on)	12	6	7	17	8	17	18
No opinion	5						

*Totals superior to 100 percent since the respondents could give two answers.
Source: Survey by SOFRES, 30 June–7 July 1972, published in Metra, vol. 11, no. 4, p. 747.

> Bourdin may need a psychiatrist, but he had fixed on a
> rationalization that no one could dispute. Most of the
> farmers of Peyrane felt the same way about the system.
> . . . The very protection given the small farmers for
> decades proved their undoing. . . . Faced with the compe-
> tition of the Common Market, the Bourdins of France
> cannot survive.[5]

In the summer of 1972, a survey offered a wide range of
choices with regard to priority objectives for economic development, ranging from "reduction of social inequalities" to "development of consumer goods" to the economic power of France and
many other choices. Very striking is the fact that in every
group, whether political or occupational, the reduction of
inequalities (largely the equivalent of reducing differences in
income and wealth) figured so prominently. Again, ideological
differences are more prominent that occupational ones, and, not
surprisingly, Leftist voters are more committed to redistribution
than those of the Right.

There is in fact much evidence that the French in the early
1970s viewed the prevailing distribution of wealth as failing to
meet the requirements of justice. Thus differences in the
standard of living were not considered legitimate by a sample of
French blue-collar workers surveyed in 1971 and 1972.[6] Moreover, such an opinion prevailed not only among blue-collar
workers, but among most groups of French society.[7]

Next on the list of objectives for economic development came
the protection of the environment and the reduction of working
time. On these two issues, there is again a clear polarization
along the political spectrum. Voters from the Right give greater
emphasis to environmental protection (as long as it does not
conflict with economic growth? In the present survey question
there certainly is no hint of such a conflict); they are also
relatively less interested in the reduction of working time. On
the left, and particularly among the Communists, reducing the
time of work is given greater importance than environmental
protection. This orientation receives its strongest support quite
clearly from blue-collar workers and (to a much lesser extent)
from employees; it also is very strong among respondents under
the age of 35.[8]

It is interesting to note that the relative emphasis given to
environmental protection does not correspond to respondent's
perception of industrial and technical progress. Respondents
from the Left are in fact more likely to express worry about the
dangers of pollution or to be opposed to the construction of a
nuclear power plant near their homes, and quite generally are
more pessimistic about the prospects of industrial civilization.
Again this tendency is particularly pronounced among blue-collar

TABLE 5.3
Opinions on Technical Progress, Pollution, (in percent)

	Total	UDR (Gaullists)	Rep. Indep. (Giscard)	Centrists (Lecanuet)	Noncommunist Left	Communists
Do you think that because of pollution, technical and industrial progress will bring more advantages or more disadvantages?[a]						
More advantages	23	26	32	33	25	16
More disadvantages	48	48	42	42	52	52
Do you think that pollution is: not so serious/an underestimated danger?[b]						
Not so serious	18	19	19	20	14	10
Underestimated	77	76	76	73	77	90
Are you personally worried about the damages inflicted by our industrial civilization? (1974)[c]						
Yes	80	73	73	82	85	86
No	14	20	20	15	10	6
Would you be opposed to a nuclear power plant built within less than 15 kilometers of your house?[d]						
Opposed	57	53	53	55	68	70
Not opposed	28	38	38	33	24	21

[a]Survey by IFOP, 9–16 November 1971; published in Sondages, no. 3(1972), p. 120.
[b]survey by PUBLIMETRIE, March 1973 (published in R. Muraz, La parole aux Francais [Paris: Dunod, 1977], p. 102.
[c]survey by PUBLIMETRIE, 25–26 April 1974 (Muraz, La parole aux Francais, p. 101).
[d]survey by PUBLIMETRIE, 5–8 April 1975 (R. Muraz, La parole aux Francais, p. 99).

workers. This phenomenon is all the more remarkable since it clashes with the official line of the Communist leadership, which takes a very optimistic view of these matters.

On the list of objectives for economic development, the expansion of public services and investments is an important goal, cited twice as often as the development of private consumption. But while support for public services and investments is spread fairly evenly among the different categories of respondents, private consumption gets a different reception. Here it is occupational distinctions which bring out the greatest differences. Shopkeepers and artisans, farmers and blue-collar workers attach a relatively greater importance to consumption. But on the whole, it must be noted that this is a low priority for all groups. Even among blue-collar workers, the reduction of the work effort is given much greater emphasis; such a reduction may take the form of earlier retirement, reduced taxes, or equal pay with less work.

TABLE 5.4
Images of Economic Progress

What does economic progress represent to you?	Total	Employees	Blue-Collar Workers
Earlier retirement	51	41	65
Pay less taxes	41	31	39
More interesting, less tiring work	28	37	18
Make as much money with less work	26	30	34
Be able to buy more things	20	23	19
Have more leisure	17	30	16
No opinion	5	2	2

Note: Respondents could make two choices. Total less than 200% since some respondents only made one choice.
Source: Survey by IFOP, June 6-12, 1972.

What about the goal of increasing the economic power of the French nation? On this point there is the strongest political polarization in the whole survey. Support for this objective falls dramatically as one moves from the Gaullists to the Communists. It is noteworthy that even for the Gaullists, the objective is given somewhat less importance than that of protecting the environment (a stark contrast with the priorities of the Gaullist leadership at that time). Another survey shows that this result is not just accidental or insignificant. In the same year, a poll of students at the Grandes Ecoles, the training ground for the French technostructure in business and the state, showed similar thinking. A majority of these students held that the actual goals of growth in France were the pursuit of international power and the increase of business profits. But for the most part, the future elites voiced their disagreement with this emphasis. Growth, most of them thought, should serve instead to promote well-being and social justice.[9]

It is interesting to compare the above survey results with the policies followed (or advocated) by the different political groups. Pompidou's emphasis on industrialization, economic growth, and individual prosperity (and also on French economic power) clearly had only limited appeal, though they drew stronger support from the Right than from the Left. This orientation was evident from other signs and developments as well. Poujade, the first French minister of the environment, noted a big change in 1971. He wrote that all of a sudden, the rush into industrialization came to a halt and gave way to hostility.[10] In many communities, industrial projects were held up by energetic local opposition groups; this movement did not start with nuclear power plants, though that is the area where it soon became most visible.[11]

In terms of their attitudes towards economic policy or generally economic development, the Centrists and the Socialists did in fact occupy the middle ground in the early 1970s. This may not be surprising; however, it shall be noted here since it was no longer true, by the late 1970s, for the "Centrists" (the liberal Right). The next chapter will show this. Could such a similarity of views have served as the basis for a political coalition? This seemed to be ruled out by the political commitments of both Centrist and Socialist political leaders. The institutions of the Fifth Republic contributed to discourage centrist experiments.

Respondents whose political sympathies go to the Communist party are most likely to resist economic modernization. They (and the Socialists) give the greatest emphasis to the reduction of inequalities and the reduction of working time. They also care least about French economic power. In addition, they are most pessimistic about the future of industrial society and in particular about technical progress. On this last point their views clash directly with those of the Communist leaders, who stress the untapped potential of technical progress and the need to free it from its current constraints and distortions which, they argue, result entirely from the current capitalist environment. As a whole, the Communist electorate appears much more interested in social protection than in aggressive policies of growth and modernization.

As to the nationalizations, an essential point of the Common Program, they were quite popular in the mid-1970s, as Table 5.5 shows.

TABLE 5.5
Nationalization of Key Firms

Personally, what is your position on the nationalization of the big firms in the following sector — are you for or against?[a]

	For	Against	Do Not Know
Private banks	42	38	20
Insurance companies	52	34	15
Electronics industry	45	34	21
Chemical and pharmaceutical industry	61	25	14
Iron and steel industry	49	31	20
Automobile industry	48	36	16

Are you for or against the nationalization, in the near future, of certain key sectors of French industry (for example, iron and steel, automobiles, electronics, chemicals, banking sector)?[b]

For	Against	Do Not Know
48	39	13

Source: [a]Survey by IFOP, 6 January 1976 (published in L'Humanité, 8 January 1976); [b]survey by IFOP, 24-25 February 1976.

In sum, the political strength of the Gaullists during this time period was probably not based on the popularity of their economic and social policies. The Gaullist goal of grandeur through effort, though considerably scaled down by Pompidou, was still very ambitious, and met with only lukewarm support even among many Gaullist voters. The blue-collar workers, though they were meant to benefit from some of these growth policies (absorption of unemployment and continuous wage increases resulted mainly from this rapid growth) were not attracted to the Gaullist camp. Pompidou failed to regain the support that de Gaulle had received from blue-collar workers, at least before 1968.[12]

By contrast, the Common Program of the Left responded to some very important (and possibly quite deeply felt) preoccupations — the reduction of inequalities, the reduction of working time, and so on. However, its strongly pro-growth orientation must have disappointed many voters in the center who sympathized with the Left. In particular, the nascent ecology movement (which met with considerable sympathy in the country, though it could not translate this into political support)[13] was strongly repelled by the Common Program's emphasis on growth and its blindness to the attendant problems; this despite the fact that the "ecologists" were also highly critical of the government's growth policies and were generally closer to the Left (in its autogestion version). Quite generally, the Left had been out of power for so long that there must have been considerable doubts about its ability to handle the affairs of the French nation. Finally, it was handicapped by the fear of Communism. The renaissance of the Socialist party was still so recent, its strengths so fragile, and the organization of the Communists apparently so much superior, that there were widespread doubts as to whether the Socialists could hold their own in a coalition government with the Communists.[14]

This leads to an apparently paradoxical conclusion — namely, that the Right maintained itself in power despite its economic policy, while the Left kept losing electoral competitions even though it had a policy that might have been more attractive to most French voters if it could have been separated from the political problems that surrounded its application. In any case, the results of the 1974 elections were close, much closer than those of 1973, and in the following years a victory of the Left was increasingly perceived as a realistic possibility. This perception in turn greatly influenced the economic policy of Giscard (at least in the first two years of his presidency) as well as the political behavior of his Gaullist coalition partners.

NOTES

1. Stanley Hoffmann, "Paradoxes of the French Political Community," pp. 39-43 and 61-65; Charles P. Kindleberger, "The Postwar Resurgence of the French Economy," pp. 156-58; both in Stanley Hoffman et al., In Search of France (New York: Harper & Row, 1963). Also S. Hoffmann, "Conclusion: The Impact of the Fifth Republic on France," in Andrews and Hoffmann, The Fifth Republic at Twenty, pp. 451-52.

2. Science, Growth and Policy (Paris: OECD, 1971), p. 26. See also, Suzanne Berger, "Politics and Antipolitics in Western Europe in the Seventies," Daedalus, vol. 108, no. 1 (1979).

3. Gerard Adam, L'ouvrier francais en 1970 (Paris: Colin, 1971). His surveys show that few workers consider changing professions (38 percent) or moving to a different area (35 percent) in the wake of economic change; see p. 244.

4. The Delouvrier report mentions in particular small farmers, shopkeepers, small industrialists and artisans as those who "will

feel threatened by the modernization of the country . . . and tend to act as if they were under siege." Paul Delouvrier, et al., 1985, La France face au choc du futur, p. 166.

5. Laurence Wylie, "The New French Village, hélas," New York Times Magazine, 25 November 1973, pp. 65 and 67. See also Henri Mendras, Sociologie de la campagne française (Paris: Presses universitaires de France, 1971); and "Le paysan français," Dossiers et documents no. 25, Le Monde, November 1975, p. 2.

6. Duncan Gallie, "Trade Union Ideology and Workers' Conception of Class Inequality in France," West European Politics, vol. 3, no. 1 (1980), p. 14, shows the following results regarding the legitimacy of differences in standards of living among French and British workers:

	French workers	British workers
Completely just	10	46
Should be less great	60	38
Should be much less great/ no difference	30	16

7. IFOP survey cited in Sondages, no. 3 (1972), p. 128.

8. Among respondents ages 21 to 34 years, "reduction of working time/more leisure" was listed by 35 percent; this figure declined considerably with greater age. Survey by SOFRES, 30 June-7 July 1972, published in Métra, vol. 11, no. 4, (1972), p. 747.

9. SOFRES survey cited in Philippe d'Iribarne, La politique du bonheur (Paris: Le Seuil, 1973), pp. 160-61; and Robert Lattès, Pour une autre croissance (Paris: Le Seuil, 1972), p. 122.

10. Robert Poujade, Le ministère de l'impossible (Paris: Calmann-Lévy, 1975), p. 194.

11. Christian Garnier-Expert, L'environnement démystifié (Paris: Mercure de France, 1973), in particular pp. 63-87. The movement against nuclear power intensified (and may have reached its peak) in 1976-77, with a series of demonstrations and local "referenda" expressing their opposition. Only one single town voted in favor of nuclear power — Flamanville, a fishing village in Normandy. Pierre Samuel, Le nucléaire en questions (Paris: Editions Entente, 1975), p. 100; and Jean-Philippe Colson, Le nucléaire sans les Français? (Paris: Maspéro, 1977), p. 184 and passim.

12. Priouret, Les Français mystifiés, p. 108.

13. Francoise Bonnal, "L'évolution de l'opinion publique à l'égard de l'écologie au travers des sondages," paper presented at the symposium "Ecologisme et politique," Foundation Nationale des Sciences Politiques, Paris, September 1970, p. 31; and Daniel Boy, "Le vote écologiste en 1978," Revue française de science politique, vol. 32, no. 2 (April 1981).

14. Roger Priouret wrote in 1973 that the P.S. could count on 100,000 militants — who were largely amateurs in the field; the P.C.F. on the other hand had 400,000 "professionals" at its disposal, who could easily swamp the Socialists. Priouret, Les Francais mystifiés, p. 261.

PART II
FRANCE UNDER GISCARD D'ESTAING: EXTERNAL CONSTRAINTS AND INTERNAL DIVISIONS

6

STOP AND GO WITH JACQUES CHIRAC

Since 1974, five major approaches have been tried out in an attempt to cope with the seemingly intractable problems of the French economy. Under President Giscard, a brief period of deflation was followed by an equally short period of reflation. This was followed by a period of stabilization. In 1981, the Socialists made an effort to reflate again while avoiding the pitfalls of such a policy. In addition, they undertook major changes in the distribution of income, wealth, and economic power. In 1982 however, they had to embark on an austerity program that may last for several years. Such "stop-go" policies are quite uncharacteristic of French economic management in the postwar period.[1] One of the purposes of this book is to explore the conditions, political and economic, which led to the adoption of such policies.

In the 1970s the economy, in France as in many other industrial countries, entered a period of trouble. In fact, this trouble started in the 1960s, even if in retrospect that period was still marked by comparative stability. But it was in the 1960s that the American balance of payments problem began to significantly fuel inflation in Europe.[2] Several countries took measures to cope with this problem; in France one such measure was finance minister Giscard's plan de stabilisation, which in turn contributed to the explosion of 1968. International trade and monetary problems became increasingly serious in the early 1970s; inflation was on the rise, in France and in many other countries as well. Yet for a time, the French government was remarkably successful in achieving its goals. The years of the Pompidou presidency were marked by record growth rates,[3] and even the balance of payments showed a slight surplus from 1970 to 1973.[4] Finally, unlike many other major industrial countries,

GRAPH 6.1

France: Economic Growth, Industrial Production
and the Balance of Trade, 1969–1981

Economic Growth

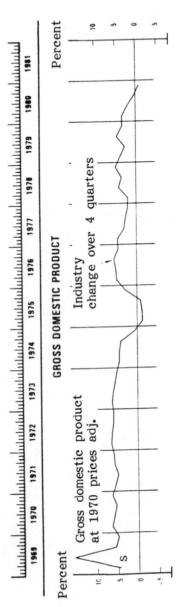

Index of Manufacturing Production

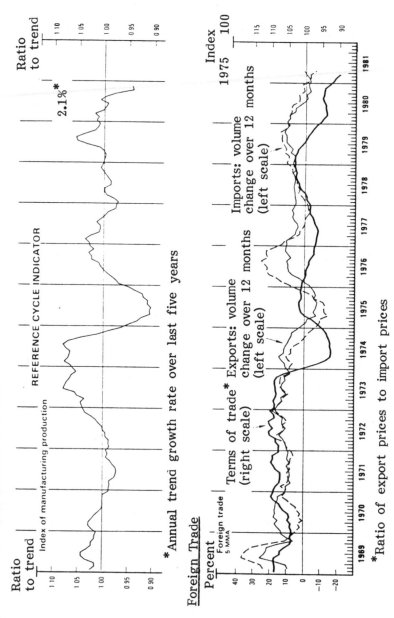

Ratio
to trend

1.10
1.05
1.00
0.95
0.90

Index of manufacturing production

REFERENCE CYCLE INDICATOR

Ratio
to trend

1.10
1.05
1.00
0.95
0.90

2.1%*

*Annual trend growth rate over last five years

Foreign Trade

Percent
Foreign trade
5 MMA

40
30
20
10
0
-10
-20

Terms of trade*
(right scale)

Exports: volume
change over 12 months
(left scale)

Imports: volume
change over 12 months
(left scale)

Index
1975 = 100

115
110
105
100
95
90

1969 1970 1971 1972 1973 1974 1975 1976 1977 1978 1979 1980 1981

*Ratio of export prices to import prices

Source: OECD, <u>Main Economic Indicators</u> (Paris: OECD, August 1981), pp. 46 and 47.

France did not experience an important unemployment problem,[5] and there was no decline in the rate of profit until 1973.[6]

The year 1974 marked the turning point. The quadrupling of oil prices, and considerable increases in the prices of other raw materials, created an important deficit in the balance of payments; at the same time, inflation (and thus interest rates) reached record levels. The first policy of Giscard, then newly elected president, was to deflate the French economy with his plan de refroidissement (cooling-off plan) of June 1974. It was thought that this would bring down interest rates, slow wage increases, and finally improve the balance of payments situation (as a recession would reduce imports more than exports).

The immediate results were considerably worse than expected. Exports did stay ahead of imports, but economic growth fell below zero. The fall was particularly marked for industrial production (Graph 6.1). Unemployment, which had been advancing slowly for some years, soared;[7] investment, which had grown with great continuity over the preceding decade, suddenly collapsed. Businesses sank deeper into debt still,[8] and bankruptcies more than doubled (Graphs 6.2 and 6.3). But while in most major industrial countries wage increases slowed down, in France the progression of real wages continued at a rapid rate.[9] This was probably due to the narrowness of the victory of Giscard over Mitterrand in 1974.[10] In any case, the position of labor was strengthened in other ways as well, as when the government in late 1974 proposed a law providing for unemployment compensation at 90 percent of the previous salary for one year and expanded restrictions upon business that inhibited dismissals of wage-earners at a time when production was falling and costs were rising.[11] As a result, the distribution of value added in industry (that is, the shares of value created going to labor costs, profits, and taxes, respectively) changed even more in favor of labor, whereas the share of capital (profits) fell to its lowest point since 1954.[12] The transfer of wealth from France to the OPEC countries, itself the inevitable result of the first choc pétrolier (oil shock) of 1974, was thus paid for almost entirely by French business firms. Their profits fell, while household incomes and consumption were maintained.[13]

As the negative effects of the plan de refroidissement became clear (the plan coincided with international developments which aggravated the deflationary impact), the government made a complete turnaround. The 1975 budget as passed by Parliament was balanced, but by early 1975 the government decided to speed up spending. In February 3.6 billion francs were released for the lowest-income groups. In March 4 billion were granted to business firms. In April another 16 billion were added to stimulate the economy; this was supplemented in June by the creation of 15,000 public service jobs, and grants for job creation in the private sector. Finally, in September, a plan de relance was launched, this time at a cost of 30.5 billion francs; roughly half of this was for investment.14 This process of reflation, and especially the plan de relance, was inspired by Jacques Chirac, then prime minister. This time the cost of adjustment to the oil shock was transferred from the business firms to the state; not surprisingly, this led to the large budget deficit of 1975 (38.2 billion francs).15 Within a brief period, the policy showed its results. Industrial production and economic growth started up again suddenly (Graph 6.1). The rise of unemployment came to a (temporary) halt in 1976.16 Profitability rose and the number of business bankruptcies declined (Graph 6.3); however, business indebtedness kept rising.17 Finally, not much was changed in the distribution of value added; there was only a slight shift from labor to capital.18 But the one single factor that doomed the relance Chirac more than anything else was the massive foreign trade deficit which it produced, and which upset the balance of payments, as economic stimulation led to a great increase of imports which was not paralleled by a similar increase in exports.19 Chirac seems to have realized as early as January 1976, only a few months after the plan de relance was started, that the situation would soon be untenable. Anticipating a deterioration of the situation which was bound to come (and would probably call for a new period of austerity), he urged Giscard to hold early parliamentary elections before the year 1978. Delay, he felt, would spell certain defeat for the Right.20 Giscard disagreed with this political analysis, counting on the break-up of the Leftist coalition and also on an improvement of the international economic situation. In early 1976 the trade gap widened; a policy reversal became unavoidable. In the summer, Chirac resigned, the plan de relance was scrapped, and Raymond Barre — at the time minister for foreign trade — was appointed prime minister, a charge that he cumulated at first with that of minister of finance and the economy. "France's best economist," as Giscard called him when he presented him to the nation, was to come up with a plan that would be closer to the inclinations of the president himself. At the time, Barre was not expected to stay in office very long. Since 1968, prime ministers had succeeded each other quite rapidly. Barre however lasted well beyond the three years which he had claimed were necessary for the success of his policy. Altogether he stayed for five years, the second longest term of any prime minister under the Fifth Republic (the longest one being that of Pompidou, from 1962 to 1968).

TABLE 6.1
France: Principal Foreign Trade Statistics

	1974	1975	1976	1977	1978	1979	1980
Cost of oil (billion francs)	43.9	39.7	49.4	55.6	52.0	65.5	107.6
Total cost of energy (billion francs)	49.7	45.3	57.7	64.7	62.3	78.3	125.5
Trade balance (billion francs)	-16.9	+6.8	-20.9	-11.5	+2.2	-13.6	-60.4
Balance of current account (billion francs)	-29.1	-0.3	-28.4	-14.8	+16.9	+4.9	-31.1
Exports (evolution in volume terms)	10.3	-3.0	9.6	8.5	6.4	7.3	3.4
Imports (evolution in volume terms)	5.5	-8.8	18.7	1.3	5.3	10.9	5.5
Foreign exchange reserves in December of each year (billion dollars)	3.7	7.4	4.4	4.7	8.3	9.9	14.1

Source: Raymond Barre, Une politique pour l'avenir, p. 78.

TABLE 6.2
France: Budget Deficits and Surpluses, 1973-1980
(excluding IMF and currency stabilization funds)

	1973	1974	1975	1976	1977	1978	1979	1980
Billion francs	+2.1	+5.5	-38.2	-20.2	-18.3	-34.3	-37.6	-30.3
As percent of GDP	+0.2	+0.4	-2.6	-1.2	-1.0	-1.6	-1.5	-1.1

Source: Raymond Barre, Une politique pour l'avenir, p. 78.

GRAPH 6.2
Investment of French Business Firms, Evolution 1963-1980
Logarithmic table
(investments in millions of Francs, at 1970 value)

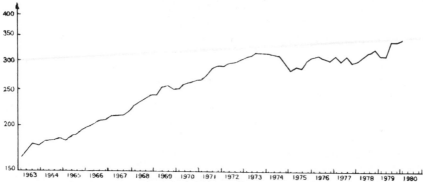

Source: Jacky Fayolle, "Le comportement d'investissement depuis 1974," Economie et statistique, No. 127 (November 1980), p. 34.

GRAPH 6.3
Bankruptcies of Industrial Enterprises in France, 1971-1980
Logarithmic table; number of bankruptcies per month.
Corrected for seasonal variations

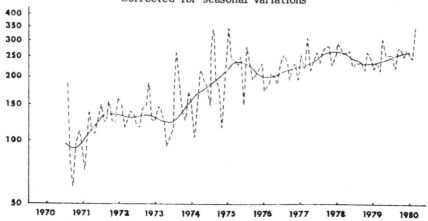

Based on data from the INSEE.
Source: Bulletin du Crédit National (January 1981), p. 26.

NOTES

1. But then the economic crisis of the 1970s has changed many things. Britain was long famous for its "stop-go" policies, but Margaret Thatcher seems to have put the British economy quite clearly in "reverse." See Graph 7.2.

2. David P. Calleo and Benjamin M. Rowland, America and the World Political Economy (Bloomington: Indiana University Press, 1973), pp. 88-93.

3. This was the time of the optimistic predictions made by the Hudson Institute, Paris; see Edmund O. Stillman, et al., L'envol de la France dans les années 80 (Paris: Hachette, 1973); see Chapter One of the present volume.

4. Paul Dubois, "La rupture de 1974," Economie et statistique, August 1980, p. 18.

5. Eurostat Review, 1970-1979 (Brussels: October 1980), p. 138.

6. Dubois, "La rupture de 1974," p. 16.

7. See Graph 7.3.

8. See Table 7.3.

9. Eurostat Review, 1970-1979, p. 148. From 1971 to 1973, Germany, Britain, the United States and Japan all had small increases in real wages. Among the major industrial countries, only Italy had rates comparable to France.

10. Pierre Cohen-Tanugi and Christian Morrisson, Salaires intérêts profits dans l'industrie française, 1968-1976 (Paris: Presses de la F.N.S.P., 1979), pp. 157-63.

11. Ibid., p. 146; and Yves Meffredi, "Quelle stratégie économique à moyen terme?," Projet, March 1978, pp. 327-36.

12. See Table 7.1. Also see Cohen-Tanugi and Morrisson, Salaires intérêts profits, p. 39 (citing C. Pheline), and pp. 219-20.

13. Raymond Barre, Une politique pour l'avenir (Paris: Plon, 1981), pp. 23 and 61.

14. Economic Surveys: France (Paris: OECD, January 1976), pp. 29-30.

15. Barre, Une politique pour l'avenir, pp. 25 and 61.

16. See Graph 7.3.

17. See Table 7.3.

18. See Table 7.2.

19. See Graph 6.1. Also, J. G. Mérigot, "Le plan Barre," Défense nationale. November 1976, pp. 99-109.

20. According to Arthur Conte, "Giscard m'a dit," Paris-Match, 6 March 1981, pp. 38-41, excerpting passages from Conte, L'homme Giscard (Paris: Plon, 1981).

7
THE BARRE POLICY:
RATIONALE AND RESULTS

Looking back to the time when he took office, Barre repeatedly stressed how much the situation in 1976 was approaching disaster. The balance of trade was seriously disturbed; inflationary wage settlements had created pressure throughout the economy; even if inflation rates themselves had not yet risen to a considerable extent, all the "symptoms of strong inflation" were present,[1] he stated. The consequences of the 1974 oil shock had not yet been faced adequately. In 1974, business firms had carried the main cost; as a result, Barre said, they had drastically cut back on their investments. Chirac's plan de relance transferred the cost to the State instead; this led to an increase in investments but to a strong budget deficit, and a weakening of the franc. Such a policy could not last; sooner or later discipline would have to be reimposed if French industry was to be able to confront the intensified competition in the world markets that was to characterize the decade to come.

In his public statements, Barre stressed the theme of inflation; initially this had a certain appeal with the public.[2] But disinflation for Barre was a very comprehensive process, and prices were not at the core of the Barre policy. Its main goal was to gradually strengthen French business firms through increasing their profitability, in particular by holding down wage increases,[3] a policy which would also have the result of holding down imports. The heart of the problem lay in the distribution of value added; here Barre tried to reverse a tendency which had started in the late 1960s. From 1959 to 1968, France's political stability (apart from the Algerian conflict) had its counterpart in the economic sector. The attitude of government towards business and labor during this time period was stable and consistent for a whole decade. The distribution of value added

TABLE 7.1
Distribution of Value Added, 1954-1973
(exclusive of agriculture; in percent)

	1954	1955	1956	1957	1958	1959	1960	1961	1962	1963	1964	1965	1966	1967	1968	1969	1970	1971	1972	1973
Wage and social costs	61.9	62.2	62.2	60.4	60.7	59.3	58.7	59.9	60.9	61.6	60.9	61.7	61.2	61.2	61.7	60.1	61.0	61.4	61.4	62.0
Global profit	14.5	15.3	15.5	17.0	15.4	18.4	19.7	19.3	18.8	18.3	19.1	18.7	19.5	19.7	20.3	21.8	21.2	20.6	20.7	20.2
Interest and dividends						5.3	5.3	5.3	5.2	5.2	5.2	5.3	5.1	5.1	5.5	5.9	6.6	6.7	6.7	6.9
Remuneration of individual entrepreneurs						9.2	9.2	8.7	8.5	7.8	7.7	8.0	7.8	8.5	8.0	7.3	7.2	7.2	7.1	6.8
Retained earnings						3.9	5.2	5.3	5.1	5.3	6.2	5.4	6.6	6.1	6.8	8.6	7.4	6.7	6.9	6.5
Other charges	23.6	22.5	22.4	22.6	23.9	22.4	21.6	20.9	20.4	20.1	20.0	19.7	19.3	19.0	17.9	18.1	17.8	18.0	17.8	17.8

Source: C. Phéline, "Répartition primaire des revenus et rentabilité du capital (1954-1973)," Statistiques et études financières, no. 19, 1975, p. 3.

by industry showed that the relative share of the state was declining, while the shares of labor and capital remained roughly stable, or rather increased in a parallel way (Table 7.1). This stable evolution was interrupted by the events of May 1968. Since that time, redistributional conflicts (under the heading inégalités sociales) have occupied a prominent place in French politics, from Chaban-Delmas' years as prime minister (1969-72) to the Common Program of the Left (1972), the presidential election of 1974, the goals of the Seventh Plan (1976-80) and the plan Barre. In the Grenelle agreements which settled the industrial conflict after May 1968, wages were increased dramatically. It was widely expected that this would bleed French business white. As a result, the government accorded exceptional assistance to private enterprise (including the devaluation of the franc). These measures went so far that in retrospect the years 1968 and particularly 1969 appear as years of extremely high profits; they even led to an overheating of the economy.[4] But the effect of the 1968 wage increases was only delayed. The years 1970 and 1971, marked by the socially progressive policies of Premier Chaban-Delmas, saw an important increase in the share of labor at the expense of that of capital. This process was slowed down under his more business-oriented successor Pierre Messmer, who governed from 1972 until Giscard's election in 1974. The year 1975 brought important changes in this distribution, again to the advantage of labor, and 1976, though reversing the trend, did not bring significant change. Business was far from regaining the ground which it had lost in the preceding year, and did not even approach the situation that had prevailed throughout the 1960s (Table 7.2).

Barre's reasoning was as follows: If wages could be held constant in real terms, then any increases in productivity would lead to higher profits (or more competitive prices), thus strengthening the financial situation of French firms in a durable way. Stronger and more export-oriented firms (as Barre stressed in 1978, 40 percent of all jobs in industry depended on exports[5]) would then proceed to make new investments and thus create new employment. In this way the French economic apparatus would be adapted to the changed international division of labor required both by the oil price increases and by French plans to become one of the world's leading industrial powers, on an equal level with West Germany. Success of the plan Barre would mean that more orders, more profits and more industrial employment would all converge on France. It was in the best interest of the French nation to practice a policy of economic liberalism on the international level; France would benefit from it by increasing her exports and by becoming one of the heartlands of the industrial world. Liberal rules also represented a most valuable help in enforcing the necessary discipline on French economic actors. Protectionism by contrast permitted the nation to fall behind without at first realizing it; its impact was therefore negative, no matter what the pretext. The only legitimate function for the state in the area of international competition was to smooth transitions in order to allow for an orderly adaptation, an orderly growth of international trade; it could never be to hold up change and adaptation altogether. The knowledge that they would have to succeed in the difficult international competition would prod French firms into an even better economic performance. Such a process of renovation would in time make France one of the victorious powers to emerge from the trade wars of the late 1970s and the 1980s.[6]

TABLE 7.2
Distribution of Value Added, 1973-1979 (in percent)

	1973	1974	1975	1976	1977	1978	1979
Rate of value added (i.e. relation of value added to business volume)	37.1	36.3	35.5	35.8	35.3	35.0	34.9
Personnel costs	68.3	66.5	74.2	72.5	73.5	74.0	72.7
Indirect taxes after deduction of subsidies	5.6	4.9	5.1	5.0	5.2	5.4	5.3
Financial costs after deduction of financial yields	5.7	7.0	7.8	6.5	6.6	6.0	5.5
Current gross profits before taxes	20.4	21.6	13.0	16.0	14.6	14.5	16.2

Note: The data basis for Table 7.2 is not identical with the data base for Table 7.1. What matters is the evolution in the distribution of value added, not the absolute figures.
Source: Pierre Muller and Philippe Tassi, "1979, année favorable pour les entreprises industrielles," Economique et statistique, February 1981, p. 10.

The measures taken in the implementation of the plan Barre can be grouped into three distinct time periods. The first period lasted from September 1976 to March 1978; it was marked (as became clear later) by relative moderation, out of concern for the 1978 legislative elections.[7] After the victory of the

Right in 1978, the path was cleared for serious action; Barre felt that he was now free to impose his policy without restrictions. Practices which had been established for decades were overthrown in a short time span. A third period, marked by a new tightening of policy, began in 1979, in response to the second oil crisis.[8] The presidential election of 1981 on the other hand does not seem to have had much impact, a point that will be taken up again later.

The core of the Barre plan was thus to strengthen the financial situation of French business enterprises. In the first period, when prices were still controlled by the government, this was achieved (after a temporary price freeze until December 1976) by letting industrial prices rise faster than earlier,[9] and by other measures such as accelerated tax write-offs. In addition, Barre promised, in his electoral program for the 1978 elections (the Programme de Blois), to halt the increase in taxes and social welfare contributions, a promise which he claims he largely kept since central government taxes did not increase much during this time period. However, local taxes (in particular the taxe professionnelle) kept on rising. The social welfare charges or contributions of the business firms rose even more, due to the fact that they finance much of the rising cost of unemployment insurance (see Table 7.3). Barre claimed though that in terms of global wage costs (direct wages plus social welfare contributions) the French firms were still doing extremely well in European terms, and thus had no reason for complaint.[10]

More dramatic change came after the 1978 elections. Prices on industrial products were decontrolled for the first time since the war, and the decree of 1945 on which price controls had been based was abolished altogether.[11] As a result, the stock market went up steeply[12] (in part, undoubtedly, also because of the defeat of the Left), and indebtedness of French firms receded for the first time in years (Table 7.3). Soon afterward, governmental controls of dismissals of the work force for reasons of redundancy were greatly relaxed; the government itself showed the way when it took control of the ailing iron and steel industry and imposed, as part of its rescue operation, a program of extensive layoffs. Similar "shake-outs" followed throughout French industry, despite increased profitability. These developments were further accentuated during the third period; Barre called for a "liberation" of entrepreneurship, an economy in which responsible entrepreneurs would make their decisions freely, without being burdened (or manipulated) by inefficient state regulations. After 1977, profits clearly recovered (Table 7.3).

In Barre's view, the progressive slowdown of wage increases was central to the improvement of the financial situation of French business. Again, the more energetic measures were only taken after 1978. Barre announced then that any business which

TABLE 7.3

The Financial Situation of French Business, 1973-1981

	1973	1974	1975	1976	1977	1978	1979	1980	1981
Profitability[a]									
Gross profits before taxes as percent of value added	20.4	21.6	13.0	16.0	14.6	14.5	16.2		
Gross profits after taxes as percent of own capital	22.6	26.6	14.6	20.5	19.1	20.0	22.0		
Indebtedness[a]									
Medium- and long-term debts as percent of permanent capital	30.5	34.4	39.0	41.0	42.0	42.8	41.8		
Gross disposable income of business enterprises (excluding nationalized firms, small business, and banks). Taken as indicator of profitability.[b]									
Yearly variations corrected for inflation (in percent)		-15.0	-1.1	+7.8	-0.7	+13.3	+5.8	-8.0	
Taxes and social contributions collected by the state expressed as percent of gross domestic product[c]									
Taxes		22.3	22.1	23.5	22.9	23.0	23.4	24.0	23.9
Social contributions		14.0	15.3	15.9	16.6	16.6	17.6	18.0	18.0
Total		36.3	37.4	39.4	39.5	39.6	41.0	42.0	41.9

*estimated

Source: [a]Pierre Muller and Philippe Tassi, "1979: année favorable pour les entreprises industrielles," Economie et statistique, February 1981, pp. 9, 10, and 12; [b]Le Monde, 10 March 1981, p. 24; [c]ibid., p. 22.

94

gave inflationary wage increases (that is, real wage increases exceeding approximately 2 percent) could not count on getting loans, contracts, or protection against imports from the state. Again this broke with a well-established practice, dating back to at least 1945.[13]   To take the edge off these measures, he promised that the lowest income groups would still be allowed to make further progress, and the government repeatedly acted to increase (though quite modestly) the purchasing power of the SMIC (the French minimum wage), of old-age pensions, and of family allowances.   In early 1981, Barre pointed with pride to the results of this policy.   In real terms, the SMIC (minimum wage) had increased between 1976 and 1980 by 10.7 percent; monthly salaries for blue-collar workers by 7.4 percent; for employees, by 6.9 percent; for technicians, 4.2 percent; and for executives, by only 2 percent.   Minimum retirement pensions had also been increased by 27.3 percent in real terms during the same time period, and family allowances by about 15 percent for each child.   In addition, indirect taxes (with their disproportionate impact on lower incomes) had been reduced, while the share of direct taxes in the State's fiscal revenues had gone up by 1.3 percent (from 21.1 percent to 22.4 percent).   Such a policy, Barre said, was dictated by considerations of solidarity in front of the hardships that French society faced, and also showed the government's concern for greater social justice.[14]

These measures were justified in part also by the need to keep consumption constant; it was important that it should not fall, since a recession (which would be damaging to business, and might also produce a "social explosion", the euphemism for a repetition of the events of May 1968) was to be avoided.[15]   If necessary, the government would increase expenditures in such a way as to keep overall consumption constant.   This explains in part the increasing budget deficits after 1976.   Barre stated that he did not view himself as a "narrow-minded liberal," and that he preferred the Swedish social democrats to Margaret Thatcher of Britain or the economists of the Chicago school, who in his view could hardly formulate an effective economic policy on the basis of their principles.[16]

However, the liberalism of Barre did mean abstention of the state in two areas: unemployment and private investment.   With regard to unemployment, his attitude was consistently one of "benign neglect."   He argued throughout that only healthy firms could create viable jobs.   For that reason he listed measures designed to increase business profits as measures to fight unemployment.   When in 1977 and 1978 the number of unemployed went up, he said that the situation should not be made to look worse than it really was — after all, he argued, some increase in unemployment was only to be expected, after the earlier years of over-employment.[17]   In the way of illustration, he added (more than a year before the government took over that sector) that a profitable iron and steel industry employing 100,000 people was much preferrable to a sick one employing 150,000.[18]   A higher growth rate, he admitted, would reduce unemployment but would not lead to more solid business firms; thus any such "improvement" was illusory because temporary.   The only real answer consisted in stronger exports and stronger profits.[19]

Unemployment figures kept creeping up every year that Barre was in office (Graph 7.3 below), but the prime minister remained unruffled.   The year 1979 brought massive dismissals, most conspicuously in the ailing iron and steel industry, where 22,000 jobs were suppressed.   Several of the "national champions" (firms such as Saint-Gobain-Pont-à-Mousson, Rhône-Poulenc, or Péchiney-Ugine-Kuhlmann) practiced a similar policy, and (partly as a result) increased their profits during this time period.[20] Barre however kept insisting that in no way did all unemployment constitute real hardship; he pointed in particular to the large percentage of unemployed women to say that in the past many of them would not even have looked for employment.[21]   In 1979, when the calculations by the INSEE (National Institute of Statistics and Economic Studies) projected the possibility of 2 million unemployed by 1985, and 3 million by 1990, Barre only scoffed at those figures, kept on arguing that France had "quasi-full employment" and that in any case, full employment could only be the byproduct of healthy business firms.[22]   Above all, he stressed, the situation of the 1980s must not be compared to that of the 1930s, when the unemployed received neither compensation nor professional training.   Because of a variety of factors peculiar to France, unemployment would not subside until 1985. He cited the large generations entering the labor market while particularly small generations, the result of the birth deficit of World War I, went into retirement; the number of women entering the labor market (many of whom would not have worked at all in the past); the maladaptation of many people due to a lack of appropriate training; the slowdown caused by the oil shock; and the industrial restructuring which necessitated a painful transition period.[23]   In 1985 there would be a turnaround for demographic reasons.

Happy the government in power at that time, who, like [the rooster] Chantecleer who thought that he had caused the sunrise with his cock-a-doodle-doo, will be able to congratulate itself for having strongly reduced the number of people looking for work!   Provided that the French economy will not, by then, have been weakened and thrown off balance by inappropriate policies![24]

This was another important point: no measures must be taken that might be irreversible (such as introducing early retirement except as a temporary measure, start another bout of inflation, create make-work programs or reduce working hours without pay cuts). In the meantime, there would be a few difficult years ahead. One other measure that Barre suggested was to have civil servants contribute to unemployment insurance; another, to use greater care in monitoring abuses of the system.25

Until the end of the Giscard presidency, not only Barre but other Giscardiens as well stuck to the view that economic stimulation could only artificially and temporarily absorb unemployment and was bound to lead in turn to an even deeper recession.26 The only direct measures in favor of employment consisted in training and employment programs for the young (for whom the state subsidized jobs) and in a program organizing (sometimes in a quite repressive way) the return of immigrant workers.27 In addition, there was the proposal to reduce the retirement age for particularly difficult kinds of work, a proposal to be implemented by negotiation and agreement between the social partners.

Private investment, too was the exclusive province of the business firms. Strong firms would not only be able to make investments, they would also know themselves which ones were best; the main task of the state therefore was to improve their financial strength. Again this broke with the well-established tradition according to which the French state took an active role in orienting investment (this had been one of the central tasks of the successive five-year plan). In fact, the reluctance to invest did cause worry in the U.D.F.'s own ranks.28 Particularly when in 1979 profits rebounded but did not lead to a significant increase in private investment, this criticism became more intense. Yet Barre insisted that it was up to business to decide on this; that there was no point in having the state encourage investment by specific measures since such a practice could only lead to bad practices. In any case, no such measures were taken.29 In late 1980, Barre noted that France had still one of the highest investment rates among industrial countries, and that its capital stock was on the average more modern than that of the Federal Republic of Germany.30

The rate of growth of the national economy, once (like investment) at the core of the five-year plans, was no longer dealt with in a direct way either; like employment and investment, it would be the result of other variables in the economy. A sound economy, Barre never failed to repeat, was more important than one with high growth rates (though he did note with satisfaction that France was still among the leading countries in this respect). It must be added that Barre, and particularly Giscard, were both concerned about the socially disruptive effects of an excessively high growth rate. This preoccupation was more relevant in the early 1970s than towards the end of the decade.31 However, it is possible that they thought that slow growth also had its good side, and certainly Giscard used this argument to appeal to the "ecology" vote, an element which was far from negligible in France in the past decade. On the other hand, Barre also expressed his belief that France stood in need of a somewhat higher growth rate than was desirable from the point of view of her economic equilibria (inflation, balance of payments). Only a somewhat higher growth rate could contain unemployment within tolerable levels.32

Since so much of the success of the plan Barre depended on the growth of exports, one might expect to see some measures that would have stimulated them, such as a devalued franc (after all, undervaluation of the national currency had been a crucial element in Germany's success).33 But in contrast to the policy conducted under President Pompidou, Barre made it clear to industrialists that he would never — never — accept such a measure, and that they better make their calculations without it. As a result, industrialists felt that they had to recoup their losses, or insufficient profit margins, by increasing prices in the home market (this had been practiced in Germany too, despite the long undervalued mark, but with a stronger domestic market).34

In recent years, there has been much discussion of a "political business cycle," in the sense of a stimulation of the economy just before major elections. Some of the actions of the Barre government clearly show sensitivity to electoral considerations, as for example the postponement of a real "tightening" of the plan Barre until after March 1978 (when the parliamentary elections were out of the way), or the delayed increases of public tariffs in 1981. But on the whole, Barre adamantly stuck to his principles: there would be no stimulation of the economy for the sake of Giscard's reelection, whether the president liked it or not.35 When the 1981 elections came around, the French economy found itself in the trough of the recession which resulted from the 1979 oil price increase (see also Graph 7.2). The short-term growth of the indices of production for all industry (excluding building) showed a negative evolution for every one of the 12 months preceding the presidential election. The worst figures were in the two months preceding the election; the trend changed direction in June. See Industrial Short-Term Trends (Eurostat), June 1981, Table II, and October 1981, Table 2. The figures are as follows:

1980

May	June	July	Aug.	Sept.	Oct.	Nov.	Dec.
-0.4	-1.4	-2.2	-1.2	-1.3	-1.8	-3.2	-1.5

1981

Jan.	Feb.	Mar.	Apr.	May	June	July	Aug.
-1.9	-1.9	-4.5	-3.2	-1.5	+0.1	+0.8	+1.1

As a result, Giscard's last-minute plan on the reduction of unemployment was not particularly credible.36

RESULTS

In judging Barre's policy, one has to remember that the international environment was particularly disruptive during this period (oil "shocks" of 1974 and 1979, fluctuation of the dollar, rise of export-oriented industries in some third world countries, and so on). The following tables must be read with this element in mind. Nonetheless, several things emerge quite clearly from the graphs and statistics.

As to the financial strength of business enterprises, Table 7.3 shows a mixed picture. There was considerable improvement of profitability from 1977 to 1979 (after the catastrophic year 1975, the plan de relance of 1976 brought a relatively good year). But 1980, when the effect of the second oil crisis came to be felt, saw renewed deterioration. In other areas, furthermore, there was little or no improvement. Thus indebtedness kept on rising; taxes and social contributions also continued their upward trend. The rise in social welfare contributions was felt as a particular hardship by business; it reflected the increasing unemployment (the French unemployment insurance system relies heavily on employers' contributions). It must also be noted that business bankruptcies further increased above the level which resulted from the 1975 deflation, and were rising again by 1980 (Graph 6.3).

This continued financial vulnerability of business, combined with the absence of any prospect for expansion given Barre's policy, helps explain the investment behavior depicted in Graph 7.1. The graph shows that from 1960 to 1970, both the investment rate and the financing of investments from retained earnings (autofinancement) were relatively high. In 1971, the invest-

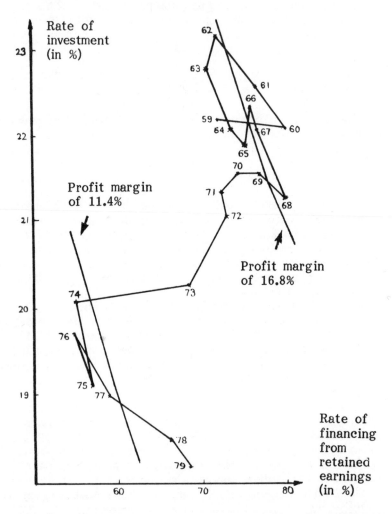

GRAPH 7.1
Profit Margins, Investment Rates and Financing of
Investments From Retained Earnings, 1960–1979

Investment rate defined as gross fixed capital formation as percent of value added. Rate of financing from retained earnings defined as gross savings expressed as percent of gross fixed capital formation. Jointly they show the profit rate; two points located on the same hyperbola correspond to an identical profit margin. Data based on French National Accounts.

Source: Jacky Fayolle, "Le comportement d'investissement depuis 1974," Economie et statistique, No. 127, November 1980, p. 33.

ment rate began to fall, and so, for some time, did auto-financement. From 1976 onwards however, the share of invest-ments financed from retained earnings increased considerably; yet at the same time, the investment rate itself continued its long-term decline since 1970 (except for a brief reversal in 1976, due to the relance Chirac). French business had become very cautious about investing. The investment "gap" which had opened in the early 1970s remained wide, even if there were modest signs of improvements towards the end of the 1970s (Graph 6.2).

The government could not claim particular success with infla-tion; during Barre's tenure, inflation rates in France remained consistently above those of a reference group of Western indus-trial countries. It was unavoidable that sooner or later this would have an impact on the franc's relation to other currencies. Real wages, despite the spartan rhetoric of the government, in fact progressed at a faster rate in France than in the European community, the United States or Japan.[37] However, there was a marked slowdown as the Barre years wore on (Table 7.4). The share of personnel costs in the distribution of value added seemed more or less stabilized (Table 7.2).

The balance of trade showed improvement in 1977 and 1978; in 1979 and 1980 the deficit at least seemed not too large when compared to the disastrous results of 1976. A return to equilib-rium, Barre argued, would necessarily take time. In addition, he stressed (at the end of his term in office) that the service balance made up for any deficit in the balance of trade; even with such countries as Germany, the United States or Japan, France had a surplus in the current balance, despite a trade de-ficit with all three countries.[38] This relative emphasis on a balance of payments in equilibrium had its counterpart in a rela-tively lower rate of growth; there was a clear downward trend in the rate of growth of the gross domestic product. True, in comparative terms the French performance was not all bad for the years 1974-1981; among the major industrial countries, only Japan had a higher growth rate during this period. But after 1978, France began to fall behind, in particular behind West Germany, which also had a considerably lower unemployment rate (Tables 7.4, Graphs 7.2 and 7.3).[39] To leaders preoccupied with Franco-German economic rivalry, Barre's performance fell scandalously short of long-held ambitions.

In the fall of 1981, Barre published a book with the title Une politique pour l'avenir.[40] Except for the foreword, it was a collection of articles, essays and speeches from his last year in office, summing up and justifying his own policy while criticizing and condemning the alternatives offered by his critics. He re-peatedly underlined the reasons for which he believed a grad-ualist policy was necessary. Disinflation was an objective that could only be achieved over time; it could not be obtained by

TABLE 7.4
Macroeconomic Data in International Comparison, 1974-1981

	1974	1975	1976	1977	1978	1979	1980
Inflation[a]							
In France	15.2	9.6	9.9	9.0	9.7	11.8	13.7*
Average in reference group	12.7	12.3	9.6	8.8	6.1	7.5	10.6*

(United States, West Germany, Japan, Britain, Italy, Canada, Belgium, Netherlands)

Yearly progression of real wages (in percent)

	1974	1975	1976	1977	1978	1979	1980
France before the crisis: 5-6 percent[b]			3.75	2.8	3.0	2.0*	1.6*
European community (weighted average)[c]	3.7	2.7	1.4	-0.3	2.1	0.6	-0.4

GDP volume growth (in percent)[d]

	1974	1975	1976	1977	1978	1979	1980
France	3.2	0.2	5.0	2.8	3.8	3.2	1.3*
Germany	0.5	-1.8	5.2	2.7	3.2	4.6	2.1*
European community (weighted average)	1.7	-1.4	5.0	2.3	3.0	3.4	1.3*

Public debt expressed as percent of GDP[e]

France	16.7	(30 November 1980)
Germany	22.6	(31 December 1979)
United States	25.6	(31 August 1980)
Japan	28.6	(31 August 1980)
Italy	58.1	(31 August 1980)

1980 budget deficits expressed as percent of GDP[f] (budgets of central administrations)

France	1.1
Germany	3.5
United Kingdom	4.8
Netherlands	4.8
Belgium	9.0
Italy	10.6

Growth rates in international comparison (1974-1981) — figures corrected for inflation[g]

Japan	33.8
France	21.3
Italy	21.0
West Germany	17.6
United States	15.7
Britain	4.8

*estimated

Sources: [a]OECD, cited in Le Point, 1 December 1980, p. 46 — for 1981, see European Economy, supplement A, No. 7 (July 1981), table 3.

[b]Jean-Michel Lamy, "Le redressememt de l'economie . . .," Les Echos, 24 August 1979; and Le Monde, 21 May 1981, p. 10.

[c]European Economy, No. 8 (March 1981), p. 20 (N.B.: The data basis for the two series above may not be strictly identical).

[d]Ibid., No. 7 (November 1980), p. 139.

[e]Raymond Barre, Une politique pour l'avenir,, p. 87 (relying on statistics from the OECD and the Internatinoal Monetary Fund).

[f]Ibid., p. 86 (relying on statistics from the European community).

[g]Le Monde, 10 March 1981, p. 24.

quick, dramatic action. In addition, there were special reasons why a policy of brutal deflation was inappropriate for France. There was the political constraint, particularly before 1978; it made it impossible, Barre said, to take too many strong measures from the very beginning. There was a psychological constraint — the French had become accustomed to continuous increases in their standard of living, to a high level of employment, and so on; they would therefore not accept sudden setbacks in these areas. Third, there was a demographic constraint: the fact that such numerous generations entered the labor market at a time when the departing generations were so small meant that French policy had to respect certain limits in order to maintain a sufficient level of employment. Finally, there was the social constraint; essentially this meant the need to maintain relative labor peace. During the last ten years, Barre stated in 1980, a dialogue had developed between the social partners in France; it had led to numerous agreements, often with a lifetime of several years. Some of these agreements contained inflationary elements; but it was better to respect them than to disrupt a development (cooperation between social partners) which was an essential part of social peace. That peace in turn was a fundamental condition for disinflation and business efficiency.[41]

What of the alternatives offered by his critics? First and foremost, there was the possibility of a "voluntarist" policy, promoting rapid growth and full employment while relying on authoritarian wage and price controls, protectionist measures and a "selective" industrial policy in which the state would decide what was best for business firms. Such a policy, Barre stated, corresponded to a certain intellectual tendance in France, the dirigisme centralisateur et planificateur (centralizing, Plan-oriented dirigisme, or leadership by the state), and had its supporters both among the Left and among the "Jacobin and nationalist Right."[42] Nevertheless he rejected this policy out of hand; experience had shown, he said (presumably a reference to the Gaullists) that it always led to "industrial disasters, profound economic distortions, social explosions, external disequilibrium, recession and unemployment."[43] Within 12 to 18 months (and here he made a clear reference to Chirac) it had to come to an end, and had to be replaced by a rigorous stabilization, leading to even greater and more painful unemployment.[44]

Barre was unwilling even to practice the traditional Gaullist rhetoric of austerity, with its celebration of will and effort. In an address before the Economic and Social Council, he declared that the ritual required him to put forward "noble verbal assurances" and include in his speech "a vibrant appeal to national mobilization." But what good would it do to resort to "generous illusions, profound emotions and fallacious incantations?" Such words were only stereotypes that "no one could in all conscience take seriously."[45]

GRAPH 7.2
Industrial Production Trends for the Major Countries
of the European Community
(Basis: 100 in 1975)

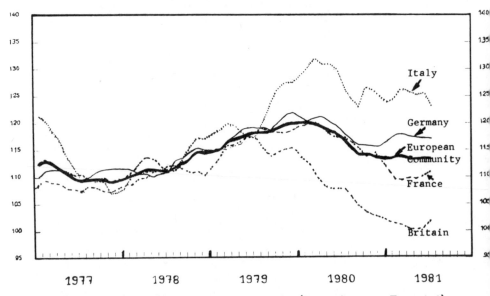

Source: Industrial short-term trends (Luxemburg: Eurostat),
October 1981.

He was particularly critical of Chirac's sudden conversion to
"Reaganism," to the fashionable supply-side economics and the
emphasis on reducing taxes and public expenditure in order to
stimulate growth, hold down inflation and reduce unemployment.
Such a policy was understandable for a country which had a budget deficit representing 2.3 percent of the GDP (France, he
pointed out, had a deficit of only 1.1 percent during the same
year, that is, 1980); a public debt vastly higher than the French
one; where taxes on households were extremely high and had not
been adjusted for inflation in three years, and where amortization rules for business were numerous and complex.   But
France had little to learn from such an approach. Her government, he stated, had practiced an authentic supply-side policy
since 1976 and had even supported demand during the same time,
though it had done so (a clear barb for Chirac) "insufficiently . . . in the eyes of those very same people who demanded
reflation and strong growth before they became the advocates of
a massive reduction of public spending."46

GRAPH 7.3
Labor Force and Unemployment, 1969-1981[*]

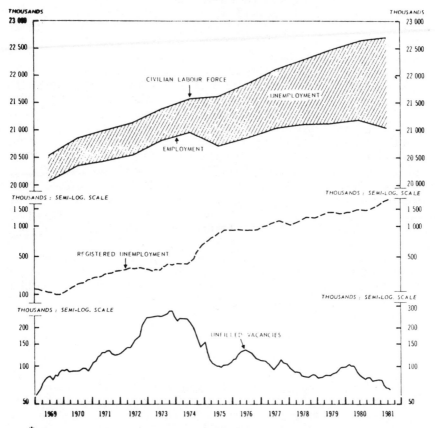

*Based on data from the INSEE.
Source: OECD Economic Surveys: France (OECD: Paris,
January 1982), p. 16.

Finally, Barre also rejected the suggestion that a more drastic ("massive and brutal") deflation was the answer to the economic problems of the French nation. Such a policy, while correct from the perspective of neo-liberal and monetarist theories, simply ignored the economic, political and social realities that every government must take into account.[47]

Of all the major political leaders, Barre was decidedly the most liberal (it is true that Chirac's profile was somewhat fuzzy after his conversion to "Reaganomics" in early 1981). The state, he argued, had a circumscribed role; there are limits to what it could successfully carry through in the economic sphere. One of its tasks was to ease transitions and thus contain social tensions. It could also make competition work, and eliminate inefficiencies and free rents. It could play an educational function and help in shaping expectations and attitudes. It could promote the dialogue between social partners and thus pave the way for more contractual relations. Finally it could show the way by practicing financial rigor and discipline in its own sphere. But in the end, its main task was to make people, wage-earners, businessmen, and farmers, more responsible and more self-reliant in their economic intercourse.[48] In Barre's view, the resulting discipline was bound to make France one of the world's economic leaders. The question was whether a majority of the French were prepared to accept this discipline — in thought, in politics, social reform and economics — for the sake of their country's international standing. In any case, this was the way in which Barre defined the stake of the 1981 elections; and he had no doubts about what the outcome would be.

NOTES

1. Barre, Une politique pour l'avenir, p. 116.

2. Immediately after it was announced, the plan Barre had majority support among French public opinion. This did not last (see surveys at the end of Part II).

3. Some of the leading French economic journalists pointed that out from the very beginning. See Roger Priouret, "Barre, ce qui manque," L'Express, 4 October 1976; Jean Boissonnat, "Le veritable objectif du plan Barre," L'Expansion, October 1976; also Philippe Lefournier, "Plan Barre: un succès inavouable," L'Expansion, October 1977.

4. Cohen-Tanugi and Morrisson, Salaires intérêts profits, p. 35.

5. Interview with Raymond Barre, L'Expansion, September 1978, p. 163.

6. Barre, Une politique pour l'avenir, pp. 157-59; 179-80; 228-30.

7. Barre admitted this freely in a speech he gave in New York, in February 1980. When he took power in August 1976, there were only 18 months left to the legislative elections; all the surveys and nearly all the political observers anticipated a victory of the Left. "For this reason, I discarded in 1976 measures which would have been perfectly justified from a theoretical point of view: I am thinking, e.g., of the immediate deregulation of prices or massive increases in public tariffs." Barre, Une politique pour l'avenir, pp. 118-19.

8. Roger Priouret, "Le feu de 'bois mort' de Raymond Barre," Le Nouvel Observateur, 24 April 1978; and Bruno Dethomas, "Le 'vrai' plan Barre," Le Monde, 13 July 1979.

9. Lefournier, "Plan Barre," p. 110.

10. Programme de Blois (Paris: Fayard, 1978), pp. 39-40. For the results, see Table II-6. For Barre's argument in retrospect, see his Une politique pour l'avenir, pp. 161-63.

11. European Economy, no. 8 (March 1981), p. 63.

12. Herbert Rowen in the International Herald Tribune, 2 October 1978; and Rolf E. Wubbels, "The French Economic Miracle: What a Different Leadership Makes," Financial Analysts Journal, July-August 1978, pp. 23-27.

13. Paul Lewis in the International Herald Tribune, 14 September 1978; and Alain Vernholes in Le Monde, 15 May 1981.

14. Barre, Une politique pour l'avenir, pp. 62-63.

15. This was a constant concern to the government, and a threatening prediction used by the opposition. See, for example, Barre cited by Alain Rollat in Le Monde, 10 January 1981.

16. Interview with Barre, L'Expansion, September 1978, pp. 154-63; and Marc Clairvois, "Le frisson keynesien de Barre," L'Expansion, 7 September 1979, pp. 28-29,

17. Interview with L'Expansion, September 1978, p. 159. He stressed this point repeatedly, stating that a situation of overemployment had in fact prevailed in France since the 1950s, or that the full employment that France experienced since that time was "largely artificial." Barre, Une politique pour l'avenir, pp. 39 and 43.

18. Jean Boissonnat, "Raymond Barre m'a dit . . .," L'Expansion, April 1977, p. 30. The number of people employed in the iron and steel industry fell from 230,000 in 1974 to 193,000 in 1976 and less than 165,000 in 1980. Olivier Marchand and Jean-Pierre Revoil, "Emploi et chômage: bilan fin 1980," Economie et statistique, Feb. 1981, p. 33.

19. Interview with L'Expansion, September 1978; similarly Giscard d'Estaing in a speech on 20 September 1978; Le Monde, 22 September 1978.

20. "How the Barre plan is making its mark," Financial Times, 11 January 1980.

21. "Premier ministre des temps difficiles," Le Monde, 5 September 1979.

22. The projections are listed in detail in Bilan économique et social, 1979 (Supplement aux dossiers et Documents du Monde, January 1980), pp. 50–51. For the government's reactions, see Jean Boissonnat, "La 'sagesse' de Barre," La Croix, 13–14 January 1980; Hobart Rowen, "The success of France Inc.," International Herald Tribune, 15 May 1980; and Henry Bussery, "La vérité est bonne à dire," Projet, September–October 1980, pp. 904–07.

23. Barre, Une politique pour l'avenir, pp. 40–41.

24. Ibid., p. 50.

25. Ibid., pp. 45–53.

26. Thus, just before the elections, Jean-Pierre Fourcade (one of the leaders of the UDF): "L'économie et l'emploi," Le Monde, 16 April 1981. Interestingly, he does not once mention Barre's name.

27. Starting in 1977, there were three National Employment Pacts which subsidized employment in a variety of ways, mostly by facilitating job training or by exempting employers from social welfare contributions. The number of beneficiaries was 579,000 in 1977/78 (first Pact), 313,000 in 1978/79, 455,000 in 1979/80 and a planned 534,000 for 1980/81. The employers did not need to commit themselves to maintain the beneficiaries in their jobs once the subsidies were terminated, and often did not do so (most of the employers taking advantage of this formula were small businessmen and artisans). As to the premiums for immigrant workers who left France (instituted in May 1977), only 23,000 persons took advantage of it by the end of 1978. Olivier Marchand and Jean-Pierre Revoil, "Emploi et chômage: bilan fin 1980," Economie et statistique, February 1981, pp. 40–42.

28. For example, Maurice Blin, a centrist senator and budget rapporteur: "Mon inquiétude, le refus du futur . . .," La Croix, 10 October 1979. For the previous practice and tradition, see Andrew Shonfield, Modern Capitalism (New York: Oxford University Press, 1969), pp. 134–40. Much of this apparatus was still in place in the 1970s.

29. "Premier ministre des temps difficiles," Le Monde, 5 September 1979; and Pierre Locardel in Les Echos, 20 February 1980.

30. Barre, Une politique pour l'avenir, p. 129.

31. Colette Ysmal, "Nature et réalité de l'affrontement Giscard–Chirac," Politique aujourd'hui, nos. 3–4, 1978, p. 14. Giscard expressed this concern already in 1972; see his contributions in Economie et société humaine (Paris: Denoel, 1972).

32. Barre, Une politique pour l'avenir, p. 74.

33. Michael Kreile, "West Germany: The Dynamics of Expansion," in Peter J. Katzenstein, ed., Between Power and Plenty (Madison: University of Wisconsin Press, 1978), pp. 208–17.

34. Wolfgang Hager, "Germany as an Extraordinary Trader," in Wilfrid L. Kohl and Giorgio Basevi, eds., West Germany: A European and Global Power (Lexington, Mass.: D. C. Heath, 1980), p. 6. For the different situation in France, see Le Point, 1 December 1980, pp. 46-47. Barre was aware of the industrialists' criticism, but considered it essentially irrational — see Barre, Une politique pour l'avenir, p. 76.

35. Alain Rollat, "M. Barre affirme que le budget de 1981 ne sera pas inspire par des 'considerations electoralistes'," Le Monde, 9 July 1980; and Dominique Audibert, "Des lendemains qui divergent," Le Point, 24 November 1980. See also Jacques Lecaillen, "Entrons-nous dans un nouveau cycle electoral?," La Croix, 30 July 1980; Jean-Gabriel Fredet, "La relance économique au secours du 'bon choix'," Le Matin, 8 April 1980; and Bernard Hartemann, "L'économie 'electorale' de 1981," La vie francaise, 9 June 1980.

36. For his plan, see Le Figaro, 28-29 March 1981 and 31 March 1981.

37. For the comparison with the United States and Japan, see Eurostat Review, 1970-1979 (Luxemburg: European Communities, 1981), p. 148.

38. Barre, Une politique pour l'avenir, p. 74.

39. At the end of 1980, unemployment in Germany was 4 percent, compared with approximately 6.3 percent in France. Bilan économique et social, 1980. (Paris: Le Monde, January 1981), p. 17.

40. Raymond Barre, Une politique pour l'avenir (Paris: Plon, 1981).

41. Ibid., pp. 118-20; also pp. 30 and 71.

42. Ibid., p. 117.

43. Ibid., pp. 117-18.

44. Ibid., p. 74.

45. Ibid., pp. 127-28.

46. Ibid., p. 167.

47. Ibid., p. 118.

48. This orientation was already outlined in his "Perspectives pour la présente décennie," presented on 10 January 1980; reprinted in Une politique pour l'avenir, pp. 95-98.

8

GAULLIST RESPONSES TO BARRE

Whatever the intrinsic value of Barre's policy, the fact remains that it came to be disapproved, soon after its inception, by three of the four major — and in the 1978 elections roughly equal[1] — political parties. In addition, there were some mild reservations even in the ranks of the U.D.F., Barre's own party. They concerned mostly the question of national solidarity in times of economic hardship; too much of the burden, so went the reservations, was carried by the unemployed and by wage earners; something had to be done to alleviate their condition, for example, a solidarity tax on the very wealthy, on inheritances, and so on, to finance public works, retraining, and relief.[2]

The attitude of the R.P.R. (the Gaullists, renamed by Jacques Chirac when he reorganized them in late 1976) was quite different. It evolved from support for Barre's policy in the first year to open criticism before the 1978 elections, and finally to increasingly bitter, even vicious attacks (though Chirac took on a more statesmanlike tone after 1979, presumably in preparation for the 1981 elections). True, not all Gaullists participated in this; many of them thought that the first duty of the party was to support the action of the government, even if they did not agree with it in important respects. In addition, some Gaullist leaders served in the Barre government as ministers; they were not the only ones though to support its economic policy openly.[3] As a result, there was no coherent Gaullist line, especially as Chirac himself changed his own position considerably over the years. In addition, there was a practical problem: what could be done to change Barre's policy? Some Gaullists went so far as to propose voting a censure motion against the government; but in the end the party shrank back from what most members must have perceived as an act close to regicide.[4]

111

Given the economic philosophy of Barre and Giscard, a conflict with the Gaullists was unavoidable sooner or later. One of the principles of the General (and of Gaullism after him) was that the political goals of the state would be set down first; the state would then intervene in the economy in such a way as to achieve the desired results. Prominent among the goals of the state were national greatness, national cohesion, and active modernization; for Gaullists, these notions implied political action on investments, employment, wages, and economic growth. After the withdrawal of the general from public affairs, Gaullist rhetoric became more subdued; but a strong interventionist practice remained. It is true that some Gaullists began to see excessive state involvement as a cause of economic inefficiency.[5] Nonetheless, the old reflexes and practices persisted among most of the leaders of the movement, in particular Chirac. The plan de relance of 1975-76 had been his brainchild, and under his leadership, the R.P.R. made it increasingly clear that if only the Gaullists had more power, they would never accept that the nation be turned over to, or martyrized by, market forces.[6] They would not stand by as she suffered in the international crisis, with her investments and growth rate falling (a setback for national greatness) and her unemployment rising (endangering national cohesion and thus power). Unsuccessfully they pressed again and again for a more active economic policy, and criticized not only the government's programs (consisting mostly of inaction, in their view) but also its soothing rhetoric. Barre and Giscard, they said, were lulling the country into a false optimism, with their statements to the effect that things were not really all that bad and would in any case improve before long. The Gaullists wanted to awaken the country from this "anesthesia"; they wanted to mobilize, to galvanize it by stirring appeals to action, sacrifice and solidarity.[7]

Chirac's resignation in 1976 had taken place against a background of differences with Giscard regarding both economic strategy and political analysis.[8] At first, Chirac remained quiet, and the Gaullists supported Barre's policy; they became more critical with the plan Barre bis in the fall of 1977. Criticism mounted with the approach of the 1978 elections. Forceful proposals were advanced in favor of another relance, or massive reflation, through a promotion of both investment and employment by the state and big industry.[9] The Keynesian nature of this strategy was made even clearer by a proposal calling for a "new Marshall Plan," one that would use the surpluses of Arab oil producers in order to finance the development needs of African countries; this would in turn result in an increase in the demand for industrial goods produced and exported by Western Europe.[10] Inflation would be held down by improving productivity (through lower unit costs; French industry was running below capacity).

By the fall of 1979, however, the idea of a reflation (relance globale) was abandoned in favor of a "new growth" (nouvelle croissance) based on a massive investment campaign.[11] These investments were to prepare France for the coming years of international economic warfare; they would develop exports, reconquer domestic markets for French industry, increase the growth rate, and in due course create new jobs.

There is one main point over which the Gaullists and Barre disagreed most strongly: the role of the state in private investment. Barre was leaving the matter up to the entrepreneurs, arguing that intervention by the state could only distort economic efficiency. Such a proposition is quite unacceptable to Gaullists: to them it is the duty of the state to guide investment. They claim that liberal capitalism has simply proven inefficient; the nation pays for what business cannot do, or does not do correctly and swiftly enough.[12] Chirac resorted to strong language: he compared business investments to armaments. In 1979 he declared that under the conditions of economic warfare in which France found herself, one could of course rearm (read: invest) slowly — as France had done in 1938 — while others rearmed rapidly; but if France continued down this road, she was headed for another débâcle along the lines of 1940.[13] These appeals for vigorous action by the state on the investment front (to restructure French industry and agriculture) were repeated with the rapport Méo in the fall of 1979. This report became for some time the centerpiece of Gaullist thinking about the economy.[14] Journalists noted however that the Gaullists had little to say about how these investments would be financed, since they at the same time disapproved of Barre's budget deficit, causing a minor political crisis at the end of 1979.[15] Chirac made an effort to answer those questions in an interview with Le Monde in April 1980.[16] The necessary funds (10-15 billion francs for investment alone, public and private) would be obtained, he argued, by reducing state expenditures on personnel, on unemployment compensation (by reducing unemployment from 1,500,000 to 500,000), an exceptional tax on wealth, and other measures. He was also more specific about where the investments should go. Overall, his policy (in all areas) called for an additional expenditure of 30 billion francs per year (6 percent of the national budget). But the idea that such funds could be raised without increasing the budget deficit or aggravating inflation was again received with skepticism.

To Gaullists, private business has a public function; this is what justifies intervention. Business may need to be encouraged, even prodded, to make the right investments; it may also need to be helped and protected. Even Debré, who outdid all other Gaullists in his appeals to sacrifice in what he saw as one of the great national crises in French history,[17] rejected Barre's policy of letting the weaker firms go bankrupt as unfair.[18] He and Chirac both proposed resorting to protective measures in order to save French industries endangered by imports.[19]

Employment, like investment, cannot be left to market forces in the Gaullist view of things. Nor do they like to oppose wages to profits, or employment to investment, as Barre was doing; thus at first the policy of reflation. Propositions pour la France, the party's program for the 1978 elections, stated that unemployment is morally and socially unacceptable and economically unjustifiable, no matter what experts might say; it also proposed an aggressive strategy of job creation.[20] Later statements, starting with the rapport Méo (perhaps in response to the oil price increases of 1979), stressed investment-led growth and left out consumption-led growth altogether. But even then Gaullists were persuaded that some progress in terms of wages was necessary for the sake of national unity. As Méo (Chirac's economic advisor) put it, "one could not lead the country from tunnel to tunnel".[21] To do so was to invite a social explosion along the lines of May 1968.[22] But the most important proposal in the direction of wage earners, apart from the promise to reduce unemployment, was the rediscovery of de Gaulle's participation after years of oblivion. Chirac talked about it with fervor and enthusiasm. Participation was the main avenue of social progress, all the more so since real wage increases had become more difficult.[23] However, neither the Giscardiens nor the employers, not to speak of the unions or the parties of the Left, thought much of that idea.

Just as investment and employment, a high rate of economic growth is also, in the minds of the Gaullists, to be promoted by political intervention. Barre played down its importance, would set no targets and seemed happy with modest percentages. It is true that at one point Chirac seemed to have espoused Giscard's views on the subject, that is, that high growth rates ("much above four percent," as he said in 1975) were not only unrealistic, but also socially disruptive.[24] However, even in 1975 Chirac was ambiguous on this point. When addressing himself to the Gaullists, he used a different language; in particular he was critical of the idea of "gentle growth" (a reference to Giscard). On the occasion of the party convention of the Gaullists (then still called the UDR) in Nice, in 1975, he wrote in the introduction to L'Enjeu, the booklet which summed up party doctrine:

We want a dynamic and prosperous society, one that is capable of producing a regular amount of goods and wealth. A few years ago such a statement would have seemed superfluous. Recent theories of moderate growth make it necessary for us now to reaffirm our choice in favor of a balanced but strong economic growth without which there can be no progress.[25]

Three years later, the new Gaullist (now R.P.R.) program Propositions pour la France mentioned an annual growth rate of 5-6 percent as an urgent national goal, and Chirac soon made bitter attacks on Giscard's idea of a croissance douce ("gentle growth"); it was gentle, he said, only for the rich.[26] Jean Méo in 1979 proposed a target of 5 percent, double the growth rate at the time; and Chirac argued that in any case the French growth rate must be higher than that of France's main trading partners.[27]

As already mentioned, not all the Gaullists shared the critical attitude of their party leader; many remained loyal to the government. There were other confusing elements. Thus, Chirac changed his strategy repeatedly. This was true in the more strictly political arena, where he tried to give his party a new identity, that of a new movement which was not just an extension of Gaullism. While successful in revitalizing electoral support for a party that had badly suffered in this area during the two years after the 1974 presidential election, Chirac failed in his plans for a new identity and a new doctrine. In the fall of 1977, the Union of the Left collapsed, contrary to Chirac's expectation that the two parties would cooperate until (though not after) the election. As a result, the electoral strategy of the RPR had to be revised again. This led to a return in full force of traditional Gaullism.[28]

In the economic area too, Chirac did not advocate a consistent strategy. He shifted from the advocacy of massive reflation (relance globale, the kind he had practiced in 1975-76) to a strategy of investment- and export-led growth, discovering in the process small and medium-sized businesses as agents of superior economic vitality (a discovery that probably had something to do with the discussion, fashionable in those days, of Italy's "underground economy"). In April 1980 he was calling for a spending program of altogether 30 billion francs (10-15 billions for investment alone) and praised President Carter for his refusal to tighten credit for certain sectors of the economy; that, he said, was the way of wisdom (he generally expressed his admiration for the creation of jobs in the U.S. economy from 1974-1978). It is true that he also called for deregulation to "liberate" small and medium-sized firms, and generally for a reduction of state expenditures, particularly on personnel.[29]

Chirac made another sharp change in the economic strategy he proposed when in early 1981 he suddenly discovered "Reaganomics." In February of that year, only ten months after arguing for a counter-cyclical (rather than a "purely inflationary") budget deficit, he announced that if elected to the presidency, he would cut back the budget by 30 billion francs and liberate business from excessive taxes and regulations. He also seemed to repudiate his earlier proposal of an exceptional wealth tax.

It was all in blatant contrast with what he had said (and, in 1975-76, done) earlier on. No wonder that René Monory, the minister who introduced industrial deregulation and price decontrol in 1978, called it pure demagogy. Le Monde in turn dismissed it as so much fantasy.[30] Whatever the merits of the economic strategies proposed by Chirac, consistency was clearly not a major consideration for him.

Some of the shifts in Chirac's position could perhaps be explained as a result of internal divisions among the Gaullists. It was clear in any case that unanimity did not reign in the party. This was illustrated by Debré's efforts to get the RPR (and above all, the government) to follow a more nationalist and protectionist line. Debré became the advocate of even greater discipline and austerity (something that Chirac on the whole rejected). With regard to foreign economic policy, Debré called with growing insistence for selective protectionist measures. Propositions pour la France, to be sure, had contrasted Europe's open borders with those of the United States and Japan, which were declared to be protected by tariffs and technical regulations; the dangers resulting from the low-cost exports of the new industrial countries were also stressed. But there was no call for substantial protection; instead, it was recognized that only adaptation to these phenomena could bring a durable solution.[31] This point of view was repeated by Chirac in 1980.[32] Debre on the other hand took an entirely different approach.

The 1970s, he argued, and in all likelihood the years beyond as well, were characterized by a situation of economic warfare; battles were taking place over currency, energy, trade, investment, and indebtedness. In this war, no longer were the legitimate needs of all countries respected; national egoism became the rule. Some countries exported at any cost while protecting themselves against imports; others over-invested in order to wipe out all foreign competition. In such a situation France had to remember that politics was above all a struggle for power; the pursuit of happiness (and social reform) had to remain secondary to this.[33] The situation amounted in fact to a great national emergency. On the one hand, this called for sacrifices; on the other, it also justified the recourse to protectionist measures.

In all those sectors where the industrial capacity of France must be affirmed, there has to be a protection of the market, by action both on the (European) Community and on the national level. The official (free trade) doctrine which is proposed to us is deathly. In times of economic peace, when all grow at the same time, one can and should lower trade barriers. In times of economic war, the opposite approach must be taken.[34]

A similar, collective Gaullist program declared that France should practice selective protectionism in order to maintain itself in those advanced industrial sectors where technology translates into power. Even if such sectors were not profitable and thus could not be justified in economic terms, the state had to support them.[35]

It is thus clear that the Gaullist camp was not unified around one policy. This was complicated by personal ambitions. The resulting confusion found its expression in the fact that in 1981, the Gaullists went into the presidential election not with one candidate but with three. (A fourth candidate, Michel Jobert, was unable to secure the necessary number of signatures endorsing his candidacy.) Before Chirac, Michel Debré had already announced his candidacy. He was followed by Marie-France Garaud, who under Pompidou and afterwards, along with Pierre Juillet, had long played the role of éminence grise of Gaullist leaders. However, they all rejected both the Left and the Barre government, and they did have at least one view in common. They all held that under Barre, the state had abdicated its proper role; only a more activist policy could save the nation from disaster.

The argument is often made that the conflict between Giscard and Chirac, from 1976 onwards, was above all a conflict of personal ambitions (rather than a clashing political beliefs). Such an argument can draw a certain amount of strength from the fact that Chirac has a record of shifting his "beliefs" and ideology in such a way as to adjust them to the political needs as he perceives them. But it must be remembered that Chirac drew much of his political strength from a movement which he had not created and which he could only partially reform. In order to be an acceptable leader to the RPR, he had to make certain concessions to Gaullism and its view of an active role for the state in economic matters. Just what this role would be was somewhat open to definition by the leadership; but it had to be an active role, in clear contrast to Giscard's and Barre's liberalism. For these reasons, ideological factors played at least as important a role in Chirac's clashes with the president as did his personal ambitions (though it would hardly be appropriate to downplay the latter). Chirac would have been more satisfied had he been able to dominate the presidential majority, as he tried to do; but the RPR's performance in the 1978 elections did not give him enough weight for this. In any case, Barre was clearly closer to Giscard's own thinking, and he frustrated his competitor's designs with skill and success — at least until May 1981.

NOTES

1. The Gaullist R.P.R. gathered 22.62 percent of the vote, the highest percentage; the Communist party the lowest percentage with 20.55 percent. René Rémond, "Les élections legislatives," Paradoxes, April-May 1978, pp. 25-32.

2. Interview with Jean Lecanuet, Les Echos, 12 September 1978; Jean-Pierre Fourcade, "Dynamisme et solidarité," L'Express, 24 March 1979; and Andre Diligent, "Le bilan," Démocratie moderne, 6 september 1979.

3. Articles by Albin Chalandon, Le Monde, 2 October 1979; and by Olivier Guichard, Le Monde, 30 October 1979.

4. Articles by André Passeron in The Guardian (weekly), 8 December 1979, p. 11, and 16 December 1979, p. 11.

5. Alain Peyrefitte, Le mal francais (Paris: Plon, 1976), pp. 404 and 440-50.

6. Propositions pour la France (Paris: Stock, 1977), pp. 173-76, 185-87, 194-95; Colette Ysmal, "Nature et realite de l'affrontement Giscard-Chirac," Politique aujourd'hui, nos. 3-4, 1978, pp. 11-23; Pierre Dabeziès, "Gaullisme et giscardisme," Pouvoirs, no. 9, 1979, pp. 27-36; and "Declaration politique du groupe parlementaire UDF, commentée par le RPR," ibid., pp. 49-52.

7. Propositions pour la France, pp. 59-61, 140-41, 165 and 230; Pierre Charpy, Lettre de la Nation, 13 July 1979; Michel Debré, Le Figaro, 18 September 1979; Jacques Chirac, Le Monde, 29-30 March 1980. These are but a few examples; the theme is constant.

8. See Chapter Six.

9. Propositions pour la France, pp. 184-89; Philippe Dechartre, "L'emploi: vouloir la relance," Le Matin, September 1978; Chirac, "Oui, la relance est possible," Le Nouvel Observateur, 14 May 1979; and Chirac, Le Monde, 5 March 1979 and 14 May 1979.

10. Propositions pour la France, p. 219; and Chirac, Le Monde, 15 April 1980.

11. Michel Garibal, "Le rapport Méo," Journal des Finances, 27 September 1979.

12. Propositions pour la France, pp. 184-89; Debré, interview in Les Echos, 6 September 1978.

13. Chirac, interview in Le Nouvel Observateur, 14 May 1979.

14. Jean Méo in Forum International, 4 October 1979 and 21 December 1979; and in Le Monde, 27 June 1980.

15. Philippe Bauchard, L'Expansion, 9-22 November 1979; Gilbert Mathieu, Le Monde, 14 February 1980; Pierre Locardel, Les Echos, 13 February 1980. For the political crisis see note 4.

16. Le Monde, 15 April 1980.

17. Debré, "Un grand dessein pour la France?," Bulletin ACADI, January-February 1978, pp. 34-58; and Debré in Forum International, 29 August 1979

18. Debre in Le Figaro, 12 June 1978, and in Le Monde, 14 February 1979; also Chirac, interview in Paradoxes, February 1975, pp. 58-59.

19. Chirac, Le Nouvel Observateur, 14 May 1979; discussed by Gilbert Mathieu in Le Monde, 16 April 1980; Debré, Forum International, 29 August 1979; and L'Expansion, 21 December 1979.

20. Propositions pour la France, pp. 177-78.

21. Méo, "On ne peut promener le pays de tunnel en tunnel," Forum International, 4 October 1979; also Chirac, interview in L'Expansion, 9-22 November 1979.

22. Méo, Le Monde, 27 June 1980.

23. Chirac, "La participation est la dernière chance de la liberté," Paradoxes, October-November 1977, pp. 75-79; Debre, "Un grand dessein pour la France?," Bulletin ACADI, January-February 1978, pp. 44-45; Propositions pour la France, p. 169; Chirac, Le Monde, 15 April 1980.

24. Chirac, interiew in Paradoxes, February 1975, p. 57.

25. UDR 1975, L'enjeu (Paris: Presses Pocket, 1975); quote from introduction by Jacques Chirac. See also p. 171.

26. Propositions pour la France, p. 181; Chirac in Le Nouvel Observateur, 9 November 1979.

27. Méo, Forum International, 4 October 1979; and Chirac, L'Expansion, 9-22 November 1979 (he talked then of 4-5 percent).

28. William R. Schonfeld, "The RPR: From a Rassemblement to the Gaullist Movement," in Andrews and Hoffmann, eds., The Fifth Republic at Twenty, pp. 97-107.

29. Chirac interview in Le Monde, 15 April 1980.

30. Monory, interview in Paris-Match, 6 March 1981; Alain Vernholes, "Faisons un rêve," Le Monde, 1-2 March 1981.

31. Propositions pour la France, pp. 56-59.

32. André Fourcans in Le Monde, 20 May 1980.

33. Michel Debré, "Un grand dessein pour la France?", Bulletin ACADI, January-February 1978, pp. 34-55; particularly pp. 36-39.

34. Michel Debré's economic program of 1979, cited in Christian Stoffaës, La grande menace industrielle, revised edition (Paris: Calmann-Lévy, 1979), p. 18.

35. Thus the Gaullist "Manifeste d'Agir pour la France," Arguments, March-April 1978, pp. 25-26.

9

ALTERNATIVES FROM THE LEFT

The year 1974 had seen the high point of Leftist unity; but towards the end of 1974, the first conflicts between Socialists and Communists set in. These conflicts gradually increased until the break of 1977. From then on, the two Leftist parties were clearly divided again. This process also led to internal divisions within the Socialist party, which broke into the open in 1979 and 1980. Many of these conflicts concerned the economic, social, and industrial policy that the Left should implement in the event it should come to power.

In the premature presidential elections which followed Pompidou's death, Mitterrand ran as the only candidate of the two big parties of the Left; he came very close to the score achieved by Giscard. Even though Mitterrand did not base his platform on the Common Program (he did not disavow it either), the Communists remained loyal throughout the campaign. Instead, Mitterrand developed more modest and more rigorous proposals, based in all likelihood on the advice of Jacques Attali and Michel Rocard. It was only in the fall of 1974 — with the Assises du socialisme, which brought new elements into the party and put Chevènement and his neo-Marxist CERES in the background — that the Communists began to be openly suspicious of Mitterrand.

In retrospect, it is clear how two different conceptions of the economy confronted each other. The Communists remained fairly stable in their views, though the compromises which they were seeking took on different forms. Among the Socialists on the other hand, views differed considerably between such "moderates" as Rocard, Attali, and Delors on one hand, and the CERES group under Chevènement on the other. Mitterrand often occupied a central position and tended to remain ambiguous in his statements and commitments in those areas where internal

121

conflict existed. His political line on the other hand was clear: make the Socialist party the strongest party of the Left and the strongest party in France, and cooperate with the Communists in order to lead a united Left to victory.

It was relatively easy for the Socialists of the different groups to agree on a common critique of Giscard and his prime ministers, Chirac and later on Barre. All were criticized for their austerity policies, even Chirac during his relance period. Rising unemployment was forecast as inevitable under such policies.[1] Already in 1975, the Socialists proposed the creation of jobs in the public sector, which they claimed was understaffed severely in several areas.

When Barre became prime minister, the Socialists at first viewed his policy as just a maneuver for the upcoming 1978 elections. Barre, they predicted, would first slow down the economy and thus hold down inflation; this would be followed by a program of economic stimulation just in time for the March 1978 elections.[2] Such a policy would not solve any of the real problems of the French economy; it would only send it through yet another stop-go cycle, after a first one in 1974-75. Obviously the Socialists miscalculated (or rather misperceived) Barre's real policy, who stuck to disinflation for a long time and excluded any preelectoral stimulation as a matter of principle. The Socialists then adjusted their criticism. No policy, they argued, could be successful unless it increased consumption and thus created stronger domestic markets. If firms were given tax breaks as incentives to invest, this was a waste of public funds because as long as they could not expect to sell their products (something that required stronger domestic markets), they would simply not invest. Since the austerity policies of the government were depressing those markets, they engaged the French economy in a vicious circle.[3] With this policy, they stated, Barre was systematically ruining French industrial power in the world. His emphasis on the external equilibrium, in the absence of decisive efforts to increase French exports by a program of large-scale investments, condemned France to slow growth and economic decline. The bourgeoisie would maintain its privileges under such a regime because of Barre's emphasis on profits (which, in any case, were not sufficiently reinvested). The working class, on the other hand, would slowly lose what it had conquered over the years since World War II. On the world level, the government's emphasis on finding an appropriate place for France in the international division of labor meant that the country would be subjected to the logic of profit of the multinational corporations; those would not hesitate to export industrial employment to cheap-labor countries, while the sectors of technological leadership would be reserved for the core countries of advanced capitalism — the United States, West Germany, and Japan.

The counterpart to this criticism was another point on which all the Socialists (or at least overwhelming majority) could agree, that is, the need for a nationalization program. The rationale for that measure was worked out in greater detail during this period. One of the most comprehensive statements (most leaders did not discuss the matter in such detail, but their views seem largely compatible with this reasoning) came from Alain Boublil in his book Le socialisme industriel.[4] (After 1981, Boublil became advisor to president Mitterrand.)

Boublil argued that full employment and the equilibrium of international payments could be achieved only if France had a strong, export-oriented industry. This in turn could only be achieved by measures that acted directly on supply, not by stimulation of demand which just resulted in increased imports. This meant that Keynesianism was largely obsolete.[5] The key to success was innovation and investment in industry. Liberal capitalism had failed in this area, mainly because in France it was dominated by finance capitalism (the banks). Finance capital was guided by considerations of short-term profitability. The highest financial rewards in France, during the 1970s, could be obtained not in industry but in real estate; as a result, most of the bank deposits were in fact channelled into that sector, while industrial investment went neglected. And when the banks did give money to industry, they did so in form of obligations, not in form of equity (new issues of stock). This led to rising indebtedness among French industrial firms and thus squeezed the investors' (stockholders') profits even further. In other words, the banks acted as a parasite with regard to industry, not as a powerful sponsor.[6] Under such conditions it was normal that industrial investments would suffer, something that quickly initiated a vicious circle: lack of investments meant lack of competitiveness, lower profits, and thus even more disinvestment.

Only industrial socialism could reverse this situation, Boublil argued. It would start out by nationalizing a few key industrial firms and the entire banking sector (which had so much distorted economic priorities in the past). Next, it would invest massively in those industries that had been selected for their potential with regard to growth, exports, and employment. In the short run, this would require going against a basic principle of the market economy, since investments would be made in sectors that might show a deficit.[7] But profitability, Boublil stressed, was a dynamic notion; it had to be looked at over time. If the firms would no longer make a deficit after a few years, if they could secure a powerful technological monopoly and provide France with exports that were relatively insensitive to international trade fluctuations, then the risk was well worth taking.[8]

On the other hand, there were limits to what could be done in this way. The state, now the main and most dynamic entrepreneur, also had only limited resources. To subscribe to too massive a program would endanger the success of the whole enterprise. The state therefore had to select a limited range of industries that were particularly promising, either because of technological leadership that would pay off economically, or because of the employment impact or a close relationship with national independence. Boublil also made it clear that any deficit must be temporary. The state must not end up subsidizing obsolete industries.[9] Thus only a concentration of means could bring the desired effect, that is, a breakthrough that would make those industries leaders in the competition for the world market.

Such a program, Boublil argued, was not at all protectionist; on the contrary, it accepted the principle of open borders and even a high level of international trade.[10] But France had to make certain that she would be placed on an equal level in such trade, instead of falling into the trap of unequal exchange, which could only lead to underdevelopment and national decline. (Nonetheless the mercantilist nature of this policy is quite clear, in fact, the reasoning is not so different from the old "infant industries" argument.[11]) The goal of this policy was to make France a core country in the world political economy, a country that would stand on an equal level with the United States, Germany, and Japan.[12] The main difference between France and the leading capitalist powers would be that in France, the advantages of industrial leadership would be reaped by society as a whole, whereas in the other countries they would presumably benefit primarily the multinational corporations. On the other hand, the fact that France would enjoy a consistent balance of trade surplus, something that Boublil specifically mentions[13], shows that this project, though it views itself as Socialist and declares repeatedly its solidarity with the countries of the third world that suffer even more from the profit orientation of international capitalism, is predatory in its own way, since its realization would mean a concentration of industrial employment in France at the expense of other areas or countries.

Boublil's general line of reasoning was identical (though more elaborate) to that of most Socialists. Even Rocard, often portrayed as the most "moderate" of the Socialist leaders (at least before Delors became more prominent), placed great emphasis on the need for nationalizations; the Left had to take control of the dominant firms so that pricing, employment, investment and production policies could be decided in the national interest, rather than be dictated by the profit considerations of the individual firms.[14] Delors, too, expressed opposition to the wholesale liquidation of French industry that took place under Barre and criticized the fact that the evolution of whole sectors was left up simply to the state of international markets.[15]

Nonetheless the nationalizations came to play a major role in the conflict between Socialists and Communists. This is best understood by the new emphasis that the Socialists now put on the market economy, which they said they would preserve (while obviously making a partial exception for the public sector). However, there was some ambiguity since different lines of argument were put forward by different Socialist leaders, usually representing the different courants, or tendencies, which made up the party.

Before the 1977 break of the Leftist alliance, these conflicts were relatively subdued. Within the P.S., there were four major courants from 1974 onward. The largest one was that of Mitterrand; it was followed at a distance by those of Rocard and Mauroy; finally, there was the CERES, led by Jean-Pierre Chevenement, which was in many respects closest to the Communist party. Until 1979, the CERES was in internal opposition (within the party), so that its voice was somewhat subdued. Under these circumstances, the weight of the "moderates" (Rocard and Mauroy) was considerably greater.

It was in 1976 that the commitments of the Socialist leaders to a market economy that would remain open internationally attracted the greatest attention.[16] Rocard tirelessly stressed the economic constraints that a Socialist government would have to face; the Left, he repeated over and over, must not fail again as it had too often in the past, when an apparently generous policy of wage gains had led to political bankruptcy within a short time period. There would be several difficult years of transition before the new Socialist policy would have an impact.[17] For this reason the Left must not promise excessive redistribution; this was simply not possible. Such a policy would create serious economic difficulties, in particular a sizeable balance of payment deficit. That in turn would put an end to the Socialist experiment, for international creditors (such as the International Monetary Fund) would be quick to impose an austerity policy, wholly at odds with the Socialist program.[18] For this reason Rocard emphasized qualitative reforms as well as changes in the distribution of power, corresponding to his philosophy of autogestion.[19]

Such a line was clearly anathema to the Communists. They were displeased by the Socialists' strong commitment to the market economy and highly critical of Rocard's emphasis on economic rigor. In addition, they viewed with growing concern the rise of a stronger Socialist party which — as Mitterrand had made clear early on — not only planned to acquire a hegemonial position of the Left, but was about to realize this objective. Since the electoral balance was turning against them, it became all the more important to the Communists to commit the Socialist party to a program which would also be acceptable to the P.C.F.

This led them to insist on an update of the Common Program in preparation for the 1978 elections. Mitterrand (and even more Rocard) disliked the idea; Mitterrand wanted as free a hand as possible, and Rocard (whose popularity was already very high) was concerned that the Communists would systematically make demagogic proposals to show that they were the only "true" representatives of the working class, and thus push the P.S. into positions which were economically untenable. But the negotiations took place anyhow; soon the expected conflicts broke out. The Socialists proposed a minimum wage (SMIC) of 2,000 francs; they quickly gave in, however, to the figure of 2,400 francs advanced by the Communists, despite Rocard's strong opposition. (Rocard in fact argued that the Communists would not mind if the wage increase drove a large number of firms into bankruptcy — the nationalized banks would come to control them, and this was just another way to enlarge the public sector.[20])

The main conflict however centered on the question of the nationalizations. The Socialists, led on this point by Rocard, wanted to stick to the list of firms laid down in the Common Program of 1972. The Communists on the other hand wished to add several sectors; in addition, they wanted to nationalize all the subsidiaries of the firms on the nationalization list. On the whole, this would have increased the number of such firms to 1,450.[21] Rocard rejected the proposal with the argument that to do so was both unnecessary and wasteful since it would require the government to expropriate minority capital that was powerless anyhow; even without such a measure the control of the parent firm meant a majority participation in the subsidiary and therefore brought effective control.[22] The Communists, it became clear, wanted a much larger public sector, and they wanted that sector to be exempt from the "logic of profit," in fact exempt from the discipline of the market. In Rocard's view, their underlying goal was a closed command economy (despite declarations about management autonomy), and they were determined to make as much progress as possible towards that goal. In any case, it was over the issue of nationalizations that the break between the two parties occurred in the fall of 1977. This break sealed the fate of the Left in the 1978 elections.

Now the mood in the Socialist party changed. For years this mood had been optimistic, based on the assumption that the Left would come to power soon. In fact, the Left had achieved a clear majority of votes at the regional elections in 1976 and the municipal elections of 1977. But the break of 1977, and the subsequent defeat in 1978, threw the Socialist party into a crisis of demoralization, recriminations and declining militantism. Rocard and Mauroy, who after Mitterrand had been the most important leaders in the party, now moved away from him. This evolution was consecrated at the party congress in Metz, in the spring of 1979, at which their two courants formed the new "internal opposition";[23] by contrast, Chevènement and the CERES returned to the party majority.

After the 1978 defeat, many of the high civil servants who had jumped on the bandwagon when the party seemed to be headed for victory dropped out again, and the morale as well as the number of militants declined.[24] There seemed to be no end to internal disagreements, even though the party was at the same time attacked from the outside by the Communists who blamed it for the break of 1977. In fact, this critique found an echo inside the party with the leaders of the CERES, who now attacked Rocard for his "economic rigor" (which brought him positive responses also from the world of business) and at one point blamed him for the breakdown of the negotiations with the Communists in 1977.[25]

It was in this atmosphere that Mitterrand developed his economic program of June 1979, which at the time met with relatively little public response. It seems that the program was not influenced by Rocard, Mauroy, or even Chevènement.[26] In many ways it was similar to the earlier programs, but it also brought some innovations. Economic stimulation via consumption still played an important role in it, but like the Gaullist program which was to be submitted a few months later, it placed greater emphasis than before on investments, more than in the adapted version of the Common Program submitted by the Socialists in January 1978. There were also proposals to reduce French dependence on international trade; from 22 percent of France's GDP, it was to come down to 20 percent, perhaps 18 percent.[27] He also proposed to eliminate generalized price controls and restrict them to those areas where competition was not effective, and to proceed with greater caution in the area of job creation. However, the program still insisted on the 35 hours week without reduction in wages as well as on reduced age limits (60 years for men, 55 for women) for retirement. The reduction of inequalities was still stressed as important, though no specific figures were given either for the minimum wage or for financing the program in general. Autogestion was not mentioned, but many of the ecology themes were incorporated. The program proposed a qualitatively different form of economic development that was to be less resource-intensive and oriented towards better consumption and more durable goods rather than towards maximization of consumption. It promised a life in which happiness, security, and the environment would not be sacrificed to the economic calculus. The return to full employment was part of the program, but here again, no time schedule or specific figures were given except for the creation of jobs in the public sector; 150,000 jobs were to be created in the civil service, and another 60,000 in local government.[28] Finally, three firms were added to the nationalization list.[29] The reception by leading journalists was similar to that given the Gaullist program a few months later: would it be possible to finance all this? Would it be possible to hold down inflation simultaneously? In addition, were the goals for reduced international trade and energy consumption realistic? But even Les Echos, one of France's most important business and financial papers, recognized that the program appeared "more realistic," even if it still contained quite a few "dreams."[30]

While Mitterrand maintained himself as the unquestioned leader within the party, Rocard (now in the "internal opposition" with Mauroy) stepped up his criticism. He was particularly critical of Mitterrand's waverings on such issues as the market economy and its precise scope; on "generous" proposals that ignored the realities of economic restraints any government would have to face; and on the "break with capitalism" that Mitterrand liked to mention, a sentence to which everyone could give a very different meaning.[31] Capitalism, Rocard argued, should not be equated with the monopolies; to do so was the strategy of the Communist party, and the P.S. had made a mistake in accepting such an interpretation of economic life. Capitalism was something much larger; it did not consist of the boards of a few dozen firms but was made up of a whole network: a system of consumer credit and of consumer behavior in the market, and the desire of many Frenchmen (including many blue-collar workers) to achieve a good place in a hierarchy based on money. All this, including the mindsets that went in hand with these phenomena, had to be questioned and needed to be overcome. But that could not be done simply by a few nationalizations, much less by redistributive reforms (which in any case were bound to be hampered by a difficult economic environment).[32]

Thus the internal divisions within the party lasted through a good part of 1980. They manifested themselves in internal party discussions over the Projet socialiste,[33] early in the year. Much of this program, it was reported, had been drafted by Chevenement, who had kept out the contributions made to the Socialist party by Rocard and the autogestion movement.[34] Rocard tried to amend the program at the party convention, but secured only about 30 percent of the delegates' votes.[35]

As the presidential elections approached, Rocard made it clear that he was interested in seeking the party's nomination, though he was prepared to yield should Mitterrand want to run again. He was more popular with the electorate than Mitterrand;[36] however, within the party the opposite situation prevailed. When Mitterrand remained aloof, Rocard finally (in October) announced his own candidacy, but he withdrew it three weeks later when Mitterrand declared that he would himself seek the Socialist nomination.[37] It was a far cry from the unity preceding the 1974 presidential elections, especially as the Communists now insisted on running their own candidate. But Rocard maintained party discipline and promised to work hard for Mitterrand's election; and as to the Communists, the Socialists had learned, since 1977, to deal more effectively with their tactics designed to weaken their chief ally the Socialist party, if necessary by insuring the defeat of the Left altogether rather than seeing the P.C.F. decline. After some hesitation, Mitterrand, who insisted on the strategy of the Leftist unity, appealed to Communist voters or sympathizers over the heads of the Communist party, a method that seemed highly successful in 1981.[38]

In that year, the Socialist position was remarkably strong. The internal conflicts of the Left had hurt it in 1978; however, by 1981 the break with the Communists showed also positive results. That break made the Socialist commitment to the market economy more credible than any reassurances that they might have given. Surprisingly, the internal conflicts of the Socialist party did not damage it before the French electorate (see Table 11.2). Increasingly it was perceived as the party who was best able to manage the economy (see Chapter 11). Prior to 1981, the Socialists were fairly consistent in the program that they presented; the major reforms which Mitterrand stressed in his campaign (redistribution and nationalization) both had solid support among the electorate. The party also made a deliberate attempt to accommodate the new social movements of the 1970s (ecology, feminism, regionalism, and so on),[39] though this accommodation may have been superficial.

Mitterrand's victory is partially explained by the strength of the Socialists (which they drew in part from the weakness of the Communists), who were able to come up with what appeared to be a credible alternative. The Left had the additional advantage of not having to deal with the many handicaps that tarnished Barre's performance, ranging from demographic problems to two oil crises. This was a luxury that only opposition status could confer. The Socialists made effective use of the INSEE forecasts that projected the rise in unemployment under Barre's policy. Even Chirac's critique of Giscard and Barre was bound to benefit the Socialists to some extent, since his proposals (at least until 1981) often had elements in common with the Socialists. Once they had concluded that Barre's policy was one of national decline, the Socialists could plausibly appeal to Gaullist voters in the name of saving the nation from disaster,[40] particularly after the first round. The standard critique that the Right had addressed to the Left in the preceding decade — that the Left would bring a collectivist, totalitarian society and economy — seemed hardly credible in 1981.[41]

GRAPH 9.1

Electoral Strength of Communists and Socialists in France,
1924-1981

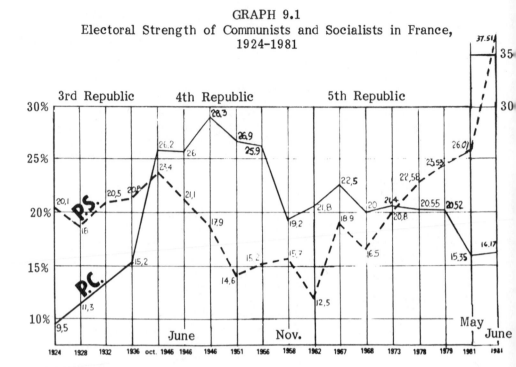

Source: Le Nouvel Observateur, 28 April 1981, p. 21;   and
Le Monde, weekly selection 7 January 1982, p. 4.   Copyright Le
Nouvel Observateur.

The evolution of the Communist party is in striking contrast
to that of the Parti Socialiste.   In the late 1960s and early
1970s, it had been the stronger party of the Left; from then on
it declined, not necessarily in absolute but at least in relative
terms, when compared to the Socialists.   To the Communist leadership relative weight was just as important, as the leadership of
the Left was at stake.   Mitterrand never made any bones about
his intentions to create a "new equilibrium" on the Left, one
more favorable to the Socialists.   As a result, as early as 1972
Marchais, the leader of the Communist party, was suspicious of
him: should the P.C. enter into an alliance with the Socialists
when their leader might end up implementing a social-democratic
policy in case he came to power?   For this reason, particular
emphasis was placed on the Common Program, which the Communists had strongly influenced (see above); it would bind the P.S.
in public and thus protect it against internal hesitations.   The
militant basis of the Communist Party (P.C.F.), several times
stronger than that of the P.S., provided an additional
guaranty.42   In the 1974 elections the Communists gave Mitter-

rand free rein though, while also giving full support to his candidacy. Misgivings arose in autumn 1974 with the Assises du socialisme, not only because they indicated that the P.S. was moving away from the Common Program but also because they showed that it was setting out to obtain a working class base through the C.F.D.T., France's second largest labor union whose leaders were prominent in the Assises; this would challenge the P.C.F. on its home turf.[43] Fears about Socialist emancipation were reinforced by the latter's emphatic commitments to a market economy in 1976, and also by the realization that electoral cooperation benefitted primarily the Socialists. The paradoxical result: even as the P.C. continued its own liberalization, marked by the abandonment of the "dictatorship of the proletarist" in 1976, its attitude towards the Socialist party became more and more rigid; by the end of the 1970s, the resulting strains effectively put an end to internal liberalization. At all costs the P.S. had to be reined in by the Common Program, which was now given an even stricter interpretation. This explains the break of 1977 during the updating negotiations[44] which formally occurred over the issue of the subsidiaries of the nationalized companies.[45] The Socialists were accused of accepting the "logic of profit." Under these circumstances, the P.C.F. leadership decided that it was better to lose an election rather than help into the saddle a Socialist party which, once in power, would "continue the policy of big capital."[46] It published an updated version of the Common Program that was much more detailed than the earlier one (of 1972); it also gave precise figures on major points (a growth rate of 6 percent every year; the creation of 460,000 civil service jobs, and so on).[47]

From that time onwards, with a brief lull in 1979, the Communists launched continuous attacks on the Socialists. In March 1980, L'Humanité, the party's daily, declared that in the end there was no real difference between the big industrialists, Barre, or even Mitterrand.[48] Events in Afghanistan and Poland fueled the conflict. In autumn 1980, the Communists even refused the long-established practice of electoral cooperation with the Socialists.[49] Their first priority became the reassertion of their own identity against an increasingly hegemonic Socialist party.

Once the ambiguous compromise of the Common Program was abandoned, the economic views of the Community party also underwent a clarification. The analysis of the economic crisis was generally in the traditional mold: it was all due to the overaccumulation of capital by national and international monopolies, causing in turn the overexploitation of the working class.[50] The oil crisis only served as alibi for the capitalist offensive against the working class conducted by the Barre government. Both Giscard and Barre were seen as acting hand-in-glove with international capital in order to dismantle French

industry in the search for higher profit rates elsewhere.[51]   If
there was an innovation, it was on the greater emphasis on
international capital rather than on "state monopoly capitalism."
The answer to the crisis — and here the French Communist party
disagreed with its Italian counterpart under Berlinguer — was
not an economic policy of "just" (that is, fairly shared) austerity
but a wholesale rejection of the logic of profit, coupled with
economic nationalism. It was the capitalist concern with profitability which led to shutdowns and layoffs. This criterion needed
to be replaced with the new one of "social profitability," which
would lead to the greater satisfaction of needs and thus to
higher output.[52]   A stepped-up demand would result from a vast
program of redistribution and rising purchasing power of all
wage-earners and peasants. If this could not be accommodated
by a market economy (where increased demand might lead to increased imports rather than increased French production), state
control over the economy would be increased, both on the domestic level (expansion of state control by nationalizations) and the
international one (protectionist measures). The issue of nationalizations was crucial since the Communist approach (state control)
was quite different from that of the Socialists. If the Socialists
were satisfied with a controlling interest in the subsidiaries, it
was because they were generally prepared to accept the
discipline of the market for these firms. To the Communists, this
meant accepting the "logic of profit", in the end that of the
monopolists and the Barre government. The conflict was replayed
in the same terms over the issue of the steel industry. Again
the Socialists, despite their opposition to Barre's handling of the
problem, were quite prepared to accept the sanction of the
market, while the Communists refused it, proposing nationalization, expansion of production, and an end to all layoffs.[53]

One of the criticisms of the Common Program had long been
that it would lead to a "closing of the borders," that is, that it
would make protectionism unavoidable and thus lead to a weakening of France's international position as well as a decline in the
standard of living. While there was always ambiguity on this
point, the Communists stepped up their nationalist rhetoric during
the late 1970s; "national" became as important a term in their
thinking and propaganda as "social." This was contrasted with
the international, and thus basically antinational ("profit is their
only homeland") disposition of "monopolistic capital."[54] The Communists tried to exploit residual anti-German feelings (a tactic
also resorted to by Chirac, while Giscard and Barre referred to
the German "model") and also racial prejudice in their campaigns
against immigrant workers. In 1980 Marchais drew the logical
conclusion from his proposal to reestablish full employment in
France. It could be necessary "in certain cases" to protect
French industry and agriculture; one must not hesitate to keep

out foreign products in those cases. But he did not discuss the problem of possible foreign retaliation.[55]

Thus the two parties of the Left had moved apart with regard to their economic policy prescriptions during the Barre era. Still there were considerable similarities: The Communists also proposed redistribution of income (though on a much larger scale than the Socialists) and advocated full employment policies. They supported the 35 hour week and earlier retirement, nationalizations and greatly improved public services and investments. On their side, the Socialists kept rejecting the suspicion that they might have become social democrats and maintained the slogan of the "break with capitalism." Mitterrand also refused to confront the Communists aggressively with their own contradictions and inconsistencies, as Mauroy and Rocard would have preferred.[56] He did not want to endanger an electoral victory by making the break irreparable. Many Communist voters were more interested in a victory of the Left than in the relative position of the Communist party within the Leftist alliance, and Marchais greatly upset party cohesion when he decided to run himself as a candidate in the presidential elections (see Chapter 14). But unlike Chirac, who refused to announce ahead of time whom he would support in the second round, Marchais announced his intention beforehand. Despite his own candidacy, he would recommend a vote for Mitterrand in the second round.[57]

NOTES

1. "Mitterrand répond à Giscard," L'Unité, 11-17 July 1975; Guy Perrimond, "Quelle relance?," L'Unité, 5-11 Sept. 1975.
2. Pierre Mauroy, "Les deux faces du plan Barre," Revue politique et parlementaire, Sept.-Oct. 1976, pp. 6-10; Jacques Gallus, "A quoi sert le plan Barre," Faire, Oct. 1976, pp. 6-8.
3. Jean Boissonnat, "Les deux stratégies," L'Expansion, July-August 1977.
4. Alain Boublil, Le socialisme industriel (Paris: Presses universitaires de France, 1977).
5. Ibid., pp. 15-17. He adds that it might work in the United States, where foreign trade plays a much more modest role (p. 62).
6. Ibid., pp. 38-46.
7. Ibid., p. 62.
8. Ibid., pp. 72-82.
9. Ibid., pp. 259-60.
10. Ibid., pp. 51-52.
11. The infant industries argument holds that tariff protection is appropriate as long as it is temporary and designed to

help industries catch up with the higher level of development reached elsewhere.

12. Ibid., pp. 77-80.

13. Ibid., p. 52.

14. Patrick Viveret, "Débat avec Michel Rocard," Faire, September 1976; and Rocard, "La gauche et les pouvoirs," Bulletin ACADI, January-February 1978.

15. Jacques Delors in Le Nouvel Observateur, 8 January 1979. Similar statements also came from Jacques Attali; Dirigeant, Feb. 1977.

16. Kathleen Evin and Roland Cayrol, "Comment contrôler l'union? Les relations P.C.-P.S. depuis 1971," Projet, January 1978, pp. 64-74. Also contributions of Mitterrand, Rocard and Attali in Faire, December 1976.

17. Michel Rocard in Le Monde, 11-12 September 1977.

18. Rocard in Faire, December 1976.

19. Viveret and Rocard, Faire, September 1976; Rocard in Le Monde, 11-12 September 1977; see also Chapter three of present volume.

20. Rocard, "La gauche et les pouvoirs," Bulletin ACADI, January-February 1978; and Ivan Levaı, "Michel Rocard fait le point," Paradoxes, February-March 1978, pp. 20-23.

21. P.C.F., Programme commun de gouvernement actualisé (Paris: Editions sociales, 1978), p. 76.

22. Rocard, "La gauche et les pouvoirs," pp. 10-12; Rocard, "Nationaliser: oui mais comment?," in Michel Rocard, Parler vrai (Paris: Le Seuil, 1979), pp. 143-49.

23. Le Nouvel Observateur, 27 Nov. 1978, p. 47; 4 Dec. 1978, pp. 62-63; 18 Dec. 1978, pp. 44 and 45; 8 Jan. 1979, pp. 28-29; 14 April 1979, pp. 32-35; Hugues Portelli, "Guerre de succession au PS," Projet, June 1979, pp. 739-42; Le Nouvel Observateur, 25 June 1979, pp. 32-33.

24. Jean-Marie Colombani, in Le Monde, 15 March 1980.

25. Attack by Laurent Fabius: George Mamy in Le Nouvel Observateur, 14 April 1979, pp. 33-35; by Jean-Pierre Chevènement: Thierry Pfister, Le Nouvel Observateur, 15 Oct. 1979. In a sample survey, 57 percent of the category "liberal professions, executives and businessmen" had a good opinion of Rocard (bad opinion: 25 percent); for Mitterrand the respective figures were 45 percent (good opinion) and 43 percent (bad opinion). Sondages, no. 2 and 3, 1978, p. 74.

26. Gilbert Mathieu in Le Monde, 10 July 1979.

27. Ibid.

28. These figures remained consistent for several years, despite the rising unemployment. Le Monde, 29 January 1976; Mitterrand in L'Unite, 2 February 1979; Le Monde, 8 May 1981.

29. The program as presented before the economic journalists is discussed in Le Monde, 23 June and 10 July 1979; it is pre-

sented in greater detail in L'Unite, 29 June 1979. The most important firm newly targeted for nationalization was Matra.

30. Pierre Locardel in Les Echos, 22 June 1979.

31. Franz-Olivier Giesbert in Le Nouvel Observateur, 30 December 1978; and Georges Mamy in Le Nouvel Observateur, 14 April 1979. When Rocard argued against increasing the minimum wage and against a reduction of the work week to 35 hours without reducing at least the higher salaries, Mitterrand reportedly responded that in these cases "politics came before economics." Rocard rejected such arguments as guimauve (marshmallow) — the typical error of a Left that fails to face reality. F.-O. Giesbert in Le Nouvel Observateur, 27 November 1978.

32. Hugues Portelli, "Guerre de succession au P.S.," Projet, June 1979, pp. 739-42; also Michel Rocard, Parler vrai (Paris: Le Seuil, 1979), pp. 91-92.

33. Projet socialiste (Paris: Club socialiste du livre, 1980).

34. Criticisms also came from Mauroy, Attali, Delors, and Lionel Jospin; on the other hand, the "Marxist" wing of the Mitterrand supporters around Pierre Joxe supported it strongly. See "Le projet du parti socialiste," Citoyens, January-February 1980.

35. Kathleen Evin in Le Nouvel Observateur, 14 January 1980.

36. See surveys in Le Nouvel Observateur, 9 April 1979, p. 46; L'Expansion, 21 September 1979, p. 91; Le Monde, 1 April 1980, pp. 1 and 8; Le Point, 17 November 1980, p. 78.

37. Le Point, 17 November and 1 December 1980.

38. Such a strategy was already proposed in 1979 by Jean-Pierre Cot (Le Nouvel Observateur, 8 January 1979, pp. 28-29), and Rocard (Hugues Portelli, "La guerre de succession au PS," Projet, June 1979, pp. 739-42). Mitterrand seems to have adopted that view in 1980 (Jean-Marie Colombani in Le Monde, 11 March 1980, p. 11; Jean Boissonnat, L'Expansion, 7 March 1980, pp. 53-57).

39. Suzanne Berger, "Politics and Antipolitics in Western Europe in the Seventies," Daedalus, vol. 108, no. 1 (1979), p. 48.

40. Gilles Martinet, "Pour une vraie politique de salut public," Faire, September 1979, pp. 3-6.

41. A large part of Propositions pour la France is devoted to this enterprise. Much of the same criticism was repeated (with less justification) in 1981; see, for example, Jean Lecanuet in Le Monde, 18 April 1981; and by Giscard himself after the first round; see Maurice Duverger, "L'épouvantail," Le Monde (weekly edition), 23 April 1981, p. 1.

42. Kathleen Evin and Roland Cayrol, "Comment contrôler l'union?," Projet, January 1978, pp. 64-74.

43. Op. cit.; Hugues Portelli, "Que se passe-t-il au parti socialiste?," ibid., pp. 45-63; J. C. Simmons, "The French Commu-

nist Party in 1978: Conjugating the Future Imperfect," Parliamentary Affairs, 32:1 (Winter 1979), pp. 79-91.

44. Evin and Cayrol, "Comment contrôler l'union?," pp. 69-73; Colette Ysmal, "Parti Communiste: Les raisons d'un durcissement," Projet, January 1978, pp. 44-54.

45. According to Rocard, Charles Fiterman of the P.C.F. had already accepted the Socialist refusal to nationalize the subsidiaries when he counted up the cost of the nationalizations in an interview with Les Echos, in February 1977; Rocard, Parler vrai, p. 148.

46. Claude Harmel, "Ce que les Communistes ont voulu," Est et Ouest, 15-31 March 1978, pp. 112-15. In 1980 the Socialist leaders were no longer taken aback by this attitude.

47. Programme commun de gouvernement actualisé, pp. 172-73. Much of this precision, there is reason to believe, was only apparent. Thus, when a large deficit appeared once the technicians calculated a budget the political leaders decided to add to the revenue side an extra budget post for "capitalist waste" that would now be avoided. See Yves Rocaute, Le P.C.F. et les sommets de l'Etat (Paris: Presses Universitaires de France, 1981), and Le Point, 19 January 1981, pp. 42-43.

48. Editorial "Remèdes à la sinistrose," L'Humanité, 1 March 1980.

49. Le Point, 6 and 20 October 1980. This was on the occasion of the senatorial elections.

50. Jean-Pierre Gaudard, "Quelle politique économique et sociale pour la France?," Cahiers du communisme, November 1977, pp. 14-23.

51. Marc Bormann, "Le démantèlement du potentiel industriel national," Cahiers du communisme, November 1976, pp. 23-30, Jean-Louis Gombeaud, "Gagner?," France Nouvelle, 2 October 1978; and (by the same author) "Appauvrir la France," France Nouvelle, 4 August 1979.

52. Bernard Marx, et al., "Avec les Communistes les moyens du changement," Economie et politique, February 1978, pp. 54-78; and Colette Ysmal, "Parti Communiste: les raisons d'un durcissement," Projet, January 1978, pp. 44-54.

53. Juliette Petit, "Sidérurgie: Le P.S. contre la nationalisation," Economie et politique, February 1978, pp. 49-51; Claude Gauche-Cazalis, "Une sidérurgie d'un type nouveau," ibid. April 1979, pp. 60-66.

54. Mireille Bertrand, "Offensive antisociale et antinationale — une même stratégie: celle du déclin," Cahiers du communisme, February 1979, pp. 4-12; Philippe Herzog in L'Express, 31 March 1979; and in Le Monde, 23 August 1979.

55. Marchais in Le Monde. 27 February 1981.

56. F. O. Giesbert in Le Nouvel Observateur, 30 December 1978.

57. On the other hand, it seems that the party gave also secret instructions to militants to help defeat Mitterrand. See, for example, Patrick Jarreau in Le Monde, 9 and 11 January 1982.

10
BUSINESS AND LABOR

The mid-1970s were a difficult time for many French employers. There were immediate economic reasons: interest rates had been rising for some time, taking up an increasing share of the return on capital; wages also progressed further, and in 1974 dismissals had become more difficult; at the same time financing of investments from retained earnings fell, indebtedness increased, and investment stagnated (particularly in large firms — it actually increased considerably in firms with less than 100 employees).[1] The political evolution added to the demoralization: the Left was showing considerable strength in polls and elections, and in fall 1976, a survey conducted by the monthly L'Expansion showed that employers expected with a ratio of 3:1 that the Left would win the 1978 legislative elections.[2] That possibility was viewed with distress by most employers of the private sector, who seemed to think that the Common Program was committed not only to redistribution but would, in the words of the Conseil National du Patronat Francais (The French Employers' Association), put an end to free enterprise and make France the home of "collectivism." Mitterrand and many Socialists might not approve of that, but they would inevitably be dominated by the Communists and their methods.[3] Not surprisingly, many employers participated actively in the propaganda battle against the Left. Some firms that were targets for nationalization entered agreements with foreign businesses in order to make that process more difficult, if not impossible. Also, some capital flight occurred just before the elections. On the whole, demoralization seemed to prevail.[4]

But with the breakup of Leftist unity in the fall of 1977, demoralization changed camp. Barre's policy was now supported and praised. At the same time the Conseil National du Patronat

Francais (which is tilted in favor of big business) came forward with interpretations and proposals which showed that in some ways its approach differed from that of government. Like Barre, this organization (abbreviated as C.N.P.F.) stressed the need to financially strengthen private enterprise; advocated complete decontrol of prices, amortization of assets by calculating them at their real value (instead of their book value, which ignored inflation), and measures to encourage stock ownership. It urged a reduction of fiscal and social charges and other, similar measures. It also joined the prime minister in the advocacy of a deflationary cure and of the need, in particular, to hold down wage increases. However, it viewed such a policy as a temporary expedient, feeling that an austerity which lasted too long was bound to weaken the economy. Consequently, as early as October 1976 the C.N.P.F. expressed worry about the decline in demand that could be anticipated, and asked for prompt supportive measures within a few months. Otherwise, it warned, there would have to be another plan Barre against unemployment by September 1977.5 France needed a high growth rate to solve her social problems;6 this in turn required a high rate of investment. In the eyes of the C.N.P.F., investment had fallen behind for two reasons: low demand (which meant that existing capacities were underused) and the fragile situation of many French business firms.7

Early in 1977, Jacques Ferry argued in his yearly C.N.P.F. report that the medicine of Barre should not last longer than one year, after which it should be possible to return to growth. He also called for a policy favorable to industry, one that would be more energetic than the one practiced by the government. This would require French enterprises that were financially strong, but it also required a framework set up by the state. The elements of such a framework were a (five-year) plan ("the affirmation of an autonomous will to promote . . . a certain rate of growth") and a solid government doctrine regarding international trade.8 Totally free trade, he argued, was unacceptable and tantamount to a surrender to American hegemony. Too many countries took advantage of such a state of affairs to practice their own kind of dumping (through undervalued currencies, low wages, and so on) in order to penetrate the French market. This was leading to untenable situations in such sectors as textiles, steel, or shipbuilding. It was very important for the government to react promptly whenever a whole sector of the French economy was threatened in its very existence and employment. Thus, the C.N.P.F., as it was quite willing to recognize, was asking for a more active role of the state. At the same time it made an effort to distinguish such a role from "interventionism," or the dirigisme to be expected from the Left. Barre did not really live up to these expectations. He believed too much in international competition and preferred to rely on measures designed to strengthen French business at the level of the individual firm without discriminating between different sectors.

The C.N.P.F. continued to call for higher expansion in the early years of the plan Barre. This was the only way to resolve the problem of unemployment, especially as the system of unemployment compensation, designed to meet the requirements of a brief emergency, was weighing too heavily on the firms and thus stood in need of revision.[9] France could not long continue with a growth rate of only three or three and one-half percent per year. The key to progress in this area was investment and an energetic industrial policy on the part of the state, which would outline the "great options" and "protect . . . without becoming protectionist."[10] In October 1979 the daily Les Echos, close to the business world, came up with a proposal to stimulate investment with an injection of 25 billion francs. This, it argued, was the logical continuation of the plan Barre, the first part of which was now "successfully completed" by deflation and the return of financial health among French firms. The 25 billion would stimulate initiative and awaken those energies which Barre's policy had necessarily discouraged in the past.[11] This proposal coincided with the Gaullist's rapport Méo (and the Socialists too had been stressing investments in their earlier June proposals). But the accommodation between the partners of the presidential coalition, clearly hoped for in business circles,[12] did not take place. Instead, Barre only tightened his policy even further, and Andre Giraud, the French minister of industry, stressed that it was not up to the state to choose those industrial sectors which should undergo the strongest expansion. The state's role, he argued, was to place each enterprise in a position which would allow it to be a winner in the international competition.[13] It is true that a C.N.P.F. spokesman supported this approach of the government; recent experience had shown, he argued, that the grand macroeconomic strategies were ill-adapted to a time of crisis, whereas individual business firms could react much more quickly.[14] In fact, some businessmen criticized the government for not going far enough in its support of private enterprise, particularly with measures improving the financial situation of business firms.[15] Overall, it seems that in business circles as in the governmental majority, there was no clear consensus on a fully "open" economy or the conditions of success.[16] These differences in approach were reflected in different electoral attitudes in 1981. Big business was on the whole favorable to Giscard, but small- and medium-sized businesses were far more likely to favor Chirac. Only a narrow majority of the big employers thought well of Giscard's economic policy by 1980. Most of the smaller ones would have preferred something else.[17]

Absence of unity on the employer side was reflected on the side of the labor unions. They also lacked unity or a common understanding of the economic situation. This should not be a surprise given the division of the French labor movement. Of the three large industrial unions, the smallest, the Force ouvrière (F.O.) is openly reformist and apolitical; the strongest, the Confédération générale du travail (C.G.T.) is for all practical purposes Communist 'and an extension of the French Communist party with which it shares some of the top leaders; and the third, the Confédération francaise démocratique du travail (C.F.D.T.) is oriented towards autogestion socialism, open towards the new social movements of the 1970s (ecology, feminism, and others), and despite its closeness with the Socialist party (since the Assises du socialisme in 1974), quite jealous of its political independence.

The C.G.T., like the Communist party, had long been relegated to the ghetto. It emerged from there in the mid-1960s. An important step in this process was an agreement with the C.F.D.T. (according to which the two unions were to coordinate their action) which corresponded to developments at the level of the political parties of the Left.18   After a period in which the unions' fortunes were better than those of the political parties closest to them (1968-72),19 the coordination with those parties reached its highest level from 1973 to the end of 1977. In 1974 both unions supported the candidacy of Mitterrand, and at one point their leaders even shared a podium with the candidate of the united Left.20   During this period, the two unions put all their hopes for a radical transformation of society (both unions challenge capitalism as well as social democracy on principle) in an election which would bring the Left to power. This led to the neglect of the more traditional labor union activities. Neither the plan Barre nor the "economic crisis" were taken very seriously at first, since the 1978 elections would put an end to all this anyhow.21   All the greater was the shock in September 1977, when the negotiations on the revision of the Common Program broke down.

As in the case of the parties of the Left, the optimistic mood of the leadership in the two "revolutionary" unions now gave way to a phase of demoralization, recrimination, and a greater divergence in their thinking.   In addition, they both developed their autonomy vis-a-vis the political parties they were close to. This was particularly true of the C.F.D.T. As early as January 1978, it prepared for the possibility of a defeat by its recentrage. The leadership announced that it had gone too far in subordinating the union's strategy to events in party and electoral politics.   Such a strategy left little initiative to the union and its members and thus encouraged passivity. It was time to remember that society was not changed by elections alone; the struggle was a much broader one, and unions had an independent role to play. Edmond Maire, the leader of the C.F.D.T., had said that much in his earlier critique of the Common Program. The C.F.D.T. now emphasized the struggle against unemployment (solidarity with the unemployed, reduction of working time); the need to increase the lowest incomes despite the crisis; the improvement of working conditions; and the new concerns such as the critique of the rapid development of nuclear power, and of "productivism" generally. By the end of 1978, the C.G.T., in turn, discovered the need for more 'trade-unionist' practices.[22]

With regard to the economic crisis that had settled on much of the Western world, the outlook of the unions diverged very sharply. F.O. argued for accepting the necessity of industrial adaptation, even though its leader, André Bergeron, was to criticise the government later on for letting unemployment rise to such high levels, reminding it that it was just such a situation which had once brought Hitler to power.[23] C.F.D.T. and C.G.T. both criticized Barre in much stronger terms. The C.F.D.T. thought that the situation was very serious. It did not simply argue for the stimulation of consumption and protectionism (and actively criticized such appeals on the part of the C.G.T.),[24] but took a more selective approach, recognizing the need for industrial restructuring to remain competitive but stressing the possibility of developing French industries in areas where imports were very high. At the same time, the C.F.D.T. argued that the cost of adaptation should be distributed differently across the population. The need to remain competitive in the world economy did not mean that social progress had to come to a halt; it merely meant that further improvements required coordination with the other countries of the European Community.[25]

The approach of the C.G.T. was different and followed that of the Communist party: the crisis was "merely" a crisis of capitalism, and perhaps just a pretext under which advantages conquered by the working class in the past were to be undermined or forcibly taken back. All that was needed, the C.G.T. claimed, was a massive stimulation of consumption and energetic measures to protect the French economy against the disruptions coming from abroad, in a framework that would generally reject the capitalist logic of profit. The way to achieve progress was to put pressure on the government and the capitalists. Thus the C.G.T. sponsored a series of mass demonstrations (journées d'action) with the intent of showing the public the massive discontent reigning among French workers. Such actions, the union proclaimed, would soon put an end to the capitalist offensive.[26]

TABLE 10.1
Days Lost to Labor Disputes
(in thousands of man-days)

1970	1971	1972	1973	1974	1975
1,742	4,388	3,755	3,915	3,377	3,870

1976	1977	1978	1979	1980
5,001	3,666	2,187	3,172	1,449

Source: Main Economic Indicators, 1960-1979 (Paris: O.E.C.D., 1980), p. 293; and (for 1979 and 1980) Le Monde (weekly edition), 12 February 1981, p. 4.

However, these mass demonstrations (which the C.F.D.T. resisted) were never quite as massive as the C.G.T. leadership was hoping. The economic crisis, reinforced no doubt by political defeat, had taken its toll on the "revolutionary" unions, particularly the C.G.T., but to a lesser extent also the C.F.D.T. (only the reformist F.O. seemed to attract a greater audience, at the expense of the two other unions). The decline started, surprisingly, in the heydays of Leftist unity, in 1974 and 1975. Union membership in some (probably quite typical) firms fell as much as 50 percent over a period of five years. The voting strength of the C.G.T. in professional elections actually declined.[27] Also declining was the number of work days lost to strikes, despite a rebound in 1979, a year in which the number of strikes was high throughout the Western world. Militancy was generally on the decline. Most of the workers were worried about their jobs and seemed more open to employers' arguments. Furthermore, the unions were unable to secure new advantages as long as the recession lasted. The employers did their best to accelerate this movement. They developed a conscious strategy of cutting down the unions by setting up mechanisms which bypassed the unions and demonstrated their "futility." The "adversary style" implicit in dealing with labor unions was to be replaced by greater "harmony" in the business firm — and greater reliance on the regular management hierarchy. Despite the resistance of the unions, that approach seemed to be quite successful.[28]

Finally, organized labor in France was increasingly handicapped by the struggle between the two main unions. The C.G.T. mirrored the P.C.F. in its attacks on the Socialists and on the C.F.D.T., which it accused of "shifting to the Right." As with the great parties of the Left, international events (in particular in Afghanistan and Poland) led to increased tensions. At one point Séguy (of the C.G.T.) even accused Maire of being in one camp with the international imperialists and capitalists[29] (just as Mitterrand was told by Marchais at one point that he too was, after all, no different from Barre or the French employers). However, just as on the level of the parties, there was no definite break, though cooperation was unimpressive. The approaching elections of 1981 did nothing to bridge the gap — perhaps because the unions did not expect the Left to win, or did not want to tie their fortunes once more to Mitterrand, whose success was uncertain; besides, there was no common candidate of the Left in the first round. The C.G.T. then became an electoral machine working on behalf of Marchais, the Communist candidate. This caused considerable tension within the union. A significant part of the membership (and many militants) greatly resented the fact that the union was used in this way. Many were also dissatisfied with Marchais' separate course, which prevented Leftist unity. Some militants started a movement that openly went against the line of the P.C.F. and supported cooperation with the Socialists.[30] After the first round, the C.G.T. leadership was less than enthusiastic in endorsing Mitterrand, pointing out that his program was too vague and not satisfactory. The C.F.D.T., though clearly favorable to the Socialist candidate, had some reservations and was still practicing its distance from electoral politics. It was very different from 1974, when both unions had actively campaigned for Mitterrand. Now neither the unions nor the employers seemed to anticipate Mitterrand's victory. The employers in particular were stunned by the event.[31]

NOTES

1. The stagnation of investments, coinciding with a rise of business indebtedness, gave rise to different interpretations. One prominent banker, Jacques de Fouchier from Paribas, argued that it was partly due to fear. Because of the threat of nationalizations, French industry had trouble raising capital in form of stock issues, and the stock market could simply not fulfill its role. See his interview in 78, si la gauche l'emportait (Paris: Ramsay, 1977), pp. 66-68. For the distinction of small firms-larger firms, see "Investissements: Remonter la pente," CNPF Patronat, September 1976, pp. 3-7.

2. Marc Clairvois, "Ceyrac vire à gauche," L'Expansion, November 1977, p. 39.

3. Interview with Francois Ceyrac, Usine Nouvelle, December 1977, pp. 48-50; and Jacques Ferry, "Les impératifs de la croissance," CNPF Patronat, February 1978, pp. 11ff.

4. Francois-Henri de Virieu, "Le patronat prépare 1978," Faire, November 1976, pp. 2-6.

5. "Le plan Barre," CNPF Patronat, October 1976, pp. 6-8.

6. "Une croissance forte est nécessaire," Notes et Arguments, CNPF, May 1976.

7. "Investissements: remonter la pente," CNPF Patronat, September 1976, pp. 3-7.

8. Jacques Ferry, "Une nouvelle politique pour l'industrie," CNPF Patronat, February 1977, pp. 19-28.

9. Interview with Francois Ceyrac, Usine Nouvelle, December 1977, p. 49. There is considerable truth to this; see the discussion of the Socialists' policy on unemployment, Chapter 13.

10. Jacques Ferry, "Les impératifs de la croissance," CNPF Patronat, February 1978, pp. 15 and 18.

11. Pierre Locardel in Les Echos, 3 October 1979.

12. Ibid.; and Michel Garibal in Journal des Finances, 27 September 1979.

13. André Giraud, interview with Le Monde, 22 September 1979.

14. Interview with Alain Chevalier, vice-president of the C.N.P.F., La Croix, 19 October 1979.

15. J. van den Esch in L'Aurore, 9 January 1980.

16. Guy de Carmoy, "Industrie francaise et industrie allemande: performances et stratégies," Politique internationale, no.6, Winter 1979/80, pp. 137-38.

17. Survey by SOFRES: L'Expansion, 17 April 1981, pp. 93-95.

18. Georges Lavau, "The Effect of Twenty Years of Gaullism on the Parties of the Left," in William G. Andrews and Stanley Hoffmann, eds., The Fifth Republic at Twenty (Albany: SUNY Press, 1981), p. 161; and George Ross, "Gaullism and Organized Labor — Two Decades of Failure?," ibid., pp. 336-37.

19. The parties of the Left entered a decline with the 1968 elections. The labor unions on the other hand progressed during this time. Jean Bunel, "L'action syndicale; crise et recentrage," Economie et Humanisme, January-February 1979, pp. 4-11.

20. "Engagées ou non, la plupart des organisations prônent la prudence et le réalisme," Le Monde, 9 May 1981.

21. Emile Favard, "Révisions déchirantes dans les syndicats," L'Expansion, December 1977, pp. 34-35.

22. Jean Bunel, "L'action syndicale," op. cit.; and Pierre Rosonvallon, "Le syndicalisme au tournant," Projet, November 1978, pp. 1033-59.

23. Claude-Francois Jullien and Lucien Rioux, "Les syndicats en ordre dispersé," Le Nouvel Observateur, 15 January 1979, pp. 35-36; and Les Echos, 18 January 1979.

24. Interview with Edmond Maire, Le Nouvel Observateur, 19 February 1979, pp. 28-30.

25. Lucien and Rioux, "Les syndicats en ordre dispersé," op. cit.

26. Ibid.

27. Dominique Pouchin, "Le syndicalisme en crise," Le Monde, 5 March 1980. The connection between the strength of French labor unions and the political fortunes of the Left has manifested itself several times during this century; see Stanley Rothman, Howard Scarrow, and Martin Schain, European Society and Politics (St. Paul: West, 1976), p. 73.

28. Pouchin, "Syndicalisme en crise," Le Monde, 6 and 7 March, 1980; "L'aveu," CNPF Patronat, December 1978, pp. 31-35; and Jean Bonis, "Nouveaux modes d'action manageriales et syndicats," Economie et humanisme, May-June 1981, pp. 31-39.

29. Le Point, 15 September 1980, pp. 40-41; and 6 October 1968, pp. 73-75.

30. See Chapter 14.

31. "Engagées ou non, la plupart des organisations syndicales . . .," Le Monde, 9 May 1981; J. M. Quatrepoint, "Les industriels dans l'expectative," Le Monde, 16 May 1981. For the political attitudes and sympathies of union members in April 1981, see Le Nouvel Observateur, 13 April 1981, pp. 26-27.

11

PUBLIC OPINION

The political mood of the country was subject to wide swings during Giscard's term of office, as the discussions of the Socialist party, the entrepreneurs and the labor unions have shown. Public opinion polls reflect these swings, but on the whole they show a picture that is quite steady and coherent. What emerges from the polls is an increasingly unpopular prime minister whose economic policy is strongly disapproved; a Socialist party which is very popular, despite an appreciation of some of its weaknesses; and a population increasingly concerned about unemployment and strongly favoring strong intervention by the state in the economic life of the country.

The figures are eloquent with regard to political leadership (Table 11.1). In the whole history of the Fifth Republic there was no more unpopular prime minister. From the beginning, those discontented with Barre were more numerous than those who were satisfied. It is true that Giscard was also the least popular of the Fifth Republic's presidents; but the popularity of French prime ministers is at best loosely linked to that of French presidents, even though the institutions of the Fifth Republic link the two office holders closely together.[1]

Despite this clear and overwhelming unpopularity there were still times when there was at least a slight plurality of respondents to hold that it was a good thing that Barre was head of the government. This may reflect the fact that austerity governments may at times be recognized as a necessary evil, though they will hardly ever be popular, as Barre well realized. In any case, by 1979 the negative opinions prevailed on this score as well. The disapproval was particularly pronounced for Barre's economic and social policies; by August 1979, even a majority

149

TABLE 11.1

Attitudes Towards Barre and the Government's Economic Policy

1. Approval of Prime Minister Barre

   A. (August 1978) Do you think it is a good thing or a bad thing that Raymond Barre is head of the government?[a]

Good thing	Bad thing
37	34

   B. (August 1979) Raymond Barre has been prime minister for three years. On the whole, has his action been rather positive or rather negative?[b]

	Rather positive	Rather negative
Overall	27	56
In slowing inflation	13	75
In combating unemployment	11	75

   C. (August 1979) Do you think that over the last three years someone other than Barre would have done better as prime minister?[c]

No	Yes
30	42

2. Approval/disapproval of the government's economic and social policy

   A. (June 1978) Are you rather satisfied or rather dissatisfied with the economic/with the social policy conducted since March 1978?[d]

	Satisfied	Dissatisfied
Economic policy	23	58
Social policy	23	54

   B. (August 1978) As to the economic policy of the government of Raymond Barre, do you approve of it, disapprove of it, or are you indifferent?[e]

Approve	Disapprove
28	44

   C. (October 1978) As to the economic and social policy of the government of Raymond Barre, would you say that you personally are:[f]

Entirely in favor	Rather in favor	Rather opposed	Entirely opposed
4	33	29	26

   D. (August 1979) Do you think that the government is pursuing a policy which in the long run will get France out of her current difficulties, or that it acts from day to day, not really knowing where it is going?[g]

		Has viable policy	Acts from day to day
Total		25	63
Distribution of negative views:	P.C.		85
(by political preference)	P.S.		76
	U.D.F.		37
	R.P.R.		57

Sources: [a]Sondages, 1978, nos. 2 and 3, p. 56; [b]SOFRES, L'Expansion, 21 September 1979, p. 96; [c]ibid., p. 97; [d]Sondages, 1978, nos. 2 and 3, p. 48; [e]ibid., p. 56; [f]ibid., p. 43; [g]SOfRES, Le Nouvel Observateur, 3 September 1979, pp. 21-24.

of Gaullist voters seemed to think that the government had no viable policy to end France's economic difficulties but was only acting day by day.

In striking contrast with the growing unpopularity of Barre (and after 1978 the declining popularity of Giscard) is the strong resistance of the Socialist party to the political erosion which affects every single one of the major parties, despite its years of disruption in the wake of autumn 1977. The Communist party's fortunes on the other hand declined even faster in the polls than those of the Right. This is all the more remarkable as in 1976, the Socialists were expected to apply the Common Program of the Left in the event they came to power. However, most of the respondents who expressed an opinion on the subject thought that the Socialists would quickly dominate such a government (Table 11.2). The image that prevailed with regard to the Common Program was not too far from reality; there was considerable skepticism even with regard to a Leftist government's ability to stem inflation, to successfully continue economic expansion, or to reduce unemployment. Nonetheless — and this appears to be the decisive element — it was the Socialist party which, by a very large margin, appeared still as the most capable of assuring success with regard to key objectives in the economic and social area. It was perceived as far superior to the U.D.F.: Gaullists and Communists trailed after another large gap. The phenomenon went so far that even U.D.F. and R.P.R. voters very strongly preferred a government made up of both of their parties plus the Socialists (a kind of "grand coalition") to the one actually in power, composed uniquely of their own parties. On the Left, the Communists were impressively loyal to a government of the union of the Left, despite the breakup over the Common Program (and perhaps for lack of an alternative that was plausible, or at least appealing, to the party's voters).[2] On the other hand, Socialist voters from 1977 to 1979 moved away from that formula, preferring an all-Socialist government or even a Centrist one (alliance with the U.D.F.). However, they showed no desire for the "grand coalition" which seemed to exert so much attraction on the voters of the Majority.[3]

As to attitudes regarding the economic situation (Table 11.3) clearly unemployment, from a place of little prominence in 1974, moved up to become the major concern. This reflected the real evolution of unemployment rates during this time period. It is interesting to note that inflation (which was also reaching very high levels and was not just a threat but a reality for all) was not as important a preoccupation. In addition, the concern over unemployment rose fairly steadily in the last year preceding the presidential elections. During the campaign itself, the problem soon became the dominant theme, though expectations regarding the government's ability to deal with it successfully may not have been characterized by great realism.[4]

TABLE 11.2
Attitudes and Expectations Regarding the Left

A. (May 1976) If the Left comes to power, what do you think is most likely to happen?[a]

The Socialists would quickly dominate the government	The Communists would quickly dominate. . .
47	22

B. (May 1976) If the Left comes to power, do you think the following things will happen?[b]

	Will happen	Will not happen
Retirement age reduced	67	17
Capital flight	60	17
Higher welfare allocations	55	27
Higher retirement pensions	53	23
Less unemployment	42	43
Slowing of economic expansion	40	36
Slowing of inflation	29	50

C. (July 1976) If Francois Mitterrand became prime minister, do you think that he would try to apply rapidly the essential provisions of the Common Program?[c]

Yes	No
55	22

D. (October 1977 and March 1979) Which of the following political parties seems to you most capable of[d]

		PS	UDF	RPR	PC
. . .assuring the good functioning	October 77	28	21	12	9
of the French economy?	March 79	31	23	12	11
. . .reducing social inequalities?	October 77	38	14	6	18
	March 79	39	15	8	18
. . .combating unemployment?	March 79	33	16	8	15
. . .defending the interests of	October 77	34	16	9	16
people like you?	March 79	32	20	9	16

E. (March 1979) There are several possibilities for forming a government. Which one of these would have your preference?[e]

	Union of the Left	Socialists alone	P.S. & U.D.F.	P.S., U.D.F. and R.P.R.	Current Majority (U.D.F. & R.P.R.)
Total	22	12	20	24	10
Political preference:					
P.C. (Communist party)	92	2	1	2	—
P.S. (Socialist party)	23	30	29	13	1
(February 1978)	(38)	(26)	(11)	(16)	(3)
U.D.F. (Giscardiens)	—	1	27	46	21
R.P.R. (Gaullists)	1	1	3	56	34

Sources: [a]Sondages, 1978, nos. 3 and 4, p. 32; [b]ibid., pp. 33-34; [c]SOFRES, cited in Projet, Nov. 1976, p. 1008; [d]SOFRES, Le Nouvel Observateur, 9 April 1979, p. 44; [e]ibid., p. 46.

TABLE 11.3
Attitudes Toward the Economic Situation

----

1. Unemployment

   A. (December 1973) Are you worried about your job, for 1974?[a]

Very worried	Rather worried	Little worried	Not at all worried
11	22	24	49

   B. (May–June 1977) What are the most dangerous threats (for the next ten years)? (Two choices possible; not all responses listed.)[b]

Unemployment	Inflation	Insecurity of energy supplies
57	37	25

   C. (August 1979) When you think of the situation in France in the next two years, which of the following are the two most important? (Not all responses listed.)[c]

Unemployment	Inflation	Insecurity of energy supplies
75	52	25

   D. (April 1981) During the electoral campaign, the candidates are dealing with several great themes: French foreign policy, unemployment, the (political) institutions. Which of these themes seem most important to you?[d]

French foreign policy	6%
Unemployment	87%
Institutions	4%
No opinion	3%

   Do you think that unemployment in France could be reduced very rapidly if one were to tackle the problem seriously?[d]

Yes	61%
No	33%
No opinion	6%

2. Responsibility for the economic crisis

   A. (February 1976) When you hear the words "French economic crisis," do you think France feels the effects of the international economic situation, or that it is mostly the French government which is responsible for the economic crisis?[e]

	International situation responsible	Government responsible
Total	56	36
Political preference:		
Majority	78	20
Opposition	40	52

3. Willingness to make sacrifices for a successful economic policy

   A. (January 1977) Would you be willing, in 1977, to accept a pause in the increase of your purchasing power in order to aid the success of the Barre plan?[f]

	Yes	No
Total	48	42
Political preference:		
Majority	73	21
Opposition	30	62

   B. (August 1979) Would you personally be prepared to accept a reduction in your standard of living for a limited time period if this would make it possible to put into place a more dynamic French economy and a more equitable distribution of wealth?[g]

	Yes	No
Total	51	38
Socialists	54	39
Communists	34	55

Sources: [a]Sondages, 1974, nos. 1 and 2, p. 11; [b]SOFRES, L'Expansion, September 1977, p. 285; [c]ibid., September 1979, p. 93; [d]ibid., Le Figaro, 18-19 April 1981; [e] Sondages, 1976, nos. 3 and 4, p. 78; [f]IFOP, Paradoxes, January-February 1977, p. 21; [g]SOFRES, Le Nouvel Observateur, 3 September 1977, pp. 21-24.

In the days when Chirac was still prime minister, most respondents blamed the international environment for the crisis; this was particularly true of the voters of the Majority, while among Opposition voters the opposite view prevailed (though less strongly). The willingness to make sacrifices for a more successful economic policy was similarly distributed, though Socialist (but not Communist) voters declared to be quite willing to even accept a temporary reduction in their standard of living, provided this would lead to a more equitable distribution of wealth as well as to a more dynamic economy. Graph 11.1 shows what distribution of incomes the French viewed as more equitable — a distribution considerably more egalitarian than the existing one.

GRAPH 11.1
Evolution of Income for Nine Professions:
Opinion and Reality in 1978

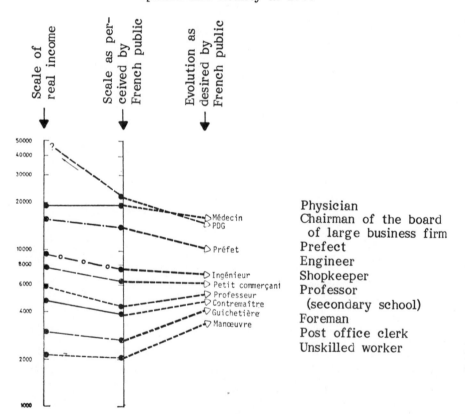

Physician
Chairman of the board
  of large business firm
Prefect
Engineer
Shopkeeper
Professor
  (secondary school)
Foreman
Post office clerk
Unskilled worker

Source: Centre d'étude des revenus et des coûts, Deuxième rapport sur les revenue des Francais (Paris: Albatros, 1979), p. 15.

It is often believed that the late 1970s brought a delegit-
imation of the state, an undermining of its authority and a
distrust regarding its active management of the economy.[5] This
may be so in other countries.   It is quite clearly not in the
case of France, at least if public opinion surveys are to be
trusted (Table 11.4).   Those Frenchmen who wanted to see an
expansion of economic intervention by the state were clearly
more numerous than those who wanted to see its restriction;   a
majority viewed nationalization favorably (such an attitude seems
to belong to Catholic countries, generally, perhaps confirming
Max Weber's — and Alain Peyrefitte's — theses about private
enterprise).[6]   The government's decontrol of industrial prices
after March 1978 met with marked disapproval even among voters
of the Majority, and both Majority and Opposition voters were in
favor of creating jobs in the civil service as a means of fighting
unemployment. Few were those who thought that the government
should stand by when unemployment spreads, leaving things up to
a general economic recovery, though many agreed that unemployment measures taken for the short term cannot replace a real
solution, which needs to come through recovery.   As to foreign
trade, the figures show that the French disapproved of the two
extreme solutions in this area: They were opposed to autarky
("closing the borders") as a means to protect France against the
crisis (a position which carried the day — though only closely —
even with Communist voters, at least in 1979).   But they were
equally opposed to unrestricted free trade, a conviction which
again clearly prevails among all political groups, even among the
constituency of the U.D.F.   Thus the figures converge to show a
political culture which strongly approves the long-standing tradition according to which the French state plays, and should play,
a key role in the nation's economic life.[7]

NOTES

1. See IFOP surveys in Le Point, 24 June 1982, p. 39
(tracing the popularity of presidents and prime ministers of the
Fifth Republic since 1958).
2. The party's tactic of weakening the Socialists even if this
meant defeating the Left altogether seems to have had very little appeal with Communist voters.
3. "Majority" as used here shall mean the "presidential majority," composed of the R.P.R. and the Giscardiens/Centrists
later united under U.D.F. — "Opposition" refers to P.S., P.C., and
the M.R.G. (Radicaux de Gauche).
4. See SOFRES survey in Le Figaro, 4-5 April 1981.

TABLE 11.4
Attitudes Towards Economic Policy Measures and Approaches

1. The role of the state in general[a]

    (October 1978) Personally, do you think that in economic matters, the state

Does not intervene enough	Intervenes just enough	Intervenes too much
40	27	16

2. Nationalization[b]

    (January 1977) As a matter of principle, do you favor or are you hostile to the nationalization of certain key sectors of industry (e.g., iron and steel, autos, electronics, chemicals, banking, oil, aircraft, nuclear, etc.)? (Responses from six European countries.)

	In favor	Rather in favor	Rather hostile	Very hostile
France	22	30	20	11
Italy	20	22	15	14
Belgium	11	29	19	13
Netherlands	12	19	26	28
Britain	6	16	27	40
Germany	4	12	35	34

3. Price decontrol[c]

    (June 1978) Do you approve or disapprove the decontrol of prices for industrial products?

	Disapprove	Approve
Total	57	23
Political preference:		
P.C.	81	8
P.S.	64	17
U.D.F.	40	38
R.P.R.	48	37

4. Creation of civil service jobs to combat unemployment[d]

	Good idea	Bad idea
Total	66	24
Political preference:		
Majority	59	32
Opposition	71	20

156

TABLE 11.4 (cont.)

5. Active employment policy in times of economic crisis[e]

(October 1978) With which of the following three options do you agree most strongly?

Fight against unemployment has priority, even at the expense of economic recovery	Economic recovery is indispensable, but the government could take more immediate measures in favor of employment	Economic recovery comes first, the improvement of the employment situation depends on it
21	46	24

6. Free trade

A. (Summer 1977) Which of the following opinions is closer to yours?[f]

	France exports a large part of its production and cannot afford to raise obstacles to its imports	France has much unemployment and cannot afford to import all products without restrictions
Total	24	51
Political preference:		
R.P.R.	31	55
P.R./Centrists*	30	45
P.S.	20	54
P.C.	14	66

*Corresponds to the later U.D.F. (P.R. stands for Parti Republicain).

B. (August 1979) If the government decided to close the borders to foreign products, do you think that this would be efficient or inefficient as a measure of protection against the international economic crisis?[g]

	Efficient	Inefficient
Total	25	56
Political preference:		
R.P.R.	22	61
U.D.F.	18	66
P.S.	28	61
P.C.	39	41

Source: [a]Sondages, 1978, nos. 2 and 3, p. 44; [b]different institutes in different countries — IFOP for France: IFOP Report AV. O1-F.8.468 (January 1977); [c]Sondages, 1978, nos. 2 and 3, p. 49; [d]ibid., 1976, nos. 3 and 4, p. 78; [e]ibid., 1978, nos. 2 and 3, p. 44; [f]IFOP, Paris-Match, 16 September 1977, p. 40; SOFRES, L'Expansion, 21 September 1979, p. 94.

5. Richard Rose, "The Nature of the Challenge," in Rose, ed., Challenge to Governance (Beverly Hills: Sage, 1980), pp. 5-28.

6. Peyrefitte argues that the decisive factor is not Protestantism but the bureaucratization of public life which followed in the wake of the Counter-Reformation. Peyrefitte, Le mal francais (Paris: Plon, 1976).

7. Shonfield, Modern Capitalism, ch. 5 ("The Etatist Tradition: France") (Oxford, England: Oxford University Press, 1969), pp. 71-87.

PART III
FRANCE UNDER MITTERRAND: PLANS FOR REINDUSTRIALIZATION AND FOR SOCIAL REFORMS

12

SOCIALIST ECONOMIC POLICY

If there is a main theme that inspires Socialist economic thinking, it is that of growth, of renewal, of mobilization of all the country's productive forces. This point is not really new (it was already part of the 1972 Common Program), however it has acquired a different ring in the circumstances of 1981, after the two oil crises and nearly five years of Barre. In his first press conference as president of the Republic, Mitterrand used Gaullist and Bergsonian language of a great elan national. When he spoke of the need for all the French to wholeheartedly partici-pate in this great undertaking, he was closer to de Gaulle and his idea of burning obligation (ardente obligation) than Pompidou or Giscard had ever been.[1] Prime Minister Mauroy expressed himself in very similar terms.[2] All the Socialists, from Delors and Rocard to the left-wing C.E.R.E.S., agreed that the basic purpose of the nationalization was to encourage a new dynamism of the French economy. Even some of the social reforms (reduc-tion of working time, greater equalization of wages) were pre-sented in the same light. By reconciling the French (and particularly the French workers) with industry, these reforms are meant to remove an important psychological obstacle to greater economic vitality and reindustrialization. The new growth that should result from this is seen as the main element in the battle against unemployment. Thus, economic nationalism is an impor-tant ingredient of the new policy — a surprise only to those who thought that Socialist rule would mean above all a reckless policy of redistribution and/or bureaucratization.

A second major emphasis of Socialist policy is the shift in the distribution of power among economic actors. Not surprisingly, the role of government, and of public power generally, is in-creased. The relatively liberal stance of the Barre years is

161

reversed: government intends to play a decisive role in employment and investment. This is most evident in the case of the new nationalizations, even if the executives of the newly nationalized establishments are to retain management autonomy. By the same token, the nationalizations take some of the most powerful firms out of the private sector (and thus reduce the possibilities for economic "sabotage"). A major effort is also made to involve the labor unions to a greater degree in the formulation of economic policy. Within private sector firms however, the distribution of power is unlikely to change radically. The representatives of wage-earners will have greater influence than before, but they will not normally participate in the tasks of management.

A third emphasis of the new policy is the substantial shift in the distribution of economic burdens and benefits. This aspect of economic policy will be discussed further below, in the context of social reform.

In general, the economic policy of the Socialist government is quite pragmatic. It is not, as some have declared, just another attempt to implement a Keynesian policy, to stimulate economic activity by a massive expansion of demand. To be sure, this was part of the Socialist strategy during the first year, but it may have reached its limits at the end of that time period, about a year after Mitterrand's accession to office. In any case, there was also a substantial effort at increasing supply without relying on a previous growth in demand. Ideally, consumption, investment and employment are all to be increased at the same time, and action is taken to affect all three.[3] As a result, some have spoken of "supply-side socialism." The main dilemma consists in coordinating these three courses of action. Lack of such coordination could lead to very serious problems. Despite this expansionary orientation, there is also at least the intention to manage the money supply cautiously and to hold overall wage increases down to the level of inflation[4], intentions that undoubtedly will be put to a hard test.

THE NATIONALIZATIONS

The most controversial measure taken by the new government was the implementation of its nationalization program. Not that it lacked a popular majority to support it — on the contrary, there had long been a clear and consistent majority favorable to nationalization.[5] But the Right, and the major part of business, regarded the measure as a test of French socialism. If the government backed away from the nationalization program, it would most likely be relatively harmless and resemble other social democratic governments. On the other hand, if it went through with the program, it was matching a serious challenge to property relationships as well as taking the chance of a bureaucratized economy and "collectivism," not to speak of all the uncertainty which would be created during the period of transition, when important decisions would presumably be delayed.

Even though the French Socialist party was an early advocate of nationalizations before World War II,[6] it was on the insistence of the Communists that this measure was put into the Common Program in 1972.[7] This did not settle the issue. There was plenty of ambiguities concerning both the scope and the modalities of the nationalization program, as evidenced by the break between the Socialists and the Communists in the fall of 1977.[8] In May–June 1981, the Socialists were caught somewhat unprepared on this issue. There was a lack of experts in the party who were familiar with the companies involved[9] (partly because victory was not expected the way it had been in 1978). Pierre Joxe, the first minister of industry, appointed a commission to study the problem. It was headed by Jacques Piette, the man who had already drafted the nationalization program of 1944-46. It seems that he prepared a vast program to restructure the French economy into large sectors which would each be dominated by a state-owned company, organized along the lines of Electricité de France, Gaz de France, Charbonnages de France, and others. This "maximalist" interpretation of Mitterrand's program was soon discarded; its sponsors stepped down quite early.[10] Joxe was replaced as minister of industry by Pierre Dreyfus, the former chief executive of the state-owned Renault company. A consensus quickly developed between Dreyfus, Mauroy, and the presidential advisers to pattern the industry nationalizations on the model of Renault, a highly successful[11] car maker nationalized in 1945. The goal would then be strong competitive firms with a large amount of managerial autonomy, not unwieldy giants like Electricité de France.[12]

But many questions remained. Should the state nationalize the existing companies outright, or should it (as Rocard had argued) merely secure a controlling interest by the acquisition of 51 percent of the capital? The latter method was legally easier: the government could carry it out by buying the shares, or (in the case of heavily indebted firms) by effectively converting its loans into a participation of capital. This would not only save money and legal problems, it would also strengthen the equity basis of the corporations concerned. Finally, in terms of effective control, there would not be all that much difference, Rocard argued, pointing to the French railroads (S.N.C.F.) where such a system had long existed.[13]

At the end of the summer of 1981, Mitterrand and Mauroy decided in favor of a 100 percent nationalization for most firms, perhaps as a conciliatory gesture towards the Left wing of the

Socialist party and the Communists, and "to make for a clearer situation."[14] (Obviously, such a step could not be reversed easily.) As a result, the measure became much more controversial. The opposition, after proposing a series of amendments in the National Assembly in order to stall the bill, seized the Constitutional Council and asked that the law be declared unconstitutional.[15] To the Socialists' relief, the Council — consisting almost entirely of members of the former majority — did not strike the law down; however, it declared several of its provisions to be unconstitutional, including the provisions relating to the compensation of shareholders.[16] The government quickly remedied these problems, in particular by the introduction of a new criterion for evaluating the compensation amount (this increased the total compensation by 15 to 20 percent over the previous bill). When the opposition seized the Constitutional Council for a second time, its arguments were roundly rejected, and the bill became law with its publication on February 13. The most important nationalization measure in French history (more important than those in 1936 and 1944-46) had been enacted. Five leading industrial corporations and all the important banks were now in public hands.[17] Altogether, the enlarged nationalized sector now accounts for 75 percent of all credits and deposits in the banking area. Its industrial establishments represent nearly one quarter of all industrial employment, roughly 30 percent of industry's business volume, and 40 percent of all investments.[18]

If there was disagreement on the method, there was a broad consensus on the purpose of the nationalizations. Essentially, they all agreed with the reasoning outlined by Boublil in his book, Le socialisme industriel.[19] The close coordination between industry, banks, and the state was presented as the basis for a new economic dynamism that would spread throughout the French economy, pulling along a private sector that needed to overcome its hesitations. Such a close coordination, Mitterrand explained, was in fact one of the causes of Japan's success.[20] This dynamism was to allow a leap forward comparable to that achieved after the Liberation. Confronted with questions about the rationale for the nationalizations, many Socialists pointed to the poor investment record of private industry over the preceding decade. Figures show in fact that over the last ten years, public sector firms increased their investments at an annual rate of about 10 percent (in volume), while in the private sector investment actually decreased during the same time period. While public sector investment only represented 18 percent of all gross investment in 1973, the figure was 32 percent in 1979.[21] (See also Table 12.1.) It is true that these figures have to be read with some caution.[22] In any case, the old accusation of business "Malthusianism," though rarely made expressly, was now put forward in so many words. What was particularly stressed was the lack of venture capital for industrial investment.[23]   Observers sympathetic to the Socialists noted that many industrial firms had adopted very cautious management practices, seeking to improve their financial condition not through an expansion of sales or new product lines but through cutting costs (dismissals and disinvestment). They also noted that many of the banks were unwilling to take on even normal commercial risks.[24]   Surprisingly, some of the executives in the targeted industries readily conceded that some definite advantages would result from nationalization.   In particular, they would permit a long-term approach to industrial restructuring and free the companies from the constraints imposed by the stock market, that is, the need to show short-term profitability.[25]   Most of the executives were in fact quite loyal to the new government, even though most of them knew that they would soon be replaced.   There was one major exception — Pierre Moussa from Paribas, and he was forced to resign by the board of his bank, which is studded with the big names of French industry and finance.[26]

TABLE 12.1
Gross Fixed Capital Formation
Volume Index Basis: 100 in 1973

	1974	1975	1976	1977	1978	1979
All branches	100.6	97.9	101.3	100.0	100.7	103.2
Industry	96.1	85.3	93.2*	88.2	86.6	86.5
Public sector+	105.0	128.7	132.6	147.3	165.4	180.3

*This increase appears larger than it was in reality;   it is due to a change in the statistical basis in the calculation of the index.   In fact, the recovery of investment in 1976 was approximately 1 percent only.

+Public sector here means "Grandes Entreprises Nationales," that is, Electricité de France, Gaz de France, Charbonnages de France, SNCF, RATP, Air Inter, Air France, and PTT. The countercyclical behavior of the public sector is even stronger if one includes other firms in which the government has an important share (COGEMA, EURODIF, COPENOR, and others).

Source: Jacky Fayolle, "Le comportement d'investissement depuis 1974," Economie et statistique, November 1980, p. 23.

The argument that the newly nationalized firms would become more dynamic under public management was supplemented by another one: that such large concentrations of power were inherently suspicious, as they could easily go against the national interest. Mitterrand himself put the matter in very strong terms. Given the phenomenon of increasing accumulation and concentration of capital, he said in his press conference of September 1981, it was only normal that firms which occupy a monopolistic position in the provision of essential goods and services should be nationalized, and thus be deprived of their ability to subvert the general interest. Neither private individuals nor foreign interests should occupy key positions in the French economy.[27] This was clearly a restatement of the Leftist tradition according to which the state should be in control of the "commanding heights" of the economy (in the French contest, de Gaulle had held a somewhat similar view).[28] To Mitterrand, the nationalizations represented the famous "break with capitalism" that the Socialists had so much discussed.[29]

Mitterrand's position was not really all that different from that of Rocard or Delors, who were often portrayed as his opponents on the issue of nationalizations. Both stressed the fact that nationalizations would make it possible for the French government to go against policy trends prevailing in the international environment, to bet on growth and dynamism while other governments and economies retrenched and deflated.[30] Without the nationalizations, the same firms would in all likelihood have acted more cautiously, and not necessarily out of a desire to undercut the government or its policy. The Barre years had shown that even rising profits were not likely to change this situation. To try to achieve the government's policy goals by regulation and indicative planning would have meant a constant and not very promising struggle.[31] Given the policy goals of the Socialist government, the nationalization measures do not appear as gratuitous or primarily motivated by ideological concerns, as some of their adversaries have claimed. They are clearly connected with the "reorientation of the economy,"[32] a goal that includes domestic expansion but also redistribution and many other reforms. Only a more affluent economy could finance all these changes; that was why nationalization was essential.

The nationalization of the banks also must be seen in the same context. The Socialists' main reproach to the banks (clearly articulated by Boublil) was that they had wasted precious resources on undertakings that, though financially profitable, were nonproductive from the perspective of industry (and industry, it must be repeated, was given an absolute preference by the Socialists, who now showed for it a passion worthy of Saint-Simon). The nationalization of the banks was intended to induce a different behavior in this respect. Bankers were told to take greater risks. It may be paradoxical, but it was through nationalization that the government hoped to make them act like enterprising capitalists.

The nationalizations were thus carried out to serve fairly clear objectives set out by the government. Did this mean that the managers of the new public sector firms would be deprived after all of their autonomy which had been stressed so much in earlier statements? The Socialists do not see it in this way. Their outlook became greatly clarified when in early 1982 the new managers were appointed and given their first instructions. To Pierre Dreyfus, the minister of industry, it was essential that these executives share the basic attitude and approach of the government; this reduced the need for supervision. The executives appointed in February 1982 were remarkable both by their high level of expertise and management experience and by their commitment (in most cases) to the Socialist cause.[33] They were given letters stating their mission: to reconcile economic efficiency and social objectives. Their task is to preside over France's reindustrialization, reversing the course taken under Barre which led to the loss of 1 million industrial jobs, to maintain normal capital profitability and to search for greater economic efficiency not just by cutting costs but by the development of sales and new products, a greater effort at research and innovation, and so on. The great orientations laid down by the state are to be respected. As to details, they are to develop a plan d'entreprise for each firm which will form a contract with the state.[34] These plans, drawn up for a period of four years, are to be flexible and can be adjusted every year in response to changes in the international environment.[35] Labor Minister Auroux even stated that the firms would be free to dismiss workers in the course of their restructuring process; nationalized industry was not intended to become a protected sector that the state would keep alive in the absence of good performance.[36]

On the other hand, some shadows soon developed over management autonomy. In March 1982, Jean-Pierre Hugon, appointed director of the Charbonnages de France one month earlier, was fired from his post because of statements that criticized the government's cutbacks on the energy savings program. (The funds were cut back in order to help finance the extra cost for natural gas from Algeria, with which an accord had just been signed.) Hugon, the government stated, had violated his obligation to keep out of political controversy.[37] Two months later, another conflict developed over the question of investments for the public sector. Dreyfus and Delors asked for a large amount to wipe out recent losses in some firms and to broaden the capital base of most of them. They wanted the budget to contribute half of this amount. But Budget Minister Fabius, concerned about the growing deficit, insisted that the nationalized banks be told to come up with two-thirds of the necessary funds, a proposal that the government finally accepted but one that was hardly compatible with real management autonomy.[38]

The nationalization program was largely completed by early 1982. There remained some questions with regard to those firms on the nationalization lists which had passed to a significant part under foreign control (Roussel-Uclaf, ITT-France, and C.I.I.-Honeywell-Bull), plus the French firm Matra. For all of these firms, the idea of a 100 percent nationalization was soon abandoned. In the case of Roussel-Uclaf, controlled by the German giant Hoechst which was reluctant to yield any signifi- cant control, a solution was negotiated which will give the French government at first 34 percent of the stock; this figure will increase over time, but Hoechst is to keep at least 51 per- cent in the near future. The result is original and will set up one of very few "European" multinationals.[39] In contrast with the very successful Roussel-Uclaf, ITT-France did not do very well. The firm had not received any orders for its products for some time, and hinted that it might have to dismiss some of its workers. At the same time, it asked for a very high compensa- tion. After lengthy negotiations, the French government took over the firm, though for much less than ITT had originally demanded.[40] The situation was again different in the case of Honeywell-Bull (CII-HB). Honeywell had only a 47 percent share in the French firm, but CII-HB was tied down by many legal re- strictions that limited its freedom of action and made for a very unequal relationship with the American multinational. In addition, Honeywell had negotiated (in 1975) an agreement that provided for very favorable compensation terms in the event of nationalization. Here it was the French government that was interested in a partnership with the American firm. Negotiations led to an agreement under which Honeywell surrendered all but 19.9 percent of its stock; this meant that it could no longer veto important decisions in CII-HB. The two firms are to cooperate in product development (and CII-HB has the right to build certain types of computers developed by Honeywell in its U.S. laboratories). They also came to an understanding on markets: CII-HB will not be subject to competition from the American firm in most of Europe and the Middle East.[41] Com- pensation terms were extremely favorable. As to Matra, a firm that was put on the nationalization list because of its extensive involvement in arms production, the government agreed to a 51 percent share in the total business when it turned out that it would have been difficult to separate the arms division from the rest of the firm.[42] The aircraft manufacturer Dassault had been handled in this way earlier on.[43]

Thus the nationalization program was completed in its outline by mid-1982. No firms will be added to the nationalization list in the near future, except in cases where no private investor can be found to rescue an ailing firm that the government considers important. This was the case of the textile manufacturer Boussac-Saint-Frères.[44] Mitterrand declared that there would be no "creeping" nationalizations (a widespread fear at one point in business circles), and that another expansion of the public sector could only come after the next general election (1986 or 1988).[45]

But the completion of the nationalization program represents only the start of what was announced as a new and very different industrial strategy. The first thing the new managers were asked to do was to come up with ambitious investment plans. They were encouraged to take a bold approach and a wider view. Investment should start up in the nationalized firms during the second half of 1982, and it should continue at a rapid pace for several years. The government announced that it would spend about 10 billion francs on the big five industrial companies in 1982 and 1983 and 30 billion over the next five years. The total amount of investment for these firms (including resources coming from banks) has been put at 75 billion for the same time period.[46] But other firms have been added. The computer sector alone (essentially CII-HB) will receive about 2 billion francs before the end of 1983, and a total of 6 billion of government funds are programmed for the time period running until 1986, with the goal of making France the third industrial power in the area of micro-electronics.[47]

As the first year of the Socialist government came to its close, some doubts arose as to whether these ambitious investment programs could all be maintained. Would the new emphasis on rigor and a limited budget deficit in 1983 not present unsurmountable financing problems?[48] If it should come to severe cutbacks in this area, then the main justification for the nationalizations would have evaporated. However, first statements by Socialist leaders indicated that this would not be the case and that industrial investment (in particular in the nationalized sector) would have priority.[49] In fact, the need to save resources for investment may have been one of the major reasons for the austerity program submitted by the Socialist government in June 1982.

When will one be able to judge whether the nationalizations have been a success or a failure? Restructuring (every firm is to concentrate on major lines of production, breaking with the diversification of previous years) and investment will need to go on for several years. The government itself declared that success or failure of the new nationalizations would show within four years, counting from the time the new managers took over.[50] That would be in 1986 — at the time of the next elections to the National Assembly.

HELPING THE PRIVATE SECTOR

The nationalizations were not the only measure intended to revitalize the French economy. The private sector was also to be given a new dynamism. At the outset however, roughly during the first half year, the attitude of the Socialists towards private sector firms was ambiguous. On the one hand, these firms were viewed as a bastion of capitalism and a likely place for the class struggle to take place (this is discussed in subsequent chapters). From this perspective, it seemed appropriate to impose new taxes on business profits. On the other hand, business cooperation was clearly necessary if the government was to succeed with its economic policy, and, in fact, both Mitterrand and Mauroy avoided making any statements that might have discouraged business in this respect, and stressed that their policy of growth would have beneficial effects for business as well. The conflict between the two attitudes came out clearly when the Socialist party, at its Valence party congress in the fall of 1981, used very radical antibusiness rhetoric. Mitterrand and Mauroy quickly made it clear that this did not reflect the policy orientation of the government.[51]

There were several ways in which public policy was intended to help business performance in the areas of hiring and investment (profitability, the core of Barre's policy, was not similarly stressed). In the fall of 1981 a whole series of financial incentives were incorporated in the 1982 budget. By the end of the year, the first projects for recapturing the French market were announced. In April 1982, important concessions to business were made with regard to tax breaks and social welfare contributions. The nationalization of the banks was followed by measures designed to facilitate credit procedures and by instructions to the banks to be more entrepreneurial in their management practices.[52] The nationalizations themselves were intended to have a positive impact on business, at least as soon as the investment process would start up and distribute orders to subcontractors and suppliers. Finally, the mild reflationary policy which followed the elections was also, to some extent, a measure to help business.

The financial incentives to private sector firms contained in the 1982 budget were numerous. The government pointed out proudly that they brought a 52 percent increase of such aid over the previous year.[53] But the difference with earlier budgets was not only in the volume of the allocated funds. The new criteria for receiving such funds were considerably more selective; replacement investments, which had become the prevailing form of investment during the Barre years and often had the effect of reducing employment, were no longer subsidized. Among the measures in this category were loans at subsidized interest rates and "subordinated loans" (prêts participatifs) first introduced by the loi Monory in July 1978.[54] The government placed special emphasis on helping small and medium-sized businesses, hoping that this sector would be particularly cooperative (a hope which was disappointed early on).[55] Other measures encouraged the formation of equity capital. Thus, the tax exemption for investors in the SICAV Monory was extended (it provided a tax exemption for the acquisition of stock of up to 5,000 francs per household, and another exemption for dividends).[56] Small savers were encouraged by the institution of a passbook with a higher rate of interest. Even the wealth tax was designed in such a way as to encourage investment, though that was hardly its primary purpose. The creation of new firms was encouraged by the institution of a passbook with a higher rate of interest. Even the wealth tax was designed in such a way as to encourage investment, though that was hardly its primary purpose. The creation of new firms was encouraged in several ways.[57] Finally, the government repeatedly reduced interest rates, at least until the speculation against the franc in the spring of 1982 forced it to reverse its course. It also argued very strongly that the countries of the European community should take a common stand and defend themselves against the high interest rates coming from the United States. If European cooperation would not be achieved, Delors declared, France would adopt such a course on her own.[58]

The business world, and particularly the representatives of the employers' organization (the C.N.P.F.), showed little enthusiasm for most of these measures. They claimed that the government in fact took more from private firms in the form of additional taxes than it returned in increased subsidies. They added that the single most important measure to help business would be to stabilize or reduce its payments to the state, in the form of taxes and social welfare contributions. In particular, they asked for a suppression of the taxe professionnelle (a kind of business and occupation tax), the shortcomings of which were openly admitted by the government.

After several months of dialogue, and after convincing itself that business cries for help had a serious foundation in terms of depressed profits and business volume, the government made important concessions in April 1982. It committed itself to reduce the taxe professionnelle by 5 billion francs in 1982, and by another 6 billion in 1983; to take over the financing of programs for the handicapped (saving business another 7 billion); not to increase social welfare contributions until mid-1983; and not to reduce the legal work week any further (that is, not below the 39 hour limit introduced in early 1982) until the end of 1983. In exchange for this, the head of the employer organization "promised" that business would perform on investment and hiring.[59]

The "reconquest of the internal market" was invoked frequently in Socialist programs in recent years, though for a long time there was considerable uncertainty as to what this could mean, given the fact that the Socialists at the same time declared their opposition to protectionism. (However, they are insistent in demanding greater protection for the European community as a whole; and foreign trade minister Jobert even presented the "reconquest" as an effort that had to aim at the European community as a whole, not just at France.)[60] In September 1981, a first illustration of this "reconquest" or recapturing was given in the furniture sector. An agreement was worked out between French producers, distributors and the state to limit imports, which were programmed to fall from 21 percent to 15 percent of French sales in one year. Given the expectation of greater domestic sales, the producers could now expand and modernize production with much greater confidence. In this they were to be assisted by state aid for investment and research and development. The agreement was expected to also lead to a currency savings of 1 billion francs. The consensus of all the participants was secured quite easily, and by January 1982 the business paper Les Echos reported that the climate in this particular industry had improved remarkably.[61]

Similar plans were soon drawn up for other sectors. The machine tool industry is important for most advanced industrial countries. In France, however, it never developed very far (currently representing only 20 percent of the capacity of West Germany in that sector). Under Giscard, despite a machine-tool plan in 1976, the industry had been shrinking steadily. In early December 1981, Dreyfus announced a plan to strengthen it. Production was to be doubled in three years, import penetration reduced from 60 percent to 30 percent, and exports increased from 15 percent to 35 percent. Given the rapid worldwide increase in the use of industrial robots (computer-instructed tools that can be reset for different tasks), the stakes are high. The government promised to help in a variety of ways: by organizing specialization and competition, encouraging standardization and research, assisting with the training of specialized labor, offering contracts for the development of prototypes, using the purchasing policy of the public sector, and so on.[62]

Comparable plans followed for the textile industry, where 250,000 jobs (30 percent of the total) were lost over the last ten years (and most French textile imports did not come from low-cost labor countries but from Italy, Britain, and the United

States);[63] for the leather industry (where great problems were caused by speculation in raw materials — the state is now regularizing that supply); the toy industry; the merchant marine . . . and more are on the drawing board.[64] What these plans have in common is a determination to recapture French markets for domestic producers by measures which combine great inventiveness with remarkable flexibility in the approaches taken. The problems of each sector are dealt with individually, and then a plan is drawn up. There is no standardized prescription that applies to every situation. It is remarkable that in most of these cases, private industry was unable to take the initiative in working out such plans. In addition to these sectoral measures, the government is significantly expanding the French research budget, which is expected to grow 18 percent in volume every year until 1985.[65]

Many of the above measures will show their value only over time. In the case of the attempt to recapture domestic markets, the time frame for success is one of several years at least, perhaps a decade. Most of the other measures should have their effect much earlier, perhaps within a year. In addition, the government took one measure whose effect was almost immediate, that is, reflation. Because it affects not just business but so many other areas as well, it will now be discussed separately.

FROM REFLATION TO SOCIALIST AUSTERITY

In their economic programs during the 1970s, the Socialists had repeatedly advocated a policy of reflation by stimulating consumption. Such a policy, they argued, would promote social justice (income redistribution), further economic growth and efficiency (by a better use of existing production capacities), reduce inflation, and stimulate investment. In the late 1970s they shifted their emphasis gradually to reflation via investment, but the element of consumption remained important.[66] Once in power, the Socialists carried out their promise by a relatively modest expansion of demand. In their minds this measure was to be relayed, in the spring of 1982, by an increase in exports (resulting from an improved international environment) and the start of the investment process. However, things did not quite work out that way.

Critics of the Left — most prominently Barre — had argued for years that a policy of reflation was bound to fail. They claimed that it would simply lead to a rapid increase in imports, reduced exports, and a dramatic balance of payments deficit. To such a situation the government could either respond by austerity (which would show the futility of the whole experience) or by "closing the borders," that is, by resorting to protectionism, which would lead to a fall of living standards over the long term. Barre pointed to the relance Chirac of 1975 as evidence that any such policy was doomed from the beginning.

The Socialists were of course aware of such criticisms and problems. Part of their answer was that an equilibrium in the balance of trade should not be sought by keeping the growth rate down, since to do so amounted to a strategy of deindustrialization. A lasting solution to the dilemma of growth and trade deficit had to come from building up a few sectors for world exports (therefore the nationalizations) and from reconquering French markets. Technological leadership was the key. Another part of the Socialist answer was to concentrate reflation on labor-intensive sectors, such as construction (housing, transports, insulation and others).[67] A program of energy savings in particular would improve the balance of trade situation later on (through the reduction of energy imports[68]) and thus remove an important constraint on growth. But all these measures could only work after a period of several years. In the meantime, the Socialists placed their hopes on an improved international environment which would stimulate exports by the spring of 1982. Finally, they did not attach to the international value of the franc the same importance as the Barre government, and were more willing to resort to devaluation if necessary.[69]

Against this background, government spending was increased immediately after Mitterrand's election, and a supplementary budget was enacted in August 1981. It provided for considerably larger expenditures than had been planned, though for the most part it only adjusted for developments before the election. The immediate social welfare measures financed by an increased deficit amounted to somewhat over 5 billion francs; other new expenditures were financed by tax increases.[70] For 1982, the budget deficit was planned at 95 billion francs, or 2.6 percent of the GDP (it is likely to be closer to 115 billion by the end of 1982); these figures are still small when compared to the deficits of other countries.[71] Most of the stimulative measures were directed towards investment. The Two Year Plan formulated by Rocard provided for massive spending in the areas of housing, high-speed railroads, canals, construction related to energy savings (insulation, utilization of waste heat), urban amenities (parks, public transportation, stadiums) and many small-scale improvements.[72] There were of course measures which act directly on demand; thus the additional civil service jobs created by the government (54,000 in 1981 alone), higher family and housing allowances, old age pensions and the like, which (together with the increased minimum wage) worked to increase consumption in late 1981.

Since the idea of a balanced budget was abandoned in principle, it became necessary to put a stop to the demands that converged from the different ministries, which — had they been accepted — would have led to a budget deficit in excess of 200 billion francs for 1983.[73] In fact, there was a first attempt to limit the 1982 budget deficit in the fall of 1981, after the first devaluation of the franc within the EMS.[74] But it was only later on that the government became aware of the limits that needed to be respected. In January Mitterrand set the level of a responsible deficit at 3 percent of the GDP, a statement that he has repeated many times since.[75] Soon it became clear that some programs that were essential to reflation in 1982 would have to be cut back in 1983 (thus subsidized loans to the private sector, and perhaps even investments for the public sector).[76] By March 1982 the reflationary approach had essentially come to an end. Austerity was beginning to make a comeback, though on a modest scale at first.[77] This evolution accelerated during the months of spring 1982, and resulted in a major policy shift in May and June.

The reasons for this adjustment were twofold. First, investments in the private sector still stagnated, or rather continued their decline. Exports also decreased, as the international recession showed no signs of ending yet.[78] After a gradual improvement in early 1982, the balance of trade deficit increased very suddenly in April. Finally, inflation (which was falling rapidly in most other OECD countries) continued at high levels in France, and even showed an accelerating trend.

In May, Socialist ministers began to increasingly use such words as rigor, effort, sacrifice and so on in their public statements. Delors took the lead. Prime Minister Mauroy followed by declaring that the government had to shift gears and would continue its program at a different speed.[79] Mitterrand himself — apparently with great reluctance — spoke in similar terms, particularly at his press conference of June 9, in which he stressed the obstacles that the Socialists had encountered and the need to respond to them by an even greater effort, to which everyone, not only the rich, would have to contribute. He also stressed the need to contain expenditures on social welfare, while underlining the determination of the Socialist government to go ahead with a rapid expansion of public sector investments.[80] While Mitterrand's press conference confirmed an evolution which had been perceptible for some time, a surprise move came only two days later. The franc was devalued for the second time, and this time the devaluation was accompanied by more stringent measures. Not only a price freeze, but also a freeze on wages and other forms of income was imposed in order to stop all pay increases, even those that had been negotiated earlier on between the social partners.[81] This was certainly a form of austerity close to that of Barre; and as under Barre, the minimum wage was exempted from the freeze. Transfer payments were no longer increased as programmed earlier. They were to be held roughly at the same levels (in real terms).[82] Real wages on the other hand could only decline, at least for a limited time period. Delors declared that these measures would slow growth by 0.1-0.2 percent (the government now set a target of 2 percent for 1982, down from the 3.3 percent projected earlier), stabilize unemployment around 2 million, and reduce the foreign trade deficit by about 30 billion francs for 1982.[83]

There are definite similarities between the relance Chirac and the reflation practiced by the Socialist government, and they generally correspond to Barre's analysis. As in 1975-76, the expected improvement of the international economic environment failed to come about. However, the situation did not deteriorate as drastically as Barre had announced it would.[84] Did the measures of June 1982 amount to a fundamental policy reversal, or did the government (as Mitterrand and Mauroy claimed) simply enter a new phase in its policy, while its basic objectives remained unchanged?

The implementation of Socialist economic policy can be broken down into several time periods. First, there is the period where the only direct effect on the economy could come from reflation. This period lasted from summer 1981 to the spring of 1982. Then comes a period of transition, a time when the long-term, structural changes (particularly the nationalizations and the investment program) cannot yet take their full effect. In a third period, the public sector investments and the reconquest of French markets are expected to show their full impact. This can only start in 1983 and will possibly take even longer. Only then can the external (balance of trade) constraints on growth be lifted, as many Socialist economists (such as Alain Boublil and Jacques Attali) themselves reasoned. At that point France should be able — in the minds of the Socialists — to return to a higher rate of economic growth without running into the obstacles of surging imports and a rapid decline in foreign exchange holdings.[85] It is during that stage that the Socialist program of large-scale redistribution could be taken up again. In this case, the shift of June 1982 towards rigor and investment (away from consumption and transfer payments) need not mark a durable change in policy. It could represent merely a strategy to get through the time at which redistributive reforms will have to remain dormant. In the meantime, the first period of reflation had allowed a relative stabilization of unemployment.

On the other hand, the relaxation of economic rigor which followed Mitterrand's election (and undoubtedly that election itself, with its inevitable impact on the business world, including international lenders) had a definite impact on the French economy. The franc had reached artificially high levels during the Giscard years, partly due to an inflow of short-term deposits from the Middle East for political reasons (already, higher interest rates could be obtained in the United States or the Eurodollar market).[86] The defeat of Giscard and the Right, the steep rise of the dollar during the summer, and the announcement of a large budget deficit for 1982 all brought strong pressure on the franc. Nonetheless Delors felt that a concerted readjustment had to wait. While a unilateral devaluation right after the elections would have had the advantage of reducing the cost of intervention to the Bank of France, it would have been a blow to French prestige and would have branded France as "irresponsible." In addition, a mutually agreed readjustment within the EMS was only possible once the dollar started to come down from its record levels, especially since a strong dollar also weakened the West German currency (as liquidities were transferred from marks to dollars).[87] Like the governments of some other West European countries (but more forcefully so), the French government criticized the United States for disrupting the world's currency market and for refusing to make any effort to stabilize the fluctuations of the dollar.[88]

In early October 1981 came the first devaluation of the franc (and revaluation of the German mark) within the EMS; vis-a-vis the German currency, the franc was devalued by 8.8 percent.[89] This was expected to give the French economy a breathing space in the crucial trade relations with West Germany for a period of about one year. But due in part to the differential economic evolution in the two countries (reflation in France, austerity in Germany), in part to political reasons (Mitterrand's trip to Israel seems to have angered Arab depositors, resulting in a massive flight of capital), the franc was under a new attack in March 1982.[90] After a relative recovery, it deteriorated again in May. A large part of the foreign exchange reserves had by that time been spent.[91] This led to a second devaluation. This time, on June 12, the franc was devalued by 10 percent vis-a-vis the German mark.[92] Even at that level, there were doubts whether it could hold the line for long, given the inflation differential with other countries, in particular with West Germany. On the other hand, Mitterrand made it clear that France had no intention of leaving the EMS.[93]

Battling inflation had never been a primary objective for the Socialists, even though Delors wanted to see inflation reduced to 10 percent in his first full year in office. Only a few ministers — most prominently Delors himself — stressed that the control of inflation was a key condition for lasting success in other areas as well (for example, unemployment). The reflation of the first year, and particularly the budget deficit, did not allow for a reduction of the inflationary pressures which existed at the time of Mitterrand's election (at that time, inflation was running at an annual rate of 14 percent). The government did try to control the situation in several ways. There was an attempt to keep wage increases down; here the civil service and the public sector firms were going to serve as models. Delors had devised a scheme under which wage increases would be programmed on the basis of a rather low estimate of inflation, with the possibility of adjustment at the end of each semester if the cost of living index showed a higher percentage than the programmed wage increases. This système Delors was accepted only with reluctance by the public sector and civil service unions.[94]

By mid-1982, the success of this formula remained uncertain. From the beginning, the Socialist government had stressed that wage increases — except for the lowest categories — could do no more than preserve purchasing power, proclaiming a policy which the Socialists had attacked when Barre was practicing it (it is true though that in exchange for wage restraint they offered an active employment policy, something which was not true of Barre).[95] Even the wage increases of June 1981, and particularly the increase of the SMIC, were not large compared to the increases granted in the wake of the events of May 1968. The government also made it clear then that the increases were not to be replicated throughout the wage hierarchy. In the fall of 1981, Delors added that maintaining the purchasing power of wages on the average meant that increases in lower incomes would have to be compensated by cuts in the upper ranges.[96]

But if rigueur — financial rigor — became the new watchword of Socialist wage policy, its application remained somewhat loose. A plan was drawn up to make civil servants contribute to the unemployment insurance system which was heavily in debt. But even though it had been agreed to (reluctantly) by Civil Service Minister Anicet Le Pors and even though a majority of civil servants was prepared to accept it, the measure was temporarily scrapped, and did not surface again until the spring of 1982.[97] And when in early 1982, the work week was reduced for all wage earners to 39 hours a week, the question arose as to whether there should be at least a partial wage adjustment. Despite earlier statements to the contrary, Mitterrand and Mauroy now endorsed the principle of "full compensation," that is, no wage adjustment despite the reduced hours.[98] The decision was certainly contrary to the economic rigor advocated by Delors and some others.

As a result of these developments, wage increases soon exceeded the government's targets. In a dramatic action that had no precedent since the late 1940s, the government declared, on the occasion of the devaluation of June 1982, a freeze of all wages, incomes and profit margins, to be effective until the end of October. At that point, new and (at least that was the expectation) lower wage increases were to be renegotiated. The increases programmed for the intervening months were to be cancelled, including the pay increase for civil servants planned for July 1.[99]

Prices were also the subject of governmental policy in many different forms. During the summer of 1981, the government showed that it was determined to enforce competition in retail trade, and took some sanctions where such competition was deficient (pharmacists, bakers). It took a stronger stand on this issue than the "liberal" Barre government — a paradox easily explained when one considers the electoral implications of such measures.[100] For 1982, a reform of all retailing was on the agenda.[101] After the first EMS realignment, the government also imposed a selective price freeze, particularly for services. On the other hand, industrial prices remained deregulated; Delors was committed to that. That first price freeze lasted until January 1982. It was followed by a negotiated agreement between the government and retailers (about half of them joined) not to increase prices on certain products. This agreement was apparently successful and helped to hold down overall increases.[102] Again, the most dramatic measures yet were taken in June 1982, when price freezes were imposed on all products. Even industrial products were included this time, though Delors hoped to decontrol them soon. Only very few products (agriculture, produce, energy) were exempted. Again, the freeze was to last until the end of October.[103]

Delors had stated his goal clearly early on: An inflation rate of 10 percent or less by the end of 1982, and 7-8 percent within three years.[104] The question is how much support Delors will get from the prime minister and the president. The record on this point is mixed. In October 1981, on the occasion of the first devaluation of the franc, Delors had asked for a strong reduction of the budget deficit. He was strongly opposed by finance minister Fabius (who had just submitted the budget a short time before) and civil service minister Anicet Le Pors. Mauroy arbitrated in favor of a compromise: 10 to 15 billion (less than Delors had asked for) would be put "in reserve" to be used only under certain conditions.[105] Some of these credits were indeed cancelled in early 1982. But it was only during the spring of 1982, when the situation began to deteriorate, that Delor' approach seemed to gain greater support. The government repeatedly announced its intent to limit the deficit both of the budget and of the Social Security system. However, it remains to be seen whether these ambitious objectives will be achieved.[106]

NOTES

1. Mitterrand press conference, printed in full in Le Monde, weekly selection, 24 September 1981.
2. Mauroy in his speech before the National Assembly; Le Monde, weekly selection, 17 September 1981; in interview, Le Monde, 6 October 1981.
3. This was made very clear already in Mauroy's speech before the National Assembly on 15 September 1981; see footnote 2.
4. Jacques Delors, interview in L'Expansion, 4 September 1981.
5. See also Table 11.4.
6. Whereas the Communists were opposed at first, from 1934 to 1936; Michel Rocard in Faire, December 1976, p. 47.
7. F. O. Giesbert and J. Mornand in Le Nouvel Observateur, 11 July 1981.
8. See Chapter 9.
9. J. M. Quatrepoint in Le Monde, 25 September 1981.
10 See note 7; also Jacques Delors interview in Le Nouvel Observateur, 24 October 1981.
11. The image of Renault as a successful car manufacturer has been attacked lately. Critics claimed especially that Renault was not nearly as profitable, and did not pay as much in taxes, as its main competitor Peugeot. See, for example, Andre Fourcans in The Wall Street Journal, 18 November 1981. In fact, however, Renault paid its shareholder (the state) quite well, though more in forms of interest on capital advances rather than in dividends; the difference is only formal. Also, Renault expanded more successfully than Peugeot. C. Baudelaire in Le Point, 23 November 1981.
12. Interview with Pierre Dreyfus, L'Expansion, 6 November 1981.
13. Fifty-one percent of the S.N.C.F. are owned by the state; 36 percent by the Banque Rothschild (which, until its nationalization in 1982, was private), and 13 percent by the Groupe d'assurances de Paris. The private shareholders never exerted any control under this arrangement, and most people actually do not know that the state is not sole owner. Michel Rocard, Parler vrai (Paris: Le Seuil, 1979), pp. 145–46.
14. F. O. Giesbert in Le Nouvel Observateur, 12 September 1981.
15. This can be done under Article 61 of the French Constitution.
16. J. M. Quatrepoint and Ph. Boucher in Le Monde, 19 January 1982.
17. The two main steel producers, Usinor and Sacilor, had been nationalized earlier; this did not cause much controversy.

18. The figures quoted in the French press vary somewhat as to the exact dimensions. See J. M. Quatrepoint in Le Monde, 13 February 1982; but also Philippe Labarde, ibid., 19 February 1982, and ibid., 19 April 1982.

19. See Chapter 9.

20. Guy Sorman in The Wall Street Journal, 19 May 1982.

21. Georges Perrineau, "L'ampleur actuelle du champ des nationalisations," Revue politique et parlementaire, July 1981, p. 62.

22. Much of the investment of these firms took place in the energy sector (nuclear energy, in particular), which is so capital-intensive that its contribution to employment is minimal, in fact probably negative. This point is taken up further below.

23. Roger Priouret in Le Nouvel Observateur, 6 March 1982. Lack of investment capital was made up in part by rising indebtedness to banks. Whereas in 1974 debts in industry were about four times as large as annual profits, by 1982 they were about ten times as large. Priouret stressed an obvious point, though one that the Socialists seemed to ignore until Mitterrand brought up this subject in his press conference of June 1982, namely, that an improvement of this situation also called for a fiscal penalty on real estate investment. Some of the defenders of a capitalist order in France are prepared to admit this deficiency of private investment in industry. However, they may explain it on different grounds. Jacques de Fouchier, one of the leading private bankers, argued in 1977 that the lack of investment was due to the fear of expropriation (without full compensation) created by the Common Program of the Left. Jacques de Fouchier in 1978. Si la gauche l'emportait, pp. 66 and 68.

24. R. Priouret in Le Nouvel Observateur, 12 September 1981; and Dreyfus interview with Le Point, 5 October 1981.

25. J. M. Quatrepoint in Le Monde, weekly selection, 18 August 1981. The same point was made by Japanese critics of American capitalism (that is, that considerations of short-term profitability were an obstacle to an intelligent industrial strategy).

26. Moussa, himself sympathetic to the French Left, thought that he had assurances that the international division of Paribas would not be nationalized. When the government proceeded to nationalize it anyhow, he helped with arranging a stock transfer which made Paribas lose control over its subsidiary in Switzerland. The operation was not (not yet) illegal but Moussa had misrepresented his activities to the government. He also was clearly subverting governmental policy. F. O. Giesbert in Le Nouvel Observateur, 14 November 1981; Le Monde, 28 October, 2 and 3 November 1981. Paribas recovered some of its stake (but not a majority) after secret negotiations conducted by Jacques de Fouchier; Le Nouvel Observateur, 26 December 1981, and Les Echos, 11 February 1982.

27. Mitterrand in his press conference of September 1981, Le Monde, weekly selection, 24 September 1981.

28. See Chapter 1.

29. F. O. Giesbert in Le Nouvel Observateur, 26 September 1981.

30. F. O. Giesbert in Le Nouvel Observateur, 17 October 1981 (on Rocard); Delors interview, ibid., 24 October 1981.

31. Dreyfus interview with L'Expansion, 6 November 1981.

32. "Reorienting the economy" is the title of a chapter heading in Projet socialiste (Paris: Club socialiste du livre, 1980), a programmatic statement "for the 1980s."

33. In some cases, the technical expertise seemed to have priority (thus Jean Gandois remained at Rhône-Poulenc, despite violent attacks by the C.G.T.).

34. Philippe Labarde in Le Monde, 19 February 1982.

35. Jacques Jublin in Les Echos, 17 February 1982.

36. Jean Auroux in Paris-Match, 5 March 1982; also Pierre Dreyfus, interview in Les Echos, 18 February 1982.

37. Le Nouvel Observateur, 3 April 1982.

38. F. O. Giesbert and Jacques Mornand in Le Nouvel Observateur, 22 May 1982.

39. Les Echos, 24 and 25 February 1982; Wall Street Journal, 10 May 1982. Such a result seems to be anticipated in Boublil, Le socialisme industriel, p. 27.

40. Jacques Mornand, in Le Nouvel Observateur, 14 November 1981; and Les Echos, 12 March 1982; and Wall Street Journal, 8 July 1982.

41. Jacques Jublin in Les Echos, 15 and 22 April 1982; Jean-Michel Quatrepoint in Le Monde, 22 April 1982; Wall Street Journal, 9 June 1982.

42. J. M. Quatrepoint in Le Monde, 11 September 1981; Wall Street Journal, 25 March 1982. The government was to acquire 25.5 percent of the stock by tender offer. The remainder would be acquired in the form of new stock, issued by the company but with the government as the only subscriber.

43. Marcel Dassault, the founder of the firm, had donated 26 percent of the stock to the state, in return only for a state contribution to the Fondation Marcel Dassault. The state already owned some stock. The remainder was to be bought in the open market, Le Monde, 10 October 1981.

44. Véronique Maurus in Le Monde, 20 March 1982. (The state took 51 percent of the stock.)

45. It seems that Mitterrand would like to see a further increase of the public sector, particularly if the recent nationalizations turn out to be successful. Roger Priouret, Le Nouvel Observateur, 12 December 1981.

46. Les Echos, 18 February 1982; and Giesbert and Mornand in Le Nouvel Observateur, 22 May 1982.

47. Jean-Michel Quatrepoint in Le Monde, 22 April 1982 and Les Echos, 6 April 1982.

48. Roger Priouret, Le Nouvel Observateur, 3 April 1982; Giesbert and Mornand, Le Nouvel Observateur, 22 May 1982.

49. Christian Pierret (Socialist deputy and general rapporteur for the budget) in Le Nouvel Observateur, 5 June 1982.

50. Les Echos, 18 February 1982.

51. See Chapter 14.

52. Francois Renard in Le Monde, 18 February 1982; Les Echos, 22 April 1982.

53. Delors interview with Le Nouvel Observateur, 24 October 1981.

54. Le Monde, 17 September 1981 (citing Mauroy). Subordinated loans have a status similar to that of equity capital in case of financial difficulties of the firm.

55. The main reason may not be a reluctance to cooperate as much as the deteriorating cash situation of the firms. Les Echos, 8 February 1982.

56. Le Monde, 13 August 1981 (citing Delors).

57. Les Echos, 26 February 1982.

58. Wall Street Journal, 11 February 1982.

59. Dominique Audibert and Denis Jeambar in Le Point, 19 April 1982; Philippe Labarde in Le Monde, 19 April 1982.

60. Chandernagor (Minister for European Affairs) pressing for greater assertiveness of the European Community in international trade negotiations, Les Echos, 23 February 1982. Jobert interview in Les Echos, 22 February 1982.

61. Dreyfus interview in Le Point, 5 October 1981; J. P. Adine and D. Willot in Le Point, 7 December 1981; and P. Lamm in Les Echos, 13 January 1982.

62. Francois Renard in Le Monde, 3 December 1981.

63. In the textile and clothing industry, the government took over, for a limited period of time, part of the social welfare contributions, a measure which is important for this particularly labor-intensive sector. It was done on the condition that the firms concerned invest and hire new personnel. Les Echos, 8 February 1982.

64. J. P. Adine and D. Willot in Le Point, 7 December 1981; F. Grosrichard in Le Monde, 10 December 1981.

65. Adine in Le Point, 18 January 1982.

66. See Chapter 9.

67. Plan intérimaire. Stratégie pour deux ans, 1982-1983 (Paris: La documentation francaise, 1981), p. 67.

68. Ibid., p. 207.

69. Mitterrand's economic program of June 1979 had stated that the EMS, based as it was on freezing wages and increasing unemployment, could not be accepted in its current form. L'Unité, 29 June 1979.

70. OECD, Economic Surveys: France (Paris: OECD, 1982), p. 47.

71. In particular, it was lower than that of Germany, Japan, Italy and Britain. It compared roughly to that of the United States. Roger Priouret, Le Nouvel Observateur, 8 May 1982.

72. Rocard interview, Le Monde, 9 September 1981; F. O. Giesbert in Le Nouvel Observateur, 17 October 1982.

73. R. Priouret in Le Nouvel Observateur, 27 February 1982.

74. It is sometimes claimed that such a reduction was demanded by Helmut Schmidt in exchange for the revaluation of the mark.

75. Les Echos, 28 January 1982. It was repeated many times later, and also in the press conference of June 9, 1982.

76. R. Priouret in Le Nouvel Observateur, 3 April 1982.

77. Alain Vernholes in Le Monde, 11 March 1982.

78. Roger Priouret in Le Nouvel Observateur, 29 May 1982.

79. Mauroy interview in Le Nouvel Observateur, 29 May 1982.

80. Mitterrand press conference of June 9, 1982; see Le Monde, 11 June 1982. Mitterrand cited the following figures for investment in the nationalized industries: 10 billion francs in 1979, 11.7 billion in 1980, 12.8 billion in 1981, 16.3 billion in 1982, and about 25 billion in 1983.

81. Le Monde, 15 June 1982.

82. Ibid., article by Paul Fabra.

83. Ibid.

84. In the fall of 1981, Barre had predicted that inflation would soon reach a rate of 15-17 percent. Cited in Le Monde, weekly selection, 1 October 1981.

85. See Note 91.

86. R. Priouret in Le Nouvel Observateur, 25 July 1981; and Lemaître, Le Monde, 6 October 1981.

87. Interview with Mauroy, Le Monde, 6 October 1981; with Delors, Le Nouvel Observateur, 24 October 1981.

88. Interview with Delors, Le Point, 17 August 1981.

89. The franc was devalued by 3 percent; the mark revalued by 5.5 percent. Le Monde, 6 October 1981.

90. Wall Street Journal, 19 and 23 March 1982.

91. Altogether, foreign exchange reserves (excluding gold) had fallen 60 percent between Mitterrand's election and early June 1982. In fact, attacks on the franc had already started in February 1981, during Barre's tenure. Le Monde, weekly selection, 10 June 1982.

92. The franc was devalued by 5.75 percent; the mark revalued by 4.25 percent. Le Monde, 15 June 1982.

93. Press conference of June 9, 1982. This contrasted with earlier statements (see note 69).

94. Alain Vernholes and Jean-Pierre Dumont, Le Monde, 9 October 1981; Les Echos, 4 and 15 March 1982.

95. Paul Fabra, Le Monde, 6 August 1981; J. P. Dumont, Le Monde, 17 September 1981.

96. This is further discussed below, in the context of redistribution.

97. Le Monde, 30 August and 10 September 1981; interview with Lionel Jospin, Le Nouvel Observateur, 17 October 1981. This stance was reversed by Mauroy, Les Echos, 11 March 1982; the change was confirmed by Mitterrand in his press conference of June 9.

98. See Chapter Thirteen.

99. Under prevailing law, the government could force the social partners to abide with the freeze; Mauroy may have hoped that they would agree to the freeze voluntarily. However, the government finally decided to modify the law. J. P. Dumont, Le Monde, 15 June 1982; Alain Rollat, Le Monde, 23 June 1982.

100. Le Point, 27 July 1981.

101. J. P. Vidal, Les Echos, 14 January 1982.

102. Les Echos, 15 January and 15 April 1982.

103. Le Monde, 15 June 1982.

104. Interview with Delors, L'Expansion, 4 September 1981. He repeated this objective in June 1982; Le Monde, 15 June 1982.

105. Le Monde, 8 October 1982.

106. The OECD predicted, for 1982, an inflation rate of about 13 percent by the end of 1982. OECD, economic surveys: France (1982), p. 59.

13

SOCIAL REFORMS

One of the major claims of the Socialists was that they would be able to manage the economy more successfully, even by the traditional standards of growth, investment, the balance of payments, and the like. Another important claim was that they would reshape economic and social life and make French society more just, more humane, and more responsive to the aspirations of the French. The main features of the new type of economic growth were to be a correction of the injustices in the prevailing distribution of the material burdens and benefits; a new solidarity in the face of unemployment; the transfer of much of social control back to the people; and the development of a new way of life, one more convivial and spontaneous, deemphasizing the competitive and individualistic consumption of material goods and leading to the development of a new community.

REDISTRIBUTION OF INCOME AND WEALTH

During the second half of the 1970s, the issue of poverty and inequality received much attention in France; this was in itself a new phenomenon. A much-debated OECD report, published in 1976, showed that France was remarkable among industrial countries both for its great inequalities and its high incidence of poverty.[1] Some steps to correct this situation had in fact been taken in the wake of 1968. For some time the minimum wage increased more rapidly than average hourly wages, and even the Barre government had proclaimed that the lowest income groups must fare better than the others in times of austerity. However, this had only led to relatively modest changes.[2]

187

The Common Program of the Left, in 1972, contained a massive plan for redistribution. But as the 1970s wore on, it became clear that the program, built as it was on the assumption of record growth rates, grew increasingly incompatible with the economic situation. In response to this, the Socialists (but not the Communists) adjusted their proposals. The measures taken by the new government since 1981 show considerable moderation on this account. Concerning the redistribution of income, several measures have been taken. The most important ones concern the increase of the minimum wage, of family and housing allowances and of retirement pensions. Minimum wages were increased by 10 percent in June 1982. This was modest when compared to the massive increases granted in 1936 and 1968, and considerably less than what the Communists demanded. The government also made it clear that it did not want to see this increase replicated throughout the wage hierarchy. As a result, the measure reached a comparatively small percentage of wage-earners.[3] For 1982, the SMIC was programmed to increase another 5 percent (or 7.6 percent, if one took into account the reduction of working hours without reduction of salary). This was not affected by the austerity package of June 1982, which specifically exempted the minimum wage.[4]

In general, the government supports wage settlements which will reduce the gap between low and high wages, and has shown the way in the area of civil service pay.[5] But average real wages will rise at best slowly, held down by two main constraints. The first one consists in the need to absorb unemployment. Higher wage costs reinforce the trend to replace labor by capital. The other constraint (related to the first) consists in the reduction of working time, especially the reduction of the work week from 40 to 39 hours, which became law in early 1982 (and further reductions are planned). Wages will rarely be reduced. This in turn means that the hourly cost of labor is increased already, with its attendant (negative) effect on job creation.[6]

Family allowances were increased more drastically (25 percent in June 1981, another 25 percent in February 1982). So were other allowances and pensions, which taken together reach a large number of the needy.[7] In this area, however, further progress seemed unlikely after June 1982. Future increases will simply keep up with inflation, at least as long as the climate of austerity continues. With regard to Social Security, the government soon showed a greater concern for financial rigor. The government rejected the idea — proposed by Minister Nicole Questiaux — that the state budget should take over a growing share of the rapidly increasing expenses. Since employer contributions are already very high (and thus discourage hiring), and were not to be raised until 1983, the most likely answer to the threatening deficit would be increased contributions by wage-earners as well as curtailed benefits.[8]

Another way in which the government has acted on the distribution of income and wealth is the tax system. The first tax reforms of the Socialist government affect redistribution in several ways. A wealth tax has been introduced on assets exceeding 3 million francs, with a tax rate ranging from 0.5 to 1.5 percent. Despite campaign statements by Mitterrand to the contrary, business property will also be taxed, though exemption is possible if profits are reinvested.[9] Taxes for high incomes were increased by adding another tax bracket at the upper end (putting the highest bracket up from 60 percent to 65 percent). Another measure directed at the higher incomes called for the taxation of business expense accounts. Finally, in a first project, a limit was also placed on the tax advantages granted for taxpayers' dependents, but this was reversed later on. These reforms fell somewhat short of the grand design to shift to a much greater reliance on direct taxes. In fact, the Socialists even increased the sales tax (the TVA), and a campaign promise to abolish it completely on essential goods was only partially realized. Once these projects are implemented, they will last for the duration of Mitterrand's term in office, at least that is what the government promised.[10] Thus the scope of change is already fairly clear. In fact, some of the measures adopted to encourage the formation of risk capital are in fact likely to benefit the wealthy, though it is true that Mitterrand also created a savings booklet for small, low-income savers with a guaranteed (indexed) return.[11]

UNEMPLOYMENT: A NEW SOLIDARITY?

The policy of the government towards unemployment and the unemployed is also part of the effort to achieve greater social justice. Though it will do little to modify the distribution of income between the average wage-earners and the highest income groups, it may prevent the formation of a new underclass of the chronically unemployed and introduce greater solidarity among wage-earners. But the measures which embody this policy are also meant to improve the everyday life of the employed wage-earners. Is it possible that the necessary, the useful and the pleasant should all go together?

In the 1960s, it was commonplace for sociologists to talk about the imminent "leisure problem." Increasing productivity was supposed to progressively reduce the hours spent in work. More time would be freed for leisure (and the problem, as discussed then, was what people would do with it). As things worked out, however, the leisure problem has not become a burning issue. Productivity did increase, and hours spent in work did decline, but the general result has been unemployment, not voluntary leisure. Table 13.1 illustrates this development for France. Since 1974, the increases in the productivity of labor — resulting primarily from more capital-intensive production — were generally greater than the increases in production (in terms of value added). As a result, despite continued economic growth, the total hours worked each year decreased regularly with the single exception of 1976. This decreasing demand for labor in industry coincided with the arrival of more numerous generations on the labor market, and also with a higher rate of women seeking employment. Thus a rapidly rising supply of workers was confronted with only a slow increase in the demand for labor (see also Graph 7.3). As Table 13.2 shows, employment fell particularly strongly in industry. In 1980, the number of jobs in industry was inferior to what it had been in 1968. By contrast, the exodus from agriculture slowed considerably in the years after 1974. The same was true for artisans. Only the tertiary sector was still a major source of new jobs.

TABLE 13.1

Indicators of Activity in Nonagricultural Market Sectors
(percent changes in yearly averages)

	1968-1974	1975	1976	1977-1979	1980[*]
Gross value added (in volume)	+6.0	+0.1	+5.0	+3.1	+1.5
Apparent hourly productivity of labor	+5.1	+3.3	+4.7	+3.2	+1.7
Hours actually worked (activity)	+0.9	-3.1	+0.3	-0.1	-0.2
Variation due to: Change in work time	-1.0	-1.7	-0.7	-0.7	-0.4
Change in numbers employed	+1.9	-1.4	+1.0	+0.6	+0.2

[*]provisional results
Source: Olivier Marchand and Jean-Pierre Revoil, "Emploi et chômage: bilan fin 1980," Economie et statistique, February 1981, p. 24.

TABLE 13.2
Evolution of Labor Force Employed in Different Sectors,
1968-1980 (in thousands)

	Dec. 31, 1968	Dec. 31 1974	Dec. 31 1980*	Evol. 68-74	Evol. 74-80
Agriculture					
Self-employed	2,362	1,698	1,501	-664	-197
Wage-earners	614	448	365	-166	-83
Industry					
Self-employed	642	579	581	-63	+2
Wage-earners	6,998	7,567	6,943	+569	-624
Tertiary sector					
Self-employed	1,631	1,534	1,530	-97	-4
Wage-earners	7,811	9,235	10,506	+1,424	+1,270
Total					
Self-employed	4,635	3,811	3,612	-824	-199
Wage-earners	15,423	17,251	17,814	+1,828	+563
Grand total	20,058	21,061	21,426	+1,004	+364

*estimated

Source: Adapted from Olivier Marchand and Jean-Pierre
Revoil, "Emploi et chômage: bilan fin 1980," Economie et
statistique, February 1981, pp. 29, 31.

One of the responses of the Socialists to this situation was
to call for the reindustrialization of the country; this strategy
has been discussed here earlier. Reflation could also make a
minor contribution. But neither measure was likely to be sufficient given the continued growth of the labor force at a rapid
rate until 1985, and at a still considerable rate in the years
thereafter.[12] Thus a plausible adaptation consisted in decreasing the number of hours each wage-earner spent in work.
In fact, that had happened briefly in the years after 1968.
Until then, France had had one of the longest work weeks in the
Common Market. By 1979, it was on the low side of the Common
Market average.[13] However, most of this decline took place
before the time of the Barre government. Once Barre was in
office, the rate of decline slowed considerably[14] (probably due
to the effort to maintain competitiveness by holding down costs).
Under these circumstances, it was not implausible to argue, as
the Left did, that the unemployment problem was best resolved if
working time was further reduced. Such a measure, to be sure,
would not increase the demand for labor (in terms of total hours
worked), however, it would spread employment more evenly

throughout the population. What had been the painful condition of unemployment when concentrated on a few could be transformed into additional free time, if only it was distributed throughout the labor force. However, this was only possible if several conditions were fulfilled, the most important one being that not only work would be shared, but also income.

The most important measure which the Socialists had proposed in this context was the reduction of the work week to 35 hours. This was to be achieved in several steps by 1985.[15] A first step was negotiated between business and labor in July 1981. It reduced the work week to 39 hours and introduced a fifth week of vacations on a general basis (the agreement also restated the goal of 35 hours by 1985). The CNPF and most unions signed the agreement. The C.G.T. however refused to sign, demanding an immediate reduction in the work week to 38 hours. The results of the negotiations were sanctioned by a law which authorized the government to implement this agreement by decree. The corresponding ordonnance became effective in February 1982.[16] It was immediately followed by strikes and controversy: would the reduction of work be accompanied by at least a partial reduction of wages, or would salaries remain untouched? The decree itself provided for "full compensation" (no reduction of wages) only for the SMIC (the minimum wage). Otherwise the details were to be worked out by the social partners. However, many members of the government were at first clearly in favor of a partial reduction of wages. Prime Minister Mauroy, minister of the economy Delors, labor minister Auroux, planning minister Rocard and others argued that the reduction of the work week had to be accompanied by a partial reduction in wages if the desired effect on employment (that is, new hiring) was to be achieved. Otherwise the reduction of working time would simply benefit those who already had a job and increase the financial burden on business, which would then be unable to increase employment.[17] In fact, several agreements negotiated before February 1982 (especially in the building and construction sector) provided for some adjustment of wages due to the new work week.[18] But then Mauroy began to waver, and eventually Mitterrand made a statement that an actual reduction of wages should only be considered once the reductions reached a certain threshold (for example, 37 hours). Until then, he stated, no worker should fear for his income on account of the 39 hour week.[19] The state showed the way: in the public sector, reduced hours were not accompanied by a corresponding wage adjustment. These statements and practices made further negotiations between unions and employers more difficult. It was less likely that unions would accept pay cuts under those circumstances, even though some union leaders, most prominently Edmond Maire, had in fact argued for such cuts earlier on.[20]

Nevertheless, several such agreements were signed.[21]   Mitterrand's decision was viewed essentially as political — he would
not be outbid on his left by the Communists (the CGT, strongly
opposed any wage reduction, but then so did F.O.), especially such
a short time before the regional elections.[22]

The 39 hour week was undoubtedly popular. As a job-creation
measure, however, or as an embodiment of solidarity in the face
of rising unemployment, it was a failure. It is likely to lead to
almost no creation of jobs. In fact, its impact was to make
labor still more expensive, thus encouraging its substitution by
capital. Shortly after its introduction, the government agreed
(in April 1982) not to reduce the legal work week before the
end of 1983.[23]   This left the field open for negotiations, but
the achievement of the 35 hour week by 1985 seemed now in
doubt.

There were other ways in which the government acted to reduce working time. Also in January 1982, a decree was issued
that created financial incentives for firms to conclude "solidarity
contracts" (contrats de solidarité) that would introduce part-time
work, reduce work to 37 hours or less by January 1983, or allow
retirement even before the age of 60, provided that these measures had a counterpart in the creation of new jobs.[24]   By the
end of April 1982, close to 2,000 such contracts had been
signed. Nearly all of them provided for earlier retirement; only
a few introduced the reduction of work time. Altogether they
had resulted in the creation of somewhat over 31,000 jobs. Over
3,000 solidarity contracts were still being negotiated at that
time.[25]

The government also encouraged the introduction of part-time
work in other ways. For the civil service it proposed the introduction of a four-day week and of half-time work, with salary
cuts of 20 percent and 50 percent respectively.[26]   But much
remained to be done in this area. Within the European community, France has the lowest rate of part-time work. Just to
catch up with the European average would, according to the
claims of a former planning commissioner, result in the creation
of 1,000,000 jobs.[27] This would reduce unemployment by perhaps
half of this figure (the formula would also increase the number
of job seekers), a substantial contribution to solving the unemployment problem. Perhaps a more flexible approach is necessary, in addition to the contrats de solidarité. For executives
and supervisory personnel, in private business, the government
proposed a "sabbatical year" formula. On such a leave, the
cadres would also be encouraged to create an enterprise of their
own.

An additional measure intended to free jobs throughout the
economy was introduced by yet another decree in March 1982.
The right to retire at age 60 seems to be important and welcome

to nearly all Frenchmen.[28]   In fact, it is a right that already exists for many wage earners, both in the public and the private sector, often under special arrangements for specific situations. In addition, since 1972 wage earners dismissed after the age of 60 could claim 70 percent of their last salary (the **garantie de ressources**).   This was extended in 1977 to those who resigned voluntarily.   Thus the great majority of Frenchmen already had the right to retire at the age of 60 (and in some cases earlier than that).   However, these schemes were based on agreements between employers and wage earners (with the state also making financial contribution) that were always limited in time, and the most recent of which was to expire in early 1983.

Mauroy promised that under the new regulation everyone would have the right to retire at age 60, and at 70 percent of his or her salary.   But in fact, the government could only decide about the first 50 percent of that sum (which is to be paid out of the Social Security system); the remainder had to come from supplementary retirement funds.   The amounts to be paid out of these funds still needed to be negotiated, with the different groups (employers, the different unions) taking very different positions.[29]   Under these circumstances (and also given the new financial rigor with regard to public finance), the reform of the retirement system is likely to have only a limited impact on the job situation.

A more radical approach to the unemployment problem, advocated by some experts of the INSEE,[30]   would consist in manipulating the cost of the factors of production (capital and labor) in such a way as to make the recourse to labor more attractive than the recourse to investment, at least within certain ranges and during periods of high unemployment.   For decades, the state has granted incentives to investment, thus reducing the effective cost of capital.   Since the beginning of the economic crisis, the French state has also, de facto, taxed employment and thus discouraged the use of labor.   This is due to the fact that social welfare contributions in France are paid very largely by employers, more so than in most other Common Market countries.[31]   When unemployment went up, the contributions went up as well, making labor even more expensive and thus encouraging its substitution by capital; clearly this amounted to a vicious circle.[32]   (Wage increases and the "full compensation" for the 39 hour week only compounded the problem.)   For the individual firm, the decisive economic elements are the relative costs of capital and labor.   But for the national economy as a whole, it is a different set of figures which is relevant, since labor is not "saved" when in fact it has to be paid for out of unemployment compensation funds, not to speak of political commitments to reduce the ranks of the jobless.

In order to encourage the use of labor, it is not necessary to hold down real wages, though this is what conservative politicians usually recommend. It would be possible for the state to correct the situation which results from the distorted costs of labor and capital respectively, and which renders impossible their optimum use from the perspective of the national economy. This can be done by taxing investment and using the proceeds to subsidize labor (for example, by taking over part of the social welfare contributions). To be sure, there are important limitations. The goal is to reach the optimum level for the use of both capital and labor.[33]   In any case, the Socialists, like previous governments, continue to subsidize investment in a variety of ways. So far, they have taken only timid steps towards reducing the cost of labor, usually limited to particular situations. Thus, the Pacte National pour l'Emploi, introduced by Barre and in fact subsidizing the employment mostly of young people, has been continued and broadened as Plan Avenir Jeunes.[34]   For the particularly labor-intensive textile industry, the government has consented — under certain conditions, that is, additional hiring and/or investment — to take over part of the employers' social welfare contributions for a limited period of time.[35]   But there seems to be no intention of expanding this approach to the economy as a whole. However, the pause in social welfare contributions announced in April 1982, and the simultaneous tax breaks for business with regard to the taxe professionnelle, may be somewhat related to this approach.

There are several other measures which were taken in the effort to bring unemployment under control. Civil service jobs were created largely as promised. An effort was made to better adapt the supply of labor to demand. This led in particular to a reform of the Agence Nationale pour l'Emploi (A.N.P.E.), also to a plan to guarantee vocational training for all 16-18 year olds who are no longer in school. Trainees will divide their time between work and school, and will receive a modest sum in return.[36]   Again, this measure is likely to show its effects only over time. For the immediate future, the Socialists have accepted the idea that they cannot yet put a halt to unemployment. In April 1982, Labor Minister Auroux stated that he expected the creation of about 100,000 jobs thanks to the contrats de solidarite by the end of 1982, and almost no effect at all from the introduction of the 39 hour week.[37]   In May, he announced that unemployment compensation would have to be decreased in the future.[38]

It is quite clear that French society, and more particularly the labor unions (except the C.F.D.T.), have not contributed much to the implementation of a policy of greater solidarity. As the summer of 1982 approached, more and more commentators raised the old question of group egoisms and situations acquises. Many groups in French society did not seem willing to give up any

advantages that they had been able to secure even when a difficult situation made such an act of national solidarity more
urgent.[39]   In turn, the government did not push the different
groups very hard, except perhaps business. It now announced —
in a considerable scaling down of earlier ambitions — its new
goal for unemployment: it was to be stabilized (no more) in
1983.

THE REDISTRIBUTION OF POWER

In their programs during the 1970s, the Socialists stressed
that they would not only pursue a different policy. They would
also change the structure of power in society, a structure which
they in turn blamed for many of the evils of capitalist society.
The main approach in this area became autogestion, though its
meaning became blurred as the term was used by very different
groups.[40]   Autogestion or self-management socialism had obvious
applications in the workplace (democratization both in the private
and the public sector). It could also be applied to life outside
work (greater participation in self-government, for example,
through territorial decentralization and democratic local government).

In the context of this book, it is the democratization of
economic life which deserves the greatest attention. The authoritarian character of French business firms has often been de-
plored. In the 1970s, the government had commissioned a major
study that was to serve as the basis for reform, but nothing
came of it.[41]   Among the Left, several approaches to this problem coexisted under the rather abstract term of autogestion.
Some Socialists (particularly Maire and Rocard) wanted to see
structures under which people would collectively control their
different life spheres, according to radical-democratic principles.
The result of such change, they thought, would be a reorientation of much of economic and social life and its priorities, away
from the pattern that had developed under capitalism, but also
state-socialism or social democracy.[42]   Others identified
democratization of the economy with greater control by a
democratically elected government (this was the position taken by
the Communists). Still others were thinking of reforms that
would essentially bring France such traditional social-democratic
reforms as a greater recognition of labor unions, and perhaps
codetermination.

Among the specific measures mentioned in this context in the
Socialist party program of 1980 were the rights of workers, the
rights of women, and territorial decentralization.[43]   It is the
rights of workers which are of particular interest to a discussion
of economic policy. Specifically listed in Mitterrand's program

of January 1981 were expanded rights of the works committees (comités d'entreprise), in particular the right to a suspensive veto of dismissals decided by management.[44]   Other rights included greater freedom of expression of wage earners on the workplace, and the right to participate in some tasks that were traditionally the prerogative of management (organization of work, hiring, training, new production techniques, and so on).[45]

Proposals of this kind had the employers greatly worried when the Socialists came to power. The government moved quickly to reassure them.   The basic principle of management authority in private firms would not be challenged, it stated. The idea of the veto was expressly rejected.[46] The basic principle would be that of negotiations between social partners.[47]   Economics minister Delors put things in perspective when, in the fall of 1981, he declared that the workers were to be given those rights which they already possessed in most other European countries, "neither more nor less."[48] Obviously this was not an area where the French government was going to come forth with innovative leadership. This did not do much to calm employers; on the other hand, it considerably irritated the C.F.D.T. leadership, one of the strongest advocates of autogestion, particularly since the subject was not given the same priority as other reforms such as the nationalizations.[49]

In March 1982, the rapport Auroux containing these reforms was approved by the government. It was then submitted to the National Assembly in the form of four different bills. The loi Auroux had several key provisions. One such provision required that in each firm with a minimum of 50 wage earners, management and labor would have to negotiate at least once every year on such issues as wages, working time, and working conditions. There was no obligation to reach an agreement. However, the employers would be expected to put many management questions on the table. The point was to create contractual – rather than hierarchical — relations betweeen management and labor. If an agreement was reached with only part of the representatives of labor, it could be blocked by groups who had not signed, as long as they represented at least 50 percent of the registered voters at the last union elections.

A second key provision gives, to wage earners, the right to self-expression in the business firm, particularly with regard to work organization and working conditions. This expression takes place on the site and during the hours of work, and is to be paid as work. A third important provision gives the right, to labor union and personnel delegates, to receive all necessary economic and financial information, to circulate freely in the firm, and to be protected against dismissal. The works committees (comités d'entreprise) have the additional right to be informed about the introduction of new techniques and their impact on employment and pay schemes. Their members may ask to receive training in economics at the expense of the firm and during regular working hours. In firms with over 300 wage earners, they can also consult outside experts on management questions, again at the firm's expense.[50]

The loi Auroux thus did not bring the kind of revolution that many patrons (employers) had been afraid of. Nonetheless the CNPF and many other employer organizations protested strongly against the proposed bill. They objected to the privileged place that was given to labor union representatives, declaring that such structures obviously assumed that the firm was a place for class struggle rather than for common undertakings. Certainly the reform totally reversed the situation as it had evolved in the late 1970s, when employers tried with some success to hollow out the role of the unions within the firms, replacing them increasingly by the internal chain of command for labor-management contacts.[51] More specifically, employers complained that the requirement to negotiate and discuss everything from wages to working conditions to new technology was setting up a parliamentary system, one entirely incompatible with the conditions of business success.[52] (On the other hand, some progressive employers whose firms generally served as inspiration to much of the loi Auroux declared that they were very happy with these reforms.[53]) Perhaps the protests have to be seen against the background of a whole series of amendments put forward by Socialist deputies in the National Assembly, who, led by neo-Marxist "maximalists" such as Pierre Joxe, wanted to go further and apply the various provisions even to small firms. The government (and indeed President Mitterrand himself) had to intervene repeatedly to make them accept the law in the form in which it was submitted to the National Assembly.[54] On the basis of its content, the loi Auroux appears comparatively moderate. It is a sign of the quality of French labor relations (or perhaps of the fears of many traditioinally autocratic employers to make concessions) that it stirred up so much controversy.

In the public sector, also, the distribution of power was to be changed, and "democracy" introduced in the workplace. The main feature of the corresponding law — still in preparation in spring 1982 — was the election of personnel representatives to the boards of administration or supervision. In other respects, the situation in the public sector firms will probably resemble that created by the loi Auroux for the private sector. Codetermination along the lines of the West German or Swedish models is not very likely at present. Most of the unions reject it because it smacks too much of "class collaboration" or otherwise goes against what unions see as their appropriate role.[55]

If one sums up these developments, it is clear that they fall short of the expectations and hopes of the autogestion advocates who joined the Socialist party in 1974. With the current leadership, self-management socialism is likely to remain a distant ideal, indeed perhaps a utopian one.

ENERGY AND ECOLOGY

There were other elements that confirmed this picture — tending to show that there would not really be any fundamental change in the orientation of economic or industrial development. Perhaps this should not surprise. However, the Socialist party had encouraged such expectations during its years in opposition. In the mid- and late 1970s, the basic orientation of industrial society in such matters as economic growth, the growing concentration of economic and political power, competitive consumption as a way of life, and so on came to be questioned by a substantial sector of the French public. These were the years when the French ecology movement emerged on the political scene. Many of these people felt at home in the Socialist party, particularly in its courant autogestionnaire (CFDT, Rocard, and others).[56] In fact, the party not only proposed autogestion (a favorite theme also of the ecologists, who expect from it the abolition of the centralized, hierarchical, and technocratic society which they blame for many evils), but also a reorientation of the economy towards different priorities, including environmental ones.[57] Thus on the question of nuclear energy, the Socialist party, though divided, seemed to move closer in recent years to the views of the ecology movement. Since the late 1970s, Socialist deputies and mayors had often opposed nuclear power projects side by side with the ecologists. As long as they were in opposition, the Socialist leaders took a very strong stand against key parts of the French nuclear program. In 1979, Mitterrand, Mauroy, Rocard, Lionel Jospin and many other prominent leaders signed a petition against the reprocessing of nuclear wastes for commercial purposes at La Hague. In early 1981, the party approved a compromise energy program which provided for a significant reduction of the nuclear capacity planned by Giscard. During his 1981 campaign, Mitterrand stated that he was personally opposed to the breeder reactor and also repeated his opposition to the expansion of reprocessing at La Hague.[58] A decision on these issues, he said, would only be taken after a "great national debate" that articulated the will of the citizenry.

Soon after the Socialists came to power, they halted all work on five nuclear sites. This was seen as a first step in the reorientation of French energy policy. But in fact, the government was already engaged in an about-face on the issue. New energy commissions, this time with little or no party input, were set up to study the same questions on which the party had decided only in January. Moreover, they were to come up with reports in an incredibly short time. In La Hague a commission of local citizens was established in August to study the problems of uranium processing. It was to make a recommendation within one month.[59] A high civil servant was charged with the formulation of a new energy program in a similar time frame. The deputies were given a few days to study those recommendations before voting on a program that was not subject to significant modification anyhow, since the government decided to pledge its responsibility to the passage of the bill.

The energy program which emerged from this process in the fall of 1981 was remarkably different from anything the Socialists had discussed over the last few years. In fact, it should have pleased the opposition — and also the Communist leadership (which, unlike Communist voters, has always been strongly in favor of nuclear power). Instead of the 39,000 megawatts projected for 1990 in the Socialist energy program of January 1981, the government opted for 55,000 MW, when even its new expert only recommended 51,000. The Two-Year Plan formulated by Michel Rocard gave the rationale: it was good to have surplus capacity, so that there was no danger that a limited production of electricity might stand in the way of rapid economic expansion once investment started up again.[60] Also, the reprocessing plant at La Hague was to be expanded after all, and the whole nuclear program was defended on the grounds that it provided technological leadership and created jobs. The old objection (that alternative energy sources, being more labor- and less capital-intensive, would have created even more jobs) was pretty much swept under the rug, though the Two-Year Plan did provide for an ambitious program of energy savings.[61] Not surprisingly, many Socialist deputies were embarrassed by so much inconsistency, in fact, the government gave the National Assembly no chance to modify its energy program. Among ecologists there was talk of betrayal, and the CFDT was predictably angry.[62] Subsequent events do not show a clear picture. In March 1982, the credits for energy savings were reduced in order to finance the extra cost of Algerian natural gas, thus provoking the resignation of Michel Hugon from his energy savings post (and his firing from his position as director of the Charbonnages de France). On the other hand, in a partial reversal, April saw the creation of the Agence française de l'Energie, and the appointment of former CFDT leader Michel Rolant as chief of the new agency. One of the most outspoken critics of the reckless promotion of electric energy by Electricité de France (EDF), Jean Syrota, was also appointed to an important position.[63]

In sum, the Socialists began by reversing in many respects their earlier stand on energy, in particular on nuclear energy, though they seem to have qualified that reversal since. Also, further debate of this question may still be planned.[64] Overall though, it seemed as though in this area as in that of <u>autogestion</u>, the "realists" had triumphed over the "visionaries."

A DIFFERENT MODEL OF DEVELOPMENT

How can one sum up the actions taken by the Socialists in the area of social reform? They will certainly bring about a reduction of inequalities in France. The change is considerable in some areas (retirement pensions, family allocations, and others), but in some areas they have already reached the limits, due to budgetary constraints. Wages, except for the minimum wage, will not change much in the near future, due to the restraints resulting from an internationally open economy. In 1982 French workers received wages that were still below the average of the European community. Even total wage costs (social welfare contributions included) were still only 90 percent of what they were in Germany.[65] But for the time being, no major reforms are on the agenda. At the end of 1981, Mitterrand stated that the outlines of a more just society would emerge by early 1983;[66] thus most of the reforms in this area have already been passed or are at least known. Further change may come later if the new industrial strategy (based on the nationalizations and the reconquest of domestic markets) should turn out to be successful, but that is unlikely to take place before the mid-1980s.

One of the goals of social reform was to introduce greater solidarity into French society. Some of this has been achieved, however, the solidarity between employed and unemployed is not remarkably great, either in terms of governmental policy or of union attitudes, which in this case are essential. In other countries — thus the "models" of Germany and Austria — organized labor has accepted a stabilization of wages, partly in order to prevent the spread of unemployment. In France, however, where a considerably higher level of unemployment prevails, the government could not secure union cooperation for such a course. (It is true that in Germany and Austria the social democrats had the advantage of having come to power before the crisis years starting in 1974; it would be difficult for a newly elected Leftist government to do the same right after coming to power.) Thus, solidarity remained somewhat impressive, and very soon came to feel the imperatives of financial and budgetary rigor, resulting from a concern to protect French independence.

The measures to bring democracy to the workplace, in particular the loi Auroux, are important reforms for France, as the controversy surrounding them has shown. However, they are quite moderate when compared with social democratic reforms elsewhere, and they do not incorporate much (if anything) of the "revolutionary" traditions of part of the French labor movement, of which the idea of autogestion is perhaps the most original element.

While the above reforms will certainly change everyday life (Changer la vie was the Socialists' program at the outset of the 1970s[67]), they are likely to produce little in the way of an original model of development. Perhaps such an objective was never very important to the majority of the Socialist leaders, and became even more remote once they had to confront the problems of government. The exercise of power represents undoubtedly a major learning experience for many of them. Some Socialist leaders have changed remarkably after only a few months in the government.[68] There is more talk now about the achievement of social democratic countries such as Germany and Austria. Social democracy is no longer dismissed or even reviled, as it used to be not too long ago in some circles of the P.S.[69]

Of the current ministers, it was Rocard who had the most ideas about more far-reaching social change in the autogestion mold, but Rocard has kept a low profile after the fall of 1981 and may not reemerge for some time. Mitterrand's own views of (and hopes for) the future, which he exposed at the Versailles summit, are not primarily based on an improvement of human relations through different social and political organization. He extolled instead his faith in technical progress. Automation, reindustrialization and improved communication would "liberate men from the double constraint of space and time,"[70] at least if mankind managed to put such progress to good use. If . . . but how was this to be achieved? That question remained mostly unanswered.

In some ways, the very success of governmental policies with respect to national goals such as the absorption of unemployment, reindustrialization, and so on may be incompatible with efforts to promote more far-reaching social reforms. The business world must not be worried excessively if it is to cooperate. The controversy over the abortive pause Delors and the real pause Mauroy well illustrated this dilemma.[71] To some extent, it is the old problem of "socialism in one country." It is difficult to combat world capitalism when one is trying at the same time to compete with other capitalist countries for a share of the world market. Even the nationalizations cannot change this situation fundamentally, as the arguments of their advocates clearly showed. Thus, Boublil argued that it was important for France to become one of the world's technological leaders because only the leaders could decide on their own pattern of development; the others had to accept a type of development handed down to them (in the form of goods, production structures, and eventually a whole society and way of life) from the core countries of world capitalism, that is, the United States, West Germany, and Japan. In order to avoid such a fate, France had to . . . emulate precisely those very same countries.[72] It was a nice illustration in Ellulian logic.[73] In other words, in order to free itself from the shackles of world capitalism, France had to become an imperialist power itself, or at the very least a core country of that capitalism. It is true that the advantages derived from core country status might not, in a Socialist France, be appropriated by multinational corporations. The "monopoly rent" might be distributed more fairly among the population. A Socialist government might also be more humane in its relations with the third world — but only as long as there was no negative impact on France's international competitive standing.[74] Matters would undoubtedly improve if European countries would join together to form that "social space" that Mitterrand has called for since his election. Until such time though, "socialism in one country" remains a difficult proposition even with the best of intentions.

NOTES

1. Adrian Sinfield, "Poverty and inequality in France," in Vic George and Roger Lawson, eds., Poverty and Inequality in Common Market Countries (London: Routledge and Kegan Paul, 1980), pp. 92-95.

2. See Chapter Seven. Also Marguerite Perrot, "Le pouvoir d'achat des salaires," Economie et statistique, January 1980, pp. 41-52.

3. It affected only 8 percent of all wage earners directly (by contrast, the 35.1 percent minimum wage increase granted in 1968 affected 12.5 percent of the wage earners). Le Monde, 20 November 18.

4. Les Echos, 15 and 24 February 1982; Le Monde, 15 June 1982.

5. Le Monde, 27 February 1982.

6. See p. 189.

7. Le Monde, 10 February 1982.

8. Les Echos, 19 February and 30 April 1982; Mitterrand in his press conference of June 9, 1982.

9. M. Roy in Le Point, 31 August 1981; and Le Monde, weekly edition, 1 October 1981. Mitterrand had announced that the outil de travail would not be taxed. Application of the tax was suspended in 1982, temporarily.

10. Jacques Mornand, Le Nouvel Observateur, 27 February 1982.

11. Le Monde, 3 March 1982. Mitterrand in his press conference of June 9, 1982 announced measures to encourage formation of risk capital.

12. The surplus of arrivals over departures from the labor market is estimated at 230,000 per year for the years 1980-1985, and at 130,000 per year for the remainder of the 1980s. Interview with Michel Albert (former Commissioner of Planning), Le Nouvel Observateur, 5 June 1982.

13. Olivier Marchand and Jean-Pierre Revoil, "Emploi et chômage: bilan fin 1980," Economie et statistique, February 1981, p. 28.

14. Ibid., graph I, p. 26.

15. Le Point, 27 July 1981; goal reasserted by Mauroy, Le Monde, 17 September 1981.

16. The decree procedure (Article 38 of the French Constitution) was resorted primarily to speed things up. Le Monde, 20 November 1981; Le Monde, 8 February 1982.

17. Discussion between Christian Goux (one of Mitterrand's economic advisors) and Raymond Soubie (former advisor for Raymond Barre) on the reduction of working time, Le Point, 18 January 1982.

18. Jean-Pierre Dumont in Le Monde, 13 February 1982.

19. Les Echos, 11 and 12 February 1982.

20. Dumont, Le Monde, 13 February 1982; and A. Laurens, Le Monde, 15 February 1982.

21. Les Echos, 13 April 1982. However, they rarely led to job creation.

22. Claude Sales, Le Point, 15 February 1982; Jacques Julliard, Le Nouvel Observateur, 27 February 1982.

23. Dominique Audibert and Denis Jeambar, Le Point, 19 April 1982.

24. Les Echos, 20 January 1982.

25. Le Monde, 4 May 1982.

26. Mauroy announced such a plan in September 1981; see Le Monde, 17 September 1981.

27. Michel Albert interviewed in Le Nouvel Observateur, 5 June 1982.

28. In an IFOP survey of 35-60 year olds, conducted in March 1982, 84 percent were favorable to lowering the retirement age to 60; only 4 percent were opposed. Survey published in Le Point, 5 April 1982.

29. Claude Sales, Le Point, 5 April 1982; Jean-Pierre Dumont in Le Monde, 26 March 1982; Les Echos, 12 March 1982.

30. Patrick Artus, Henri Sterdyniak and Pierre Villa, "Investissement, emploi, et fiscalité," Economie et statistique, November 1980.

31. In France, contributions by employers and wage earners financed (in 1977) 81.5 percent of all social protection, in Italy, 71.3 percent, in Germany, 69.9 percent, and in Britain, 52.8 percent. Ibid., p. 121.

32. Ibid., p. 119.

33. The authors of the article propose an 18.5 percent tax on investment, with the proceeds of which they would finance a reduction of Social Security contributions by 5 points. They say that this would increase jobs by 300,000 to 400,000 over six years, and increase production by 1 to 1.5 percent. Ibid., p. 115.

34. The beneficiaries were around 300,000 in number. Les Echos, 19 January 1982. In the past, the Pacte National pour l'emploi had often subsidized jobs which were not permanent; this was supposed to change. Roger Priouret, Le Nouvel Observateur, 22 August 1981.

35. Les Echos, 8 February 1982.

36. Le Monde, 26 March 1982.

37. Les Echos, 16 April 1982.

38. Le Monde, 7 May 1982.

39. Roger Priouret, Le Nouvel Observateur, 15 May 1982.

40. Communists used the term of control by a "truly democratic" government.

41. The rapport Sudreau in 1974.

42. See Chapter Three.

43. Projet socialiste (Paris: Club socialiste du livre, 1980), pp. 231-302.

44. Point 60 in 110 Propositions pour la France (Mitterrand's election brochure for the presidential elections of May 1981).

45. See also Projet socialiste, pp. 236-244.

46. D. Jeambar in Le Point, 13 July 1981; and Mauroy before the National Assembly, Le Monde, 17 September 1981.

47. Mauroy, ibid.

48. Interview with Delors, Le Nouvel Observateur, 24 October 1981.

49. A. Laurens in Le Monde, 17 October 1981; also Les Echos, 3 and 5 November 1981.

50. Roger Priouret, Le Nouvel Observateur, 30 April 1982.

51. See Chapter Ten.

52. Francis Gautier (Entreprise et Progrès) in Les Echos, 30 March 1982; Rene Bernasconi (C.G.P.M.E.) in Les Echos, 30 April 1982; Yvon Gattaz, (C.N.P.F.), cited in Le Monde, 12 May 1982.

53. Thus Antoine Riboud, Le Nouvel Observateur, 8 May 1982.

54. Kathleen Evin, Le Nouvel Observateur, 8 May 1982.

55. See interview with Public Sector Expansion Minister Le Garrec, Le Point, 19 April 1982; also Roger Priouret, Le Nouvel Observateur, 20 February 1982.

56. Francoise Bonnal, "L'évolution de l'opinion publique à l'egard de l'écologie au travers des sondages," paper presented in September 1980 at the Fondation Nationale des Sciences Politiques in Paris.

57. Projet socialiste, pp. 177-79.

58. Le Monde, 22 August 1981.

59. G. Porte in Le Monde, 30-31 August 1981.

60. Plan intérimaire. Stratégie pour deux ans. 1982-1983, p. 213.

61. Ibid., pp. 207 and 209.

62. Le Point, 3 August 1981; Le Monde, 30 September, 1 and 9 October 1981; Le Nouvel Observateur, 3 and 17 October 1981. See also the series of interviews and articles in Que faire aujourd'hui, October 1981.

63. Michel Bosquet, Le Nouvel Observateur, 30 April 1982.

64. This is at least mentioned in the Motion nationale d'orientation passed by the Socialist Party Congress at Valence in October 1981; see paragraph III (1).

65. The rapport Bloch-Lainé, which drew up a kind of "inventory" of the situation in France at the end of Giscard's term in office, stated that income inequalities remained still too high, and that the relative position of French blue-collar workers vis-a-vis junior executives or employees of the tertiary sector was one of the most unfavorable within the Common Market. Cited in Le Nouvel Observateur, 2 January 1982. The figure of 90 percent for total wage costs in France as compared to those in Germany in early 1982, stems from Pierre Locardel, Les Echos, 13 April 1982. Locardel, however, stresses the fact that only three years earlier, French wage costs were only 75 percent of what they had been in Germany.

66. Mitterrand in his address of 31 December 1981; Le Monde, 2 January 1982.

67. Changer la vie (Paris: Flammarion, 1972).

68. Research minister (and former C.E.R.E.S. leader) Jean-Pierre Chevenement greatly surprised everyone by his "statesmanlike" attitude. It is assumed that he has higher ambitions, and in June 1982, when Dreyfus retired from the Ministry of Industry, Chevènement was given this portfolio in addition to that of Research. Budget minister Fabius, who once had criticized Rocard for his "un-socialist" economic rigor, became the apostle of limiting the budget deficit in the spring of 1982, to the point that he clashed with Delors. Franz-Olivier Giesbert and Jacques Mornand, Le Nouvel Observateur, 22 May 1982.

69. This criticism used to be particularly intense in the ranks of the C.E.R.E.S. In the words of Georges Sarre, social democracy was "a type of society in which capital makes sure of the voluntary integration of the working class . . . into the

established order." Sarre in Le Nouvel Observateur, 30 December 1978.

Rocard also criticized the social democratic approach, but for different reasons. First, he argued that the crucial questions that wage earners confront in industrial societies are no longer mainly related to money income, but also to qualitative aspects of life; in particular, there was a rising demand to participate, not to be administered. Social democracy, with its comprehensive welfare administration from above, could not deal with this problem; autogestion was the natural answer. In addition, social democracy produced its greatest advances during the period of rapid growth and easy affluence which followed World War II. The future was likely to be more difficult. Michel Rocard, debate with Patrick Viveret, Faire, September 1976.

70. Mitterrand's report to the Versailles summit, cited in Le Monde, 7 June 1982.

71. In late 1981, Delors called for a halt to reforms, arguing that business was unlikely to perform well if it was saddled with an unceasing flow of reforms. Mauroy and Mitterrand disagreed, at least for the time being; both sides undoubtedly had Léon Blum's experience in mind (see Chapter Fourteen). Jean Daniel in Le Nouvel Observateur, 5 December 1981. In April, the compromise with business came anyhow, as discussed above. It was commonly called the pause Mauroy.

72. Alain Boublil, Le socialisme industriel, pp. 52, 79, and 255.

73. Jacques Ellul, The Technological Society (New York: Knopf, 1964). Ellul argues that technique can only be met by similar technique, and that its structure defines its own purposes. As a result of this, he concludes that Hitler really won the war (that is, his techniques did, though in the end they were applied more successfully by his adversaries).

74. It is true that there may be some leeway. In 1982, France secured a few very large contracts from developing countries by offering particularly favorable terms on technology transfer, more so apparently than its competitors. This characterized the contract to furnish Mirage jets to India (over two-thirds of which will be built in India itself). The same approach was also taken in negotiations over telephone equipment with India and Indonesia, letting these countries produce themselves part of the equipment that France wanted to sell them. Les Echos, 8 April 1982 (telephone equipment for India), 15 April 1982 (Mirage jets for India); Wall Street Journal, 6 April 1982 (telephone equipment for Indonesia).

14

PROBLEMS AND PROSPECTS

French national politics, particularly at election time, traditionally wakes up old fears both on the Left and the Right. A whole fauna of monsters then comes alive in the French political imagination. For the Right, the prospect of a victory of the Left always conjures up a whole series of threats. The Communists would very quickly come to dominate the Socialists, many on the Right argued over the last decade, thanks to their effective control over the largest union (the C.G.T.) which would take to the streets with its well-disciplined troops if the Socialists tried to resist Communist demands.[1] Or else radicals (in or outside labor unions) might mobilize the workers and ask for a fundamental change in wages and working conditions, along the lines of what had happened in 1936 and 1968.[2] In the top-level negotiations between business, labor, and the government in the wake of such a mobilization, the Right warned, a Leftist government would in one big swoop surrender to demagogic demands and effectively wreck the French economy for a long time to come. Even if that catastrophe was avoided, a Leftist government in which the Communists had a decisive voice might do much the same thing over a longer period of time, a year or two perhaps. (This is why every time the government appeared to make a concession to the C.G.T., the event caused jitters in the business press.) Irresponsible expenditures would increase inflation to unprecedented levels, imports would increase dramatically and exports decline because of lack of competitiveness, and soon the government would find itself forced to resort to strong protectionist measures which (leading to retaliation) could only aggravate the problem in the long run. This would within a few years leave an economy bled white by excessive wage and social welfare payments,[3] internationally indebted and only artificially maintained by ever-increasing state intervention. These fears of the Right are based in part on the conservative interpretation of the record of Leftist governments in French history; and it is true that the Cartel des Gauches in 1924, and the Front Populaire in 1936-37, ended in economic failure. However, the reasons for their failure were not necessarily (and certainly not exclusively) the ones the Right likes to focus on, as shall be seen in a moment.

The fears of the Right have their counterpart on the Left. There, the favorite specter is the sabotage of progressive governmental policies by business and/or the owners of capital. Businessmen are seen as lacking all patriotic sense, prepared to move their capital abroad on the first opportunity, to halt all investment and hiring, and to generally paralyze public policy in an effort to bring down the government as quickly as possible. They will even — so goes the fear — inflict losses upon themselves as long as they can damage the government; in other words, they will resort to la politique du pire.

These questions can be put in less extreme terms. Are the Socialists likely to be successful with their economic and social policies? Will they be able to maintain sufficient political support among the major groups and organizations of the country and among the public? Will they be successful in confronting the international environment, and will their policies be successful in economic terms?

DANGERS ON THE LEFT

There are several dangers that the Socialist government may conceivably encounter because of political problems with the Left (or a part thereof). The danger most stressed by the Right before the elections was that of being swamped, either by a Communist partner (P.C., C.G.T.) that turned out to be stronger than expected (and was perhaps backed up by a strong and uncontrollable radical element among the new Socialist deputies), or by a popular mobilization movement along the lines of what had happened in 1936 or 1968. In the first year of the Socialist government, none of these dangers seemed to be very prominent. Not that the government did not experience problems with the parties and labor unions that make up the Left, but they were of a different nature. What the Socialists complained about most was a lack of support for the government among the labor unions, and even foot dragging among Socialist party militants in doing their job. Apathy and disunity of the Left seemed to present greater problems than excessive energy and assertiveness on its part.

Of the above dangers, the "Communist threat" will be dealt with first, that is, the problems that the Socialist government could experience with the PC and/or the C.G.T. Even observers sympathetic to the Left had in the past stressed this problem. But as discussed earlier, that threat had diminished considerably in the late 1970s, and the results of the 1981 elections confirmed this development. In electoral terms, the Communist party reached a catastrophic low in 1981 (15.3 percent in the presidential elections, 16.17 percent in the subsequent National Assembly elections). The number of Communist deputies fell from 86 to 44.[4] It did not show any signs of recovery in the 1982 regional elections, where it again achieved only 15.87 percent of the vote.[5] In order to have four Communist ministers in the government, the Communist party had to sign a veritable capitulation that not only condemned most of the Communist foreign policy stand of the last years but also bound the Communists to cooperate loyally with the government at all levels. Even Communist labor was to accept and respect "the choice of May 10."[6]

In general, the four Communist ministers have been models of loyalty to the government. On the other hand, the Communist party leadership clearly practices a two-faced policy. On one side is the cooperation with the Socialists, by the same people who, from 1977 to 1981, denounced them as social-democratic traitors; on the other is the purge in the party and the C.G.T., directed against those who, after the break of 1977, continued to advocate continued unity and cooperation between Socialists and Communists, and who in 1981 were openly skeptical of the leadership's "conversion" after Mitterrand's election, a conversion which in their view remained very superficial. In the Communist party, this led to the exclusion of Henri Fiszbin and his collaborators at Rencontres communistes, a weekly devoted to the discussion of these problems.[7] In the C.G.T., the relatively liberal Séguy, suspected also of a weakness for cooperation with the Socialists, was replaced by the hardliner Henri Krasucki as the P.C. tightened control over the leadership of this labor union.[8] A purge soon followed.

From such preparations among the Communists, it is not altogether far-fetched to infer that they are preparing for the possibility of renewed confrontation with their senior coalition partner. True, their support is not needed at the present time in the National Assembly, but the C.G.T. remains, despite its decline, the most important labor union. The question is whether the Communist leadership could effectively use the union to destabilize the government. At the present time — and probably for some years to come — this seems quite unlikely. The decline of the Communist party has been paralleled by a decline of the C.G.T. in union elections. Membership has been falling, and so have militancy and revenues.[9] More importantly perhaps, the union is profoundly divided internally over political questions. This showed first when the leaders used the unions to promote the candidacy of Marchais in the presidential election.[10] Dissent intensified during summer and fall of 1981, when the Communist party moved to consolidate its hold over the executive organs of the union. This resulted in the resignations of two leaders at the highest level in October 1981. Not since 1966 had such high-level resignations occurred in the union — nor was dissent limited to the upper echelons.[11] This dissent reached new and unprecedented levels during the Poland crisis in late 1981, when the C.G.T. was the only labor union not to condemn the Jaruzelski regime's crackdown on Solidarity. Discipline within the organization nearly collapsed. Whole federations sent in their collective protests.[12] While the leadership, both within the party and the union, soon reasserted itself and produced a show of relative unity, it avoided dealing with the real problems at issue.[13]

After June 1981, many observers of French political life predicted that the Communist party and the C.G.T. were unreliable allies at best, and would turn into aggressive opponents of the Socialist government as soon as that government was going to either experience economic difficulties or shift towards a policy of austerity. When Mitterrand made his statement on the 39 hour week, this was seen as a concession to the C.G.T., which strongly opposed anything but full compensation. On the occasion of the pause Mauroy, the C.G.T. predictably protested against these "free gifts" to business. But, on the other hand, the Communist leadership checked L'Humanité, the party's daily, when in Marchais' view that newspaper had gone too far in "outbidding" the government with demagogic proposals.[14] And when, in June 1982, austerity became the official policy of the government, the Communists soon pledged to support the new policy orientation, at least as long as wage earners would not be alone in carrying the necessary burdens.[15]

With the Communists, it is clearly the C.G.T. (which is under Communist hegemony, though not under exclusive Communist control) which presents potentially the greater problem. It is less troubled than the P.C. and still remains France's largest labor union. With regard to Socialist support, the problem is different. When the Socialists triumphed in the parliamentary elections of June 1981, this brought a very large contingent of new deputies to the National Assembly. Many of them were teachers. They often lacked a background in economics and — as intellectuals — were suspected of a penchant for dogmatism. In fact, the government was somewhat concerned at first about its own majority, and decided to "channel" its self-expression.[16] In this effort it was largely successful. There were not too many instances of radical rhetoric, except during the Valence

Party Congress in the fall of 1981 (which adopted very hard, neo-Marxist anti-business language, to be discussed below) and during the debate on the nationalizations.

On the whole, however, it does not seem as though the (parliamentary) Socialist party exercised much influence on the formulation of government policy. It was somewhat taken aback by the pause Mauroy and criticized it for lacking solid counterparts in the form of tangible business concessions, but received little satisfaction. It was largely ignored when the government submitted the loi Auroux. The Socialist deputies would undoubtedly have gone substantially further in their reforms than the government.[17] On the occasion of the major policy change of June 1982, a scheduled consultation with the party was postponed until the decisions were taken. The party had little choice but to acquiesce, despite a reluctance to do so in certain quarters.[18]

If the Socialist party did not make a stronger show of power in its first year after the 1981 elections, this is in part due to the institutions of the Fifth Republic. It is also due however to the particular state that the party found itself in. Undoubtedly, it suffered from the fact that most of its major leaders were now in government (it was decided early on that the ministers would not retain party functions). Militantism also fell after the elections,[19] and more difficult times yet may have set in with the announcement, in mid-1982, of policies that call for understanding and sacrifice. At Valence, the party defined its own role as that of a "force of proposition, impulsion, and reflection."[20] The government sees things somewhat differently; it wants the party to explain official policy, and criticized it for not living up to this task.[21]

Leftist parties and unions can create serious difficulties for a Socialist government not only by overloading it with excessive demands; in a time of economic difficulty, unions can endanger the success of governmental policy by resisting changes that may be required to overcome a crisis situation. (The British unions have often been blamed for this during the last decade.) The unemployment situation in France has certainly reached important proportions. The employment policy of the government relied heavily on a reduction of working hours, and generally on a greater solidarity among all citizens. That policy could only be successful if wage earners were prepared to accept a wage evolution that would take into account the reduction of working hours (that is, something less than "full compensation"), as the government had originally proposed. But from the outset, two of the three largest unions, the C.G.T. and the reformist F.O., simply rejected such an approach out of hand.[22] The result — reduced hours with full pay — did improve the situation of those who were employed, but did little if anything for the unemployed. Of the major unions, only the C.F.D.T., long the strongest advocate of solidarity among all workers without regard to their status, took a different stand.

This is not really surprising. Since 1979, the C.F.D.T. had followed a new policy (of recentrage), one that combined greater solidarity with economic realism and thus a rigor unusual for a labor union. After the Leftist victory in 1981, the C.F.D.T. made only very moderate demands. It also expressed its willingness to cooperate in a policy that would stabilize real wages as long as the lowest incomes would be increased, if necessary at the expense of the higher brackets.[23] When Mitterrand made his statement on the 39 hour week (that no wage earner should fear for his wages on account of the one-hour reduction), Maire was outspoken in his criticism. He declared Mitterrand had made a major faux pas.[24] On the other hand, he welcomed the greater economic rigor of the government when it finally arrived.

In adopting such a stance, Maire was clearly taking major risks within his own organization. After all, the C.F.D.T. had adopted its new policy of recentrage in 1979, with only a majority of 56 percent, and predictably enough the C.G.T. had accused it of collaboration with the class enemy. However, the C.F.D.T. congress of May 1982 showed that Maire enjoyed stronger support than ever in his own organization, which also pronounced itself favorably on the policy of solidarity that Maire stood for.[25]

In its first year in office, the Socialist government did not follow a clear policy toward the unions. It avoided singling out one union for special treatment, fearing that it might otherwise alienate the others. At first, it seemed to share the approach of the C.G.T., which repeated its opposition to any policy of austerity. Only during the spring of 1982 did it move more closely to the position of the C.F.D.T. However, when in June 1982 it announced its policy of austerity, all three major unions (C.G.T., C.F.D.T. and F.O.) seemed prepared to cooperate, but it remained unclear how long that support would last, particularly as far as the C.G.T. was concerned. This did not just concern the leadership at the top level. Most strikes in 1981-82 were not called by the union leadership but by local units.[26] To some observers it seemed that France could hardly avoid falling into the British pattern of the mid-1970s; after a period of restraint, union militancy would break out at the grassroots and make all coherent governmental policy impossible.[27] But the French situation is quite different from that of Britain, and at the very least, such a forecast seemed premature.

There are several respects in which the situation of French workers differs from that of their counterparts across the Channel. France has not experienced a policy of deflation that continued, with varying degrees of severity, for several decades;[28]

and French workers have seen their situation improve rather than deteriorate during that time period. Finally, it is important to remember that France has a much lower level of unionization — one of the lowest among Western countries, lower even than that of the United States and equal to that of Spain.[29] Of course, this also means that unions may be less able to control spontaneous outbreaks of discontent on the part of wage earners. This takes us to the next danger for a Leftist government: will the Socialists have to confront a mass mobilization that can only be settled by giving in to excessive and unreasonable demands?

Twice in this century, France has seen massive mobilizations. In 1936, the electoral victory of the Popular Front led to a huge wave of mobilization throughout the country. For a whole month after the election, there was a conservative caretaker government. Only after that time did the Popular Front government under Leon Blum come into office. It was during this month — partly out of impatience with the caretaker government, which blocked political change — that the mass mobilization took place. One of Blum's first acts was to call for a meeting between the leaders of business, labor, and government, in order to settle the massive strikes.[30] In May 1968, the circumstances were somewhat different, but the settlement procedure (meetings at the highest level between representatives of government, business, and labor) was similar.[31]

It should be noted that in both cases, the movement was directed against a government of the Right; also, in both cases the unions played essentially a stabilizing role. Nonetheless, many observers expected another such mobilization to take place after the victory of Mitterrand in 1981. To their surprise, no such event occurred. It is even less likely to occur after the Socialists' first year in office, except as a result of some dramatic change that can hardly be predicted. The government's pragmatic search for improvement responds to many aspirations; but there is little now to encourage the nearly utopian expectations (that is, that decisive change could be achieved in a very short time, by one great effort) that seem to have been characteristic of 1936 and 1968. More likely 1982 was to be a year of demobilization, particularly among workers and union militants,[32] after the pause Mauroy and the austerity policy of the Socialists confirmed in mid-year. (The pause in the reforms of the Popular Front government probably consecrated the decline of Léon Blum in 1937, a point to be taken up shortly). It is true that new occasions for turmoil and mobilization may arise, but the mobilization itself is more likely to be a spontaneous phenomenon, not one that can easily be predicted.

In any case, the fear of (or hope for) such a mass movement is never entirely absent from the French political scene. Especially the employers (the patronat) are nervous and see dangers in fairly small incidents, such as the relative increase in strikes or the fact that some managers were detained in their offices by striking personnel.[33]   After all, had not the Socialist party at Valence announced a possible "radicalization" of the struggle in the enterprises to make employers more pliant?

The government certainly would have liked to receive more union support for its own policy, and did encourage the unions to become more active.   But this has little to do with a mass mobilization.   First of all, the unions never really initiated these mass movements in this country, and what the government was concerned about was the reluctance of the unions to ever sub- scribe to governmental policies without important reservations. More cooperation was the government's goal, not a radicalization which (unlike the Socialist party) it had never advocated.   Even this limited goal is not likely to be achieved in the near future. The major unions, for different reasons in each case, do not want to be associated too closely with the Socialist government. The C.G.T. wants to preserve its separate identity, and hold the fort in the hope of a revival of the Communist party.   The C.F.D.T. stresses that governmental policy alone is not sufficient to bring about change, and that social movements must play a major (and relatively independent) role.   F.O., while friendly towards the Socialist government, does not want to get into politics and does not want to compromise union independence (as, for example, in an incomes policy).   For the Socialists in power, this situation is clearly disappointing.   They were hoping that the unions would support their major goals and mobilize the world of labor on behalf of governmental policies.[34]   Instead, they find organizations which are somewhat cooperative, yet maintain a critical distance.   It must be added that union agreement with governmental policy would have been a difficult feat under any circumstances, as the unions disagree among themselves on very important points.[35]   Clearly, any hope for a united front of labor is misplaced.

In sum, the government was certainly faced with problems on the Left.   But these problems were unlike the dramatic threats projected by the Right before the elections, and resembled closely the problems that any government would face in times of economic difficulties.   In some respects, and in one of those paradoxes not infrequent in politics,[36] the Socialist government is probably better placed to ask the Left for sacrifices than would be a government of the Right.

DANGERS ON THE RIGHT

On the other side of the political spectrum, the government is faced with related kinds of problems.   There is the possible threat of sabotage by business, or at least of a cooperation so hesitant or so reluctant that major policy objectives cannot be achieved. Secondly, the political parties of the Right might stage such a strong comeback as to make the government appear as ineffective, possibly even as illegitimate, before the electorate. If public opinion should massively desert the Socialist government, this would undoubtedly represent a serious setback. (The question of public opinion support will be discussed separately further on.)

In all Western countries, business leaders share in the exercise of public power, by deciding matters which are crucial for the public welfare. As Charles Lindblom put it,

> Because public functions in the market system rest in the hands of businessmen, it follows that jobs, prices, production, growth, the standard of living, and the economic security of everyone all rests in their hands. Consequently, government officials cannot be indifferent to how well business performs its functions.[37]

In order to perform, businessmen will want inducements: "income and wealth, deference, prestige, influence, power, and authority, among others."[38] Also, they will commonly demand more from the government than they really need in order to be motivated.[39] The basic principle is that in a free market system, businessmen can withhold their performance if they are not sufficiently motivated or accommodated — if they do not sufficiently get their way.

There have been several occasions in French history on which businessmen (or the holders of capital) have withheld their performance or cooperation. Not surprisingly, this was most dramatic under governments of the Left. There was substantial capital flight after the victory of the Cartel des Gauches in 1924 (the government of Edouard Herriot).[40] The most decisive episode took place after the victory of the Popular Front in 1936. A massive capital flight was followed by an equally massive investment strike. The determination to sabotage the government was quite clear. William L. Shirer, in his history of the Third Republic, writes that

> The rush by the possessors of capital to send it abroad was designed not only to protect themselves but, obviously, to sabotage the efforts of the Popular Front to regenerate the country's depressed economy by putting French capital to productive work. . . . the industrialists . . . resentful at having been pressured into raising wages and shortening working hours, made little effort to try to find new markets and increase production and investment.[41]

Blum's first attempt to deal with this problem was an effort to reconcile the business community, which led to the famous pause, in March 1937. The pause brought a policy of austerity, a halt to reforms, and at the same time the reestablishment of a free market for gold. Its main purpose was to inspire business confidence so as to end the strike of capital, but all it achieved was to alienate the Left, while the Right viewed it as a partial surrender. Only in mid-1937 did Blum decide on a course of radicalization, by trying to get control over capital exports in the form of gold or foreign exchange. At that point, however, the Senate refused him the necessary powers, and soon thereafter Blum resigned.[42] Related problems, though less extreme, occurred again in 1945.[43]

It is this history which has shaped the views of many people on the Left, and indeed the possibility of business sabotage of governmental policies is something that cannot simply be ruled out. But then the current situation is different from 1936 in more than one respect. Even if there were an effort at such sabotage, its possibilities would be considerably restricted compared to the days of the Popular Front. The exchange control legislation that Blum failed to obtain has been in place long since, even under conservative governments, and the outgoing Barre government exercised tight supervision during its last days in power.[44] There was some capital flight, but only on a limited scale. In the fall, the Socialists lifted the anonymity that had governed all transactions in gold.[45] In addition, the nationalizations restrict the possibilities of sabotage. The most powerful firms and practically the whole credit system will play no part in "withholding performance". From this perspective, the nationalizations could actually be viewed as a preemptive measure; they make a united front of business against government by far more difficult.

Is there in fact a will to sabotage the policies of Mitterrand and the Socialist government on the part of French business? Immediately after the elections, there were clearly some entrepreneurs who wanted to do everything possible to bring down the new government, advocating la politique du pire. Such cases were reported throughout the French press.[46] Lagging cooperation with the government's aims of starting up hiring and investment was evident in later months as well, though it is not clear to which extent the reasons were purely economic, as businessmen usually claimed.[47] It is a fact that businessmen made a show of studied pessimism, painting reality in excessively dark colors and thus discouraging hiring and investment.[48] On the occasion of the Valence Party Congress, with its denunciations of business and its rhetoric of class struggle, many thought they had seen the writing on the wall.[49] Hardliners in the C.N.P.F. wanted systematic opposition to the government. However, the election of Yvon Gattaz to the leadership of the C.N.P.F., in December 1981, indicated that they were in a minority, as Gattaz stands for a progressive group of employers and is known to favor dialogue with the Socialist government.[50]

The Moussa affair, in the fall of 1981, offered a test of the loyalty of big business. Pierre Moussa headed the Banque de Paris et des Pays-Bas (Paribas), and in order to protect some of the international holdings of his firm against nationalization, he made the French bank lose majority control over its Swiss subsidiary. Even though this was not illegal — a decree outlawing such actions was passed only shortly afterwards — it clearly undercut the policy of the government. In this situation, it was the board of Paribas, which lists some of France's most prominent industrialists (some of whom were soon removed from their positions, after their firms were nationalized) that forced Moussa's resignation, declaring that it would respect the policy of a democratically elected government.[51] It was a far cry from 1936, when some businessmen began to say that they would rather have Hitler than Blum.[52]

On the other hand, French businessmen were clearly unhappy with the general direction of the government's economic and social policies, and they were particularly upset with that policy under the special conditions of 1981-82. At first, they criticized the uncertainty cast over business by such measures as the nationalizations, the wealth tax, the budget deficit and the like. Clearly those criticisms did not have much, if any, impact. But soon they focused their complaints on the issue of the new financial burdens that business firms had to carry. The increased minimum wage, the reduction of working time (39 hour week, fifth week of paid vacations), earlier retirement, higher Social Security contributions and the increase in the taxe professionnelle were estimated to cost over 90 billion francs on a yearly basis (the government however came up with a substantially lower figure). By contrast, additional aids to business were put by the C.N.P.F. at a mere 11 billion.[53] Given the dismal state of the French economy, the employers' organization predicted a sudden increase of bankruptcies, a further fall in investment, and the continued rise of unemployment, unless measures were taken to encourage private initiative anew.[54] In his meetings with Prime Minister Mauroy and President Mitterrand, Yvon Gattaz (the new head of the C.N.P.F.) stressed the urgent need for some reduction in the financial burdens weighing on business, especially as the increase in these burdens coincided with a decrease abroad, and thus made French firms even less competitive.

Economics Minister Delors was himself in favor of making concessions to business, though he questioned the calculations put forward by the C.N.P.F. However, when he called for a pause in reforms in December of 1981, this caused considerable controversy among the Socialist leadership. It was clear that Mitterrand's and Mauroy's thinking were shaped by Leon Blum's experience. Important concessions to business before any of the major social reforms had been enacted carried with it the danger of alienating the voters that had brought the Left to power; at the same time it could make business (and the Right) even less yielding and willing to accommodate.[55] But after several months of negotiations (and the enactment of several social reforms by decree), a compromise was arrived at, soon termed the pause Mauroy described above.[56] Business expressed its satisfaction. It saw the pause as evidence that the government finally recognized the real problems of the business world.[57] Gattaz in turn promised that French business would do its best to help the government achieve its policy goals. Soon after the pause, the C.N.P.F. came up with a program to strengthen cooperation among French business firms in order to reduce imports, develop research and development, and achieve other goals that the government stressed in its policies.[58]

To be sure, new problems surfaced very soon once the question of financial charges was settled. Many employers were upset by the rapport Auroux and the legislation derived from it. They predicted that irreparable damage would be done to business efficiency by the attempts to introduce democracy to the workplace and the privileged place granted to labor unions.[59] But there was no longer the same feeling that had existed earlier on — that governmental policies were obviously ignorant of all business realities and would sooner or later end in disaster. After a year of Socialist government, French business seemed prepared to play its role with a certain amount of loyalty. Sabotage was not considered as a serious alternative.

Of course, this development cannot be viewed in isolation. There is another factor that restrains the leeway available to business. A radical undercutting of the government only makes sense if there is a political alternative to the group in power. In 1936-37, thanks to the instability of the Third Republic's institutions, such an alternative was available relatively easily, despite the massive mandate of the voters who had elected the Popular Front government. By contrast, the Constitution of the Fifth Republic gives the regime a stability that relegates the search for an early alternative to the realm of wishful thinking. In addition, the French political Right, in its first year after the defeat of 1981, would have been unable to offer a viable alternative even in the absence of the constitutional restraints just mentioned, despite its success at the regional elections of 1982.

After Giscard's defeat, mutually hostile feelings dominated the leadership of the two parties of the Right. The loss of the presidency of the Republic was followed by another, perhaps even more demoralizing setback in the elections for the National

Assembly. The catastrophe was particularly marked for the Giscardiens (U.D.F.), who received 19.20 percent of the vote and saw the number of their deputies fall from 120 to 64.[60] After that election the elements united by Giscard as part of his presidential majority turned into different directions as Giscard withdrew from the political scene. He did not come out of hiding again until early 1982. One of the three groups which form the U.D.F., the Centre des Démocrates Sociaux (C.D.S.), seemed eager to emancipate itself from Giscard's leadership. As to the Radicals, some of them considered an alliance with Chirac's R.P.R.[61] In the absence of a clear leader, the U.D.F. seemed to become the victim of centrifugal forces. It is probably this fact which decided Giscard to a relatively early political comeback, despite considerable doubts about his leadership in the ranks of his "own" party. In April 1982, he became a member of the party's executive bureau; in June, he was acclaimed again at the congress of the Republican party.[62] However, the U.D.F. had done little thinking about a new program, and did not develop a coherent political strategy during this time period. There was a general feeling that a renewed rivalry with Chirac could only lead to another disaster, yet there was also the recognition that the party needed a viable presidential candidate if it wanted to play a major role in French politics. Giscard seemed well on the way to persuade a reluctant party that he was in fact just such a candidate.

It was partly due to this vacuum that the Gaullists, or rather the R.P.R. under Chirac, fared somewhat better in their first year in opposition. Chirac had lost, by a wide margin, his gamble to make it to the second round of the presidential election. In the subsequent National Assembly elections the R.P.R. gathered 20.80 percent of the vote; this reduced the number of its deputies from 155 to 88,[63] despite the fact that Chirac had quickly organized a rightist coalition after Giscard's defeat. The U.D.F. deputies at that point panicked, and Chirac prevailed with his proposal of forming an electoral coalition (U.N.M., or Union for a New Majority) already for the first round; this coalition gave a better place to the candidates of the R.P.R.[64] From then on, Chirac tried to establish himself as the only viable leader of the Right, an enterprise in which he was helped by the U.D.F.'s divisions. More than ever, the R.P.R. now became the party of Chirac. In his effort to renovate it, Chirac dropped all references to de Gaulle and Pompidou; the old Gaullist leaders (including Debre) are no longer to play major roles. This development was confirmed at the Toulouse party congress in early 1982. The party is also to be given a new doctrine.[65]

In the meantime, the R.P.R. (and to some extent the Right generally) had shown a certain trend towards extremism, at least in some verbal statements. Some of its members claimed that the 1981 elections were really based on a misunderstanding, others portrayed the "socialo-communist" coalition as a first step down the road of totalitarianism.[66] Especially after the regional elections, which the Right won (somewhat to its own surprise), several of its members questioned the legitimacy of the Socialist government and even of the president of the Republic. Michel Debré declared that the "socialo-communist" government used to be legitimate, but that now it was only the legal government of France.[67] Peyrefitte spoke in similar terms. Finally, Claude Labbé, a prominent leader of the R.P.R., called publicly for the resignation of both Mitterrand and Mauroy. Chirac publicly disapproved of these statements, but he was suspected of playing a double game.[68] In the National Assembly, the Gaullists (if they can still be called that way) practiced systematic obstruction, apparently in the hope that the government would resort to special procedures in order to have its major bills passed (nationalizations, regionalization, loi Auroux); they could then have denounced it as authoritarian.[69] The U.D.F. was considerably more moderate in its opposition. Both Giscard and Barre occasionally stated their approval of certain aspects of Socialist policy.[70]

The difference between the two parties illustrated a problem that the Right did not confront in its first year in opposition. In order to return to power at the national level, a measure of agreement on a program will probably be necessary, especially for the elections to the National Assembly (in 1986). Neither opposition party has made much progress on this account. It is true that time is not terribly pressing, unless one assumes, as leaders in both parties have occasionally claimed, that the Socialist government would soon go down in disgrace. For the R.P.R., a programmatic renewal is expected to come from a series of political clubs, similar to those of the Left in the 1960s. Chirac does not seem to be committed to any particular program; in fact, there is little consistency in his programmatic thinking. He made a first about-face in February 1981, when he discovered supply-side economics. Another one followed in May, when in contradiction with his former stand he argued that it was a good idea to elect a National Assembly that would oppose the president. In the fall of 1981 he strongly criticized the Socialist government's program of economic stimulation, stating that it would lead to an import surge. Journalists pointed out that his critiques would be more impressive if he had not himself practiced just such a policy six years earlier.[71] His analysis of Socialist economic policy is limited to a categorical rejection. That policy, Chirac claims, is "archaic," "partisan," "ideological," and bound to end in catastrophe.[72] Chirac's new crusade, in fact it was nearly his economic program, consists in advocating a decisive reduction in taxes and other charges. He proposes to bring them from the current 43.3 percent (Chirac claims 45 percent) to 36 percent. This is an ambitious program. It is probably also quite unrealistic (the last time French taxes were this low was in 1970).[73] No real program has yet been formulated, but then Chirac is not in a hurry. He sees the municipal elections of 1983 as the first step in the reconquest of power at the national level. But even assuming that a leadership struggle between Chirac and Giscard can be avoided — will the two major opposition parties be able to agree on a common program?

This problem did not present itself in the by-elections of January 1982, nor in the regional elections two months later. The common attacks on the Socialist reforms provided an easy substitute. The victory of the Right in these elections came as a surprise.[74] One would probably do well not to overestimate its importance. It seems extremely unlikely that they amounted to a repudiation of Socialist policies. Public opinion polls in any case showed that on the level of national politics the government still enjoyed strong majority support throughout the country.

PUBLIC OPINION AND POLITICAL LEGITIMACY

In the first few months after Mitterrand's elections, during the famous état de grâce, support for the Socialist government seemed to be simply overwhelming. Not surprisingly, this state of affairs did not last. However, surveys show that for both Mitterrand and Mauroy positive views largely outweighed negative ones not only in August 1981 but also in February 1982. During the same time period, the Socialist government was consistently thought of by a majority as doing a good job in handling the nation's problems. The opposition could never gather more than one third of positive views and was judged negatively by nearly one half. (The most popular ministers were, with great consistency, Mauroy, Rocard and Delors.) Even on the issue of economic policy, positive perceptions of the government's action outweighed negative ones, though often only by a narrow margin. Simulated elections administered by another opinion research institute showed that this situation still prevailed even around the time of the by-elections of January, and the regional elections of March 1982 (both of which the Left lost). In these surveys, the political support for the parties of the Left, assuming that national legislative elections would be held, was roughly the same as in June 1981. Only the P.C. seemed headed for further decline, something that may indeed hold serious implications for the future. In the same surveys, the leaders of the opposition still appeared to be highly unpopular. They did not represent a credible alternative to the Socialists, and received support from only about one-fifth of the electorate (see Tables 14.1 and 14.2).

TABLE 14.1
Mitterrand, Mauroy, the Socialist Government
and the Opposition Before Public Opinion

1. Do you judge the performance of the president of the republic Francois Mitterrand, since his election in May 1981, to be overall

	Very Positive	Rather Positive	Rather Negative	Very Negative
		Positive		Negative
August 81	6	39	23	7
		45		30
November 81	5	40	26	9
		45		35
December 81	6	42	28	9
		48		37
February 82	5	40	28	8
		45		36

2. And that of Pierre Mauroy, since his nomination in June 1981?

	Very Positive	Rather Positive	Rather Negative	Very Negative
		Positive		Negative
August 81	7	40	19	6
		47		25
November 81	7	38	25	9
		45		34
December 81	6	42	26	10
		48		36
February 82	5	39	25	9
		44		34

3. According to you, does the government have the capability to handle the problems that France is facing today? And does the opposition?

	Government		Opposition	
	Positive	Negative	Positive	Negative
August 81	54	30	27	46
November 81	53	31	28	48
December 81	52	35	33	47
February 82	55	33	28	46

4. More specifically in the economic area, do you think that the government is handling the problems that confront the French well or poorly?

	Positive	Negative
August 81	47	35
November 81	44	41
December 81	45	44
February 82	42	41

Sources: For all figures of this table surveys by IFOP, published in Le Point, 31 August 1981; 23 November 1981; 4 January 1982; and 1 March 1982.

TABLE 14.2
Evolution of Support for Major Political Parties and Leaders
(February-April 1982)

1. Percentage of vote that each party would have achieved if a national (legislative) election had been held at time of interview.[a]

	Elections, June 1981	15-19 Feb. 1982	1-6 March 1982	15-20 March 1982	1-6 April 1982
Communist party	16	12.5	12	13	14
Socialist party-M.R.G.	38	37.5	42	39	38
Total Left	54	50.0	54	52	52
U.D.F.	19	18.5	19	18	20
R.P.R.	21	21.5	20	21	21
Total Right	40	40.0	39	39	41
Other	6	10.0	7	9	7

2. Altogether, do you think that Valery Giscard d'Estaing/ Jacques Chirac would do better, worse or pretty much the same as Francois Mitterrand?[b]

	Better than Mitterrand	Worse than Mitterrand	About the same	Do not know
Giscard	17	32	43	8
Chirac	21	40	25	14

3. Do you think that as prime minister, Raymond Barre would do better, worse, or the same as Pierre Mauroy?

Better	Worse	Same	No opinion
23	41	27	9

Source: [a]Survey by B.V.A., published in Paris-Match, 30 April 1982; [b]ibid., 7 May 1982.

It is interesting to place these results against the time schedule of Socialist policy. Late 1981 and early 1982 certainly represented a difficult period. The état de grâce was over. The political scene was dominated by the nationalization debate, which made the government appear in an ideological light of partisan divisiveness. Reflation was too modest to have much of an impact on the economic situation. Social reforms (many of which were quite popular) were much talked about, but no major ones were enacted until March, and many were not applicable until much later still. In addition, the austerity of spring 1982, which was officially consecrated in May-June, could hardly make the government more popular. But in mid-1982, one could think that that year might be the most difficult for the Socialists, at least in economic terms. Later in the year the first effect of the investments in the nationalized sector could be expected to show up. Private sector investment was expected to increase as a result of the pause Mauroy.[75] An improvement in the international economic situation (predicted by the OECD to take place in 1982) would further have eased the pressure.

It may be true however that a Socialist president and government will have greater problems with public acceptance than would a president or government of the Right. This too may change over the years, but for the time being, Socialist leaders may be more likely to be perceived as "partisan." Their counterparts from the Right can more easily cast themselves as "national" figures, or at least they could do so during the period of rapid economic growth. It may well be that this no longer applies in an environment where conflicts over economic policy have become more intense, as they did in France in the 1970s.

POLITICAL AND ECONOMIC VIABILITY

A good approval rating by public opinion is, however, not sufficient to guarantee the political future of the government and its policies. Electoral and economic success will also be necessary. Even if the Socialist party should continue to progress in the electorate, the weakness of its allies, particularly the Communists, may represent an increasingly serious problem. This was shown by the regional elections of March 1982. To illustrate, Table 14.3 shows the evolution of the Leftist parties in the last three regional elections. The Socialists made continuous and uninterrupted progress; the other parties and groups of the Left, however, declined, and so did the Left overall. As a result, several prominent Socialist leaders went on record to proclaim the need for the Socialist party to broaden its appeal and recruit among the political center. One of these statements came from Rocard, who would like to see the "modernist" bourgeoisie included in the Leftist coalition. The other (and more surprising) statement came from Chevènement, once the leader of the pro-Communist C.E.R.E.S. He wanted to see the party make an effort to include artisans, small businessmen, farmers, and similar groups.[76] Undoubtedly, either course will mean a change in policy. In particular, the C.G.T.'s position, often privileged by Mitterrand, is likely to suffer. But then the first year of Socialist rule has shown that economic rigor was not necessarily an unpopular position. Rocard, Delors, and Maire, all advocates of a more stringent policy, did not suffer any setbacks with public opinion for the stand they took. The regional elections may have conveyed a similar message.[77]

TABLE 14.3
Voting in Regional Elections — Cantonales
(Leftist parties and groups in first round)

	7 March 1976	18 March 1979	15 March 1982
Extreme Left	0.7	0.8	0.58
P.C.	22.8	22.4	15.90
P.S.	26.6	26.9	29.71
M.R.G.	2.4	1.9	1.72
Other Left	4.0	3.1	1.70
Total Left	56.5	55.1	49.61

Source: Le Nouvel Observateur, 20 March 1982.

Such an evolution (towards greater economic rigor) seemed to be required, in any case, by the evolution of the French economy. The reflation of fall 1981 had had a mild stimulative effect, but stagnation returned in the spring of 1982. (It is true though that France was one of very few countries, in the European Community, to show growth in industrial production during the 12 months preceding April 1982.) The major problems however were international in nature. They derived from the fact that the evolution in France took a direction opposite to that of most of its trading partners.[78] This aggravated the inflation differential between France and its international economic environment, and led to the dramatic import surge of April 1982. (During the preceding three months the foreign trade situation had shown gradual improvement.) In other words, the external constraints that rein in the French economy now came to be felt with much greater force, and threatened to undermine Socialist economic policy.

It is these external constraints which the Socialists are of course trying to lift, not with protectionism, as their opponents argue, but with liberal-mercantilist measures. The nationalizations, the reconquest of domestic markets, the program for energy savings, and the project of a "European social space" all go in this direction. France's trading partners have mixed feelings about such policies. Germany in particular stands to lose an important share of its market, and similar concern is likely to prevail elsewhere.[79] In any case, all these programs, even assuming that they will not be set back by other factors, will have their full impact only by the mid-1980s — perhaps later, certainly not earlier. In the meantime, the Socialist government will have to live with — and respect — the external constraints, hold down trade deficits and limit international indebtedness. For if international creditors (such as the IMF) should ever get a major say in French economic policy — not an immediate prospect by any means in mid-1982 — this would put a quick end to the Socialist experiment.[80]

NOTES

1. This view was expressed regularly in the conservative newspapers such as for example, Le Figaro, 2-3 May 1981.

2. The famous accords Matignon (1936) and accords de Grenelle (1968).

3. This is a staple of Rightist opinion, not only in France. "They call up the image . . . of some dying beast which, on its very death bed, feeds upon itself in a last orgy of lust and socialism" — this sentence applies to Britain. Stephen Blank, "Britain: The Politics of Foreign Economic Policy," in Peter J. Katzenstein, ed., Between Power and Plenty (Madison: University of Wisconsin Press, 1978), p. 93.

4. Le Monde, weekly selection, 7 January 1982.

5. Ibid., 16 March 1982.

6. Joint Statement by the Socialist Party and French Communist Party, 23 June 1981.

7. Denis Jeambar in Le Point, 7 September and 5 October 1981; Patrick Jarreau in Le Monde, 5 October 1981; and Le Monde, 3 December 1981.

8. Officially, Séguy retired only in June 1982. C. F. Jullien in Le Nouvel Observateur, 12 September 1981; Michel Noblecourt, Le Monde, 19 June 1982.

9. C. Mital in L'Expansion, 23 January 1981; C. F. Jullien and T. Pfister in Le Nouvel Observateur, 2 March 1981.

10. C. F. Jullien in Le Nouvel Observateur, 9 March and 30 March 1981.

11. J. Roy in Le Monde, 16 October 1981.

12. J. P. Dumont in Le Monde, 8 January 1982; D. Audibert in Le Point, 18 January 1982.

13. Confusion was still evident in May 1982. Denis Jeamber, Le Point, 24 May 1982.

14. Patrick Jarreau, Le Monde, 7 May 1982.

15. Jean-Yves Lhomeau, Le Monde, 22 June 1982.

16. Ibid., 6 May 1982.

17. Kathleen Evin, Le Nouvel Observateur, 8 May 1982.

18. Le Monde, 25 May 1982; Jean-Marie Colombani, Le Monde, 4 June 1982.

19. Kathleen Evin, Le Nouvel Observateur, 3 April 1982.

20. Motion nationale d'orientation, Valence Party Congress, para. III (2) and V (4) (b).

21. Alain Rollat in Le Monde, 17 March 1982. The P.S. responded by saying that the government should show more coherence in its policy. Jean-Yves Lhomeau, Le Monde, 6 April 1982. Also around this time, Pierre Joxe (leader of the Socialist deputies and neo-Marxist himself) made a strong attack on Prime Minister Mauroy. Franz-Oliver Giesbert, Le Nouvel Observateur, 30 April 1982.

22. Jean-Pierre Dumont, Le Monde, 8 February 1982.

23. Edmond Maire, Le Monde, 26 August 1981; Les Echos, 2 December 1981; Jean-Pierre Dumont, Le Monde, 8 February 1982.

24. Le Monde, 19 February 1982.

25. Jacques Julliard, Le Nouvel Observateur, 29 May 1982; Michel Noblecourt, Le Monde, 1 June 1982.

26. Roger Priouret, Le Nouvel Observateur, 15 May 1982.

27. Yves Guihannec, Wall Street Journal, 30 June 1982.

28. See Stephen Blank, "Britain: The Politics of Foreign Economic Policy," pp. 89-137.

29. Jacques Julliard in Le Nouvel Observateur, 31 October 1981; Hubert Landier, Demain, quels syndicats (Paris: Livre de poche, 1981).

30. William L. Shirer, The Collapse of the Third Republic (New York: Simon and Schuster, 1969), pp. 289-95.

31. Stephen S. Cohen, Modern Capitalist Planning: The French Model (Berkeley: University of California Press, 1977), pp. 243-50.

32. On the demoralization among union militants (and their letdown after a year of Socialist rule), see the articles by Michel Noblecourt in Le Monde, 21, 22 and 24 May 1982.

33. Antoine S. in Le Nouvel Observateur, 7 November 1981; and Les Echos, 17 February and 1 March 1982. The actions often came from wage earners with no union affiliations.

34. Georges Sarre, "Les syndicats ne jouent pas le jeu," Le Nouvel Observateur, 5 June 1982.

35. Thus, the C.G.T. is strongly in favor of the nationalizations (something that meets with doubts from C.F.D.T. and F.O.) and was long opposed to any austerity, in particular also to wage reductions on the occasion of the 39 hour week (similarly F.O., total disagreement of C.F.D.T.). Differences extend to all major areas of change (in particular, also the loi Auroux).

36. Thus it was de Gaulle who contained the French nationalists and their ambitions for Algeria, or Nixon who checked anti-Communism as an obstacle to detente.

37. Charles E. Lindblom, Politics and Markets (New York: Basic Books, 1977), p. 172.

38. Ibid., p. 174.

39. Ibid., p. 177.

40. Shirer, Collapse of the Third Republic, pp. 160-65.

41. Ibid., pp. 287-88 and 306.

42. Ibid., pp. 308-24.

43. Henry W. Ehrmann, Organized Business in France (Princeton: Princeton University Press, 1957), pp. 103 ff.

44. Here the contrast with 1936 was particularly strong. The capital drain started between the election and Blum's access to power. Blum then hoped to bring it to a halt by promising that he would respect liberal economic principles (that is, not impose exchange controls).

45. Announced by Budget Minister Laurent Fabius on 30 September 1981, to take effect immediately. Le Monde, weekly selection, 1 October 1981. (Fabius took no chances — he made the announcement during a press conference, but waited with this particular item until 6 P.M., when the banks were closed.)

46. Maurice Roy in Le Point, 11 May 1981; J. M. Quatrepoint in Le Monde, 16 May 1981. The phenomenon was implicitly recognized by Yvon Gattaz later on; Les Echos, 26 January 1982.

47. Philippe Labarde in Le Monde, 18 November 1981; Maurice Roy in Le Point, 23 November 1981.

48. Roger Priouret in Le Nouvel Observateur, 28 November and 12 December 1981. He cites specifically a bulletin from the Employers' Organization (the C.N.P.F.), dated November 1981. It did not in one word mention the expansion that was under way but gave all the reasons why firms should not invest, sometimes citing questionable data.

49. The document adopted at Valence spoke of the "class enemy" and of the need to carry the class struggle into business enterprises. Valence Party Congress, Motion nationale d'orientation, para. III and V. Mauroy and Mitterrand expressed their disagreement; Danièle Molho in Le Point, 30 November 1981; Le Monde, 9 December 1981.

50. Le Nouvel Economiste, 21 December 1981.

51. F. O. Giesbert in Le Nouvel Observateur, 14 November 1981; Le Monde, 28 October, 2 and 3 November 1981.

52. Shirer, Collapse of the Third Republic, p. 324.

53. Les Echos, 8 and 9 April 1982.

54. Yvon Gattaz in Les Echos, 29 March 1982.

55. Jean Daniel, Le Nouvel Observateur, 5 December 1981.

56. See Chapter Twelve.

57. Pierre Locardel in Les Echos, 21 April 1982.

58. Les Echos, 23 April 1982.

59. Undoubtedly the authoritarian structures of many business firms have shaped the mindsets of union leaders as well as of employers. It is not inappropriate to expect problems of transition.

60. Le Monde, weekly selection, 7 January 1982.

61. Irene Allier in Le Nouvel Observateur, 3 October 1981; Bernard Stasi interview in Paris-Match, 15 January 1982; Les Echos, 17 February 1982; and Le Point, 22 February 1982.

62. Les Echos, 6 and 8 April 1982; Le Monde, 12 June 1982.

63. Le Monde, weekly selection, 7 January 1982.

64. Geneviève Galey in Le Point, 25 May 1981.

65. Andre Passeron in Le Monde, 20 July 1981; report on Chirac press conference, Le Monde, 7 October 1981; and Passeron in Le Monde, 26 January 1982.

66. Georges Mamy, Le Nouvel Observateur, 13 February 1982.

67. Le Figaro-magazine, 9 April 1982.

68. Georges Mamy, Le Nouvel Observateur, 15 May 1982.

69. Laurent Zecchini, Le Monde, 31 May 1982. The most likely procedure to be applied would be Article 49 (3) of the Constitution, by which the government can impose a law unless a motion of censure is voted against it.

70. Thus, Giscard stated that he approved of the regionalization reform, and even of the fifth week of vacations (G. Mamy, Le Nouvel Observateur, 5 June 1982); Barre stated his approval of the natural gas contract with the Soviet Union and praised the Mauroy government for its policy of wage discipline (Les Echos, 1 February 1982).

71. Le Point, 2 November 1981.

72. Chirac press conference, Le Monde, 7 October 1981; A. Passeron in Le Monde, 26 January 1982.

73. Interview in Paris-Match, 5 March 1982. It should be added that of the current 43.3 percent only 24 percent are taxes in a technical sense; 19.3 percent are contributions to social welfare programs financed independently. Le Monde, 29 December 1981. It is true that fiscal pressure in France is higher than in Japan, the United States, Germany, Britain, or Italy, though not as high as in the Scandinavian countries or the Netherlands. See Les Echos, 12 February 1982 (supplement).

74. Interview with Claude Labbe, Paris-Match, 5 March 1982.

75. Increased investments were forecast by the Bank of France in June. Wall Street Journal, 22 June 1982.

76. Jean-Yves Lhomeau, Le Monde, 6 April 1982.

77. Franz-Oliver Giesbert, Le Nouvel Observateur, 27 March 1982.

78. Roger Priouret, Le Nouvel Observateur, 8 May 1982.

79. In a very strongly worded editorial, the Wall Street Journal attacked the plans for financing of investments in the nationalized sector on the one hand as inefficient, on the other

as protectionist and socialist-nationalist (and therefore a danger to "world economic health"). That they might also present a danger to U.S. interests was not mentioned, though this seemed clearly on the author's mind. The whole article seemed to represent an exercise in the free trade religion a la Cordell Hull, in which imperialist elements usually remain below the level of consciousness. "No shame in France," <u>Wall Street Journal,</u> 17 May 1982; also David P. Calleo and Benjamin M. Rowland, <u>America and the World Political Economy</u> (Bloomington: Indiana University Press, 1973).

    80. <u>Wall Street Journal</u> editorial, 9 June 1982.

15
UPDATE AND OUTLOOK

The second half of 1982 did not bring any major changes. Rather, the policy reversal operated in June was confirmed in one area after the other. The emphasis on the nationalizations as the major measure of Socialist transformation was also confirmed, though some problems appeared on the horizon. The most important change for the private sector was the announcement that the financial burdens weighing on business must now be lightened. However, this announcement had little practical impact in 1982, and may not have any for some time to come.

The new austerity policy showed its first results during the second half of the year. Inflation was effectively held down by the wage and price freeze, and finished the year roughly at the 10 percent mark which the government had set up as its target. (But then the real test always comes after the end of such freezes.) The balance of trade, which had shown such disastrous deficits in the first six months of 1982, registered some improvement. At the same time the government made clear its determination to promote exports and, if necessary, to control imports. This determination was demonstrated by some isolated measures, which probably must be viewed as symbols and signs of the new determination. The value of the franc was maintained throughout 1982, despite repeated attacks of speculation against it. However, the defense of the currency forced the government to resort to a rapidly growing international indebtedness.

The domestic political environment remained largely undramatic. After its offensive in late spring, the opposition no longer challenged the legitimacy of the Socialist government; nor did it come up with a comprehensive program of its own. Relations between Socialists and Communists remained largely as before, marked by the Communists' desire to participate in the government while at the same time marking out their own specificity by criticizing the government for yielding to the Right or to business. Employers and unions did not mount major challenges to the government, despite earlier expectations of widespread unrest. Nonetheless the president, the government, and its leading figures showed continuous losses in public opinion polls, a development which may announce serious problems ahead.

As to the international environment, it was marked by a progressive spreading of austerity policies and a recession not only among France's most important trading partners (and especially in West Germany), but among nearly all European countries and in the United States. Similar developments took place among the countries of the OPEC, which no longer showed a surplus due to the fall in oil prices, and thus had to reduce their purchases abroad. More dramatically, many developing countries met with the impossibility of repaying their debts on schedule, and had to cut back drastically on their development plans (and thus imports). Certainly such an environment would have made things difficult for any government. It did so with particular vigor for the Socialists, since they had based their policy on the assumption that the international environment would improve during 1982 (an assumption which they were not alone to hold). In the second half of 1982 the Socialists made the difficult adjustment to the new situation. Even when the year was out, the end of the international recession was not yet in sight.

For the near future, the outlook is grim. Nineteen eighty-three will be a year of slow (perhaps zero) growth for France, and Rocard's Ninth Plan shows that one must be cautious about early improvements. It is likely that unemployment will resume its upward curve. The controversy on the efficacy of the nationalizations will undoubtedly remain undecided for some time. But then one must remember that French liberalism could not be made a success under Giscard and Barre; they went as far as they could, and that was not far enough. This point shall be taken up in Chapter Sixteen. But even if it will not show great economic successes any time soon, it could be that the Socialist government will make France a more integrated country and society than she would have been otherwise, with industrial relations more similar to those that exist in other Western European countries, and with the political polarization reduced by the French Left's first durable experience with national policymaking.

ECONOMIC AND SOCIAL POLICY

In the fall of 1982, it became increasingly evident that the policy of rigor put into place in the spring of the same year was to stay around for some time to come. The budget for

1983, presented and discussed in September and October, confirmed the new course. The deficit would not be allowed to grow beyond the 3 percent target set earlier by Mitterrand, even if that meant cutbacks in spending. Around the same time, the government approved a plan drawn up by Pierre Bérégovoy, the new minister of social affairs, to balance the budget of the Social Security system by 1983. It was clear that some of the measures of the Bérégovoy plan would draw fire from the labor unions. They had been proposed years ago, but were judged excessively unpopular during Giscard's presidency.[1] Similar steps were taken to reduce unemployment payments. After much squabbling, it was finally decided that civil servants would definitely make a contribution (on a temporary basis) to an unemployment solidarity fund. (Because of their guaranteed job security, they do not have to pay unemployment insurance.)[2]

As the freeze came to its end, the government adopted a tough line with regard to wages. Prime Minister Mauroy announced the end of automatic wage indexing, and labor minister Auroux took a strong stand against it, pointing out that the practice was prohibited by a decree from 1959, and that only a steadily growing economy had allowed the neglect of this prohibition. (In fact, it would have been a political problem even for de Gaulle to enforce the prohibition in the 1960s.) The minimum wage was increased in real terms, but not by the full amount (4 percent) targeted by the government earlier on.[3] Finally, a decline of real incomes was forecast for 1983. Even in 1982, real wages had declined, but this was more than compensated for by increases in transfer payments — family and housing allowances and the like.[4] However, the practice of the government did not always fit the professed rigor. Thus, some public sector employees secured a de facto wage indexing, something that raised questions about the government's ability to carry out its wage policy elsewhere.[5] But renewed determination may come from an unfavorable international environment. In late fall 1982, Delors stated that it would take at least another 18 months of policy of rigor (the Socialists avoid the word austerity) in order to turn the French economy around, and Mitterrand seemed to be prepared to take an even longer view, anticipating an improvement no earlier than 1984 or 1985.[6]

The National Account Statistics projected the current policy and came up with an interesting forecast. As a result of the policy put into place, they calculated that the distribution of value added would be modified in such a way as to reduce wage costs and increase profits. This was the very goal that Barre tried to promote, more or less unsuccessfully, several years earlier. It is true though that in the meantime, private sector profits and internal financing of investments had hit new record lows.[7]

Even as it formulated its austerity policy, the Socialist government reaffirmed the emphasis it placed on the nationalized sector, one of the few programs essentially left intact while others had to be cut back. This priority for the public sector was repeated in the 1983 budget proposal. At the end of November, the different firms finally submitted their plans for the medium term, plans which were full of ambitions and urgent pleas for additional funds. By that time however, it had become clear that despite the government's privileged treatment of the nationalized industries, several serious problems had developed. The uncertainty about how much the government would or could contribute to the public sector, in order to wipe out its accumulated debt and build up its investment, had taken its toll. In part, this may have represented just a problem of transition. But it seems likely that the requirements of the industrial firms may clash in a durable way with the laws that govern the functioning of the state in times of financial emergency. The large investments which the public sector firms intend to make need to be planned ahead for years, while the government cannot guarantee the necessary resources for such a long time into the future.[8]

The expansion of the public sector in any case seemed to have come to an end. The question was hardly discussed except in the area of banking, where the old proposal for a National Investment Bank was reactivated by a member of the CERES, whose former chief (Chevènement) was now minister of research and industry. Delors quickly rejected the proposal, arguing that the main problem was the attitude of the bankers (their reluctance to assume industrial risks — the old problem, even before the nationalizations) and that a reform had to concentrate on that phenomenon. Another state institution, he argued, would not help the problem. Chevènement kept out of the public controversy, though he seemed to favor the idea of such a bank.[9] The issue is likely to surface again if conditions in the credit sector do not improve (and if Chevènement should be able to strengthen his position, which most likely is his ambition).

Policy towards the private sector was given a new direction by Mitterrand's Figeac declaration early in the fall. Mitterrand declared then that the highest priority in public policy was to ease the financial burdens weighing on the private sector in the form of high taxes and social welfare contributions plus high interest rates combined with high indebtedness. Mitterrand suggested a reduction in the social welfare contributions and a reduction of interest rates, against the trends prevailing in the international capital markets if necessary.[10] These declarations were translated into policy measures throughout the fall, though most of them were not applicable right away. Already the 1983 budget provided for accelerated depreciation allowances for business. Also, the applicability of the wealth tax was postponed largely until 1985. The financing of family allocations, paid so far by contributions from business, will be transferred to households (that is, taxes).[11] The stabilization of Social Security and unemployment insurance expenditures goes in the same direction; both programs are financed to an important degree by employer contributions. However, the total sum of social welfare contributions will keep on rising throughout 1983, as it kept rising in 1982 despite Mitterrand's earlier promise to stabilize them.[12] In part, this is of course due to the deteriorating economic situation. Only 1984 may thus bring the much-demanded stabilization and perhaps reverse a trend that started more than a decade ago.

Foreign economic policy was closely connected with economic policy in general. The balance of trade had experienced record deficits during the first half of 1982, due to the reflationary policy of the Socialists' first year in power. Once the policy of austerity was adopted, there was slow improvement. In October, the government decided that in addition to an austerity policy at home, some spectacular steps were necessary in trade policy itself. It adopted some measures stimulating exports but more importantly (because of the reaction they provoked) it adopted some measures which clearly stood out as protectionist; thus the requirement that all customs papers be filled out in French. In an action designed to show its determination, it slowed the import of video recorders down to a trickle by channeling them through the small town of Poitiers, with a customs office employing only two people. At the same time the government repeated its demands for measures throughout Europe to correct trade imbalances, particularly with Japan. (But as before, it encountered stiff resistance from several other European community countries, led by Germany.)[13] For the sake of perspective, it should be said that France has the most unbalanced trade structure of any European community country, and that in 1982 it had become the dumping ground for other countries' exports, being the only large country that practiced a policy of growth at least during the first half of the year.[14]

For some time to come, only continued austerity can hold down the trade deficit until French exports start growing again. In the Socialists' view of things, this will come about as a result of a new vitality in the nationalized industries. In the meantime, the decline of the dollar, by reducing the cost of energy imports, may bring some urgently needed relief.

As to the value of the French currency, it remained relatively stable after its decline (marked by two devaluations) during the first year of Socialist government. During the last three months of 1982, it even regained in value compared to the currency of France's 15 most important trading partners.[15] Nonetheless there were several attacks of speculation against the franc, and repeatedly a devaluation was expected by currency traders. But this time the government stuck to its guns, though it had to take out major international loans in order to defend the franc. In September, a 4 billion dollar loan was signed with international banks, the largest such loan ever made to a state. This was followed in December by another loan of the same size, granted by Saudi Arabia.[16] While French international indebtedness still remained low by international standards, it was now rising at a rapid rate, enough to raise the question of vulnerability to international pressures. In addition, inflation differentials with major trading partners (especially West Germany) remained high.

DOMESTIC AND INTERNATIONAL POLICY ENVIRONMENTS

No major changes occurred in the political environment during the second half of 1982, except for a definite drop in popularity of the major governmental figures and the president himself. The two parties of the Right made no breakthroughs, programmatic or otherwise, though they achieved a better understanding about cooperation. One important point though regarding their policy proposals: Both parties promised that if returned to power, they would undo not only the nationalizations recently carried out by the Socialists but also those effected right after World War II.[17] Particularly for the Gaullists, this is a major step, one that makes the ideological change announced by Chirac's 1981 election platform appear as more than just another episode. If this promise is carried out some day, it would mean another major transformation of the French economic structure, more important than the one brought about by the Socialists in 1981/82. Most likely and somewhat paradoxically, it would produce more of that damage that the Right, not without some justification, reproached the Left with: there would be another period of uncertainty and disruption of the firms concerned, perhaps along the lines of the successive British nationalizations and denationalizations. The proposed step seemed to be inspired more by ideology than by pragmatic considerations.

On most accounts though, the rhetoric of the Right (and particularly that of Chirac) seems to have calmed down. No longer was the government's legitimacy put into doubt as it had been earlier on, particularly in the first half of 1982. The leaders of the two parties of the Right (Chirac and the now reconfirmed Giscard) achieved a working understanding about the cooperation of the two parties. For the municipal elections of 1983, efforts were coordinated rather harmoniously. Though the parties of the Right are likely to win these elections, this does not mean that their national policy proposals (to the extent that they exist) have become more credible or more widely accepted. Opinion surveys showed that they hardly benefitted from the declining popularity of the Socialists.

On the Left, the picture is also one of overall continuity. There were the usual frictions between the government and the Socialist party in Parliament, and between the government and the Communist party. In neither case was there anything to indicate that these frictions would soon lead to a crisis or dramatic change. Pierre Joxe, the leader of the Socialist deputies, was known to oppose Prime Minister Mauroy and in particular his austerity policy, but he does not have the following to effectively oppose the government on this issue. André Lajoinie, chief of the Communist group in the National Assembly, seemed to rise very fast in the hierarchy of the P.C.F., apparently at the expense of Marchais. However, he seemed to stick to the policy practiced by his party since May 1981: make every effort to stay in the government, exert influence, occasionally condemn the Socialists for allegedly giving in to pressures from the Right or from business, but avoid a major confrontation. This strategy is probably dictated by the Communists' continued weakness. The Socialists and the Communists also worked out an agreement for the municipal elections several months ahead of the event. Competition between the two parties was limited to occasional "primaries," which would in those cases decide which party would lead the Leftist coalition in the second round.

The weakness of the Communist party was accentuated by that of the C.G.T., the Communist-dominated labor union. In the union elections of December 1982, its share of the vote fell (from 42.4 percent in 1979) to 36.8 percent. In industry alone, the share of the C.G.T. fell from 50 percent to 45 percent. By contrast, C.F.D.T. and F.O. progressed slightly in industry, though they stagnated overall. Together they now surpassed the C.G.T. in votes. The biggest surprise came with the success of the Confédération Générale des Cadres (C.G.C.), a largely white-collar organization which has no political sympathies for the Left. It almost doubled its representation among wage earners, from 5.2 percent to 9.6 percent.[18]

Perhaps the C.G.T. is suffering from a difficult position, in addition to the general decline of Communist organizations. On the one hand, it means to be the intransigeant defender of workers' rights, yet it has been relatively conciliatory about the government's austerity policies. (C.F.D.T. and F.O. have fewer problems explaining their stance.) But then outright opposition would hardly be a more promising strategy, and other options are blocked by the C.G.T.'s understanding of the crisis.

As to the employers, they seem to have adopted a strategy of antagonistic cooperation. They expressed mounting concern over the increasing financial burdens on business (and in fact, profits and investments had fallen further, reaching new lows), but expressed mild satisfaction at the limited concessions which they could achieve. Overall, there were few violations of the price freeze. In December, the C.N.P.F. organized a meeting of businessmen which came up with a series of proposals to the government, and which the government agreed to discuss rather quickly.[19] If antagonisms between business and the government are obvious, the rhetoric is on the whole restrained, and relations seem to be fairly pragmatic.

While the relations of the government with the major political and economic groups thus seemed characterized by a measure of stability in the fall of 1982, there was one area in which there was a dramatic deterioration — the government's standing in public opinion polls. This deterioration started in the summer, about when the new austerity policy was put into operation. It is likely to be a durable phenomenon, since no major deviations from that course now appear possible for some time to come (not before 1984 in any case). Nor do the Socialists have measures in reserve that could be implemented independently of the recession and which could mobilize public support. It will be a difficult passage for the government, which before long might find itself with an approval rating similar to that of Barre. However, it will at least have a more solid majority in the National Assembly, and probably the grudging support of the unions. In any case, the Constitution of the Fifth Republic makes for a government that is not much dependent on public opinion — not until the next major elections in any case, thus not until 1986.

But it was not the political environment in France which in 1982 raised the greatest problems for the Socialist government and its economic policy. The biggest problems came from the international economic environment, which deteriorated sharply in the course of the year. When the Socialists embarked on a course of reflation in 1981, they anticipated an upturn in international business which would stimulate French exports and thus the French economy as a whole. As a result, the phase of countercyclical spending by the government would not materialize in 1982, with the result that the French balance of trade deficit reached record levels and soon forced the abandonment of the reflationary policy altogether. It is worth noting though that these expectations regarding an economic upturn in 1982 were held not only by the French government, but by the majority of economic experts at such organizations as the OECD and the European community. They were incorporated into the economic policies of many other governments as well, who on this basis adopted deflationary policies, thinking that under the circumstances they would not do too much damage. Because the underlying assumption turned out to be wrong, those policies had a much more severe impact than had been intended, and they became themselves a contributing cause of the deepening recession. This was shown by an OECD study published at the end of 1982.[20] For the same reason, France became a target area for exports from other countries since it represented one of the few markets which was still expanding (or at least not shrinking).

The international problems were of course not limited to OECD countries. France has a very pronounced trade deficit with the most advanced industrial countries. On the other hand, relations with third world countries are characterized by a surplus. In 1982, these countries too experienced difficulties that reached new dimensions of intensity, resulting in severe setbacks for French exports. On this account, more problems must be expected as the new austerity policies are taking hold in such countries as Mexico or Brazil, and soon in other countries as well. OPEC export markets are also shrinking as the surpluses of these countries disappeared. If these conditions are to persist, for example, if the world economy should indeed find itself in a phase of a Kondratieff downswing, one wonders about the markets for the production that will come from the nationalized industries, where such massive investments are planned. However, even then it will remain urgent for French industry to reduce the market penetration in industrial goods coming from advanced industrial countries such as Germany and the United States, and to a lesser extent Japan.

The question will remain for some time whether the nationalizations were the most appropriate way to take up that challenge, that is, to counter the market penetration in the area of industrial products from technologically leading countries. There is a fairly wide consensus among French economists who have dealt with this question, that the French industrial structure is deeply problematic and that only selective intervention can help. The state cannot help all of French industry by general measures and a liberal policy but must focus on certain industries, certain particularly promising technologies selected for privileged treatment. Only in this way, they argue, can France overcome the external constraints to its economic development, a point discussed at greater length earlier in this book. This consensus includes Socialists like Boublil, but also authors closer to the Right such as Lionel Stoléru, Christian Stoffaës or Alain Cotta.[21] Disagreement among them concerns only the way in which this selectivity principle is to be implemented. Here, the Socialists' answer is nationalization. The others would resort to less drastic means.

There is, however, one line of reasoning which refuses this analysis altogether. Some observers reject the entire selectivity approach, arguing that there is no real structural problem in French industry, and that the French balance of trade deficit must be viewed as the result of growth rates higher than those of its neighbors, in particular West Germany.   Liberal measures that would apply evenly to all of French industry are viewed as a more efficacious way to deal with this problem — thus Bela Balassa, who would favor a policy such as that of Barre.   He supports his reasoning by citing statistical data showing that import penetration actually decreased in the course of the 1970s, and that there is a close relationship between French trade deficits, German surpluses, and the different growth rates in the two countries.[22]

But while trade results improved during the period studied by Balassa, they have deteriorated again since the last years of the 1970s, for reasons which economists are still guessing about, and this despite the fact that the French growth rate fell below that of Germany.[23]   Unless the nationalizations produce clear successes in the next few years, something rather unlikely given the current situation, the question of the selectivity principle will remain unsettled for a long time yet.

As to the immediate future in any case, the outlook for the French economy is grim.   The INSEE painted a dark picture for 1983.   Rocard, in his documents worked out for the Ninth Plan (1983-1988), showed that conditions will remain dismal for several years.[24]   And the French Socialists (just like other governments in the industrial world) have no strategy to deal with the deteriorating international environment.   The idea of a European social space (the project to promote social progress in Europe through coordinated social reforms) may be making very limited progress;[25] but such efforts cannot come up with a remedy for the larger problems, such as the massive transfer of industrial production from the old industrial centers (in Europe, the United States) to the new ones in the Far East and elsewhere.   There is not even the political will for a common reflation in the European community at this point.   It is unavoidable that such environmental constraints will leave deep marks on the economic evolution of any country.   French socialism, whatever its intentions, will have to come to terms with them.

NOTES

1. Le Monde, 1 October 1982; and Les Echos, 21 December 1982.

2. Les Echos, 1 October 1982.

3. Ibid., 27 August 1982; 14 October 1982 (Auroux' statements); and 29 October 1982.

4. Ibid., 4 and 6 January 1983; 9 September 1982.

5. Michel Noblecourt in Le Monde, 16 November 1982 (for civil servants). Les Echos, 16 December 1982 (for RATP-SNCF).

6. Les Echos, 25 October 1982; Le Monde, 26 November 1982.

7. Les Echos, 10 and 27 August 1982; 30 September 1982 (National Accounts forecast); and 13 and 14 December 1982.

8. Jean-Michel Quatrepoint in Le Monde, 15 November 1982. For an overview of the plans, see Jacques Jublin, Les Echos, 14 December 1982.

9. Les Echos, 13 december 1982.

10. Ibid., 5 October 1982; Le Monde, 26 October 1982.

11. Le Monde, 5 and 6 November 1982; also 9 November 1982.

12. Alain Vernholes in Le Monde, 26 October 1982.

13. Le Monde, 22 October 1982; Les Echos, 28 October 1982.

14. Les Echos, 13 August 1982.

15. According to the statistics of Morgan Guaranty Trust, cited in Les Echos, 7 January 1983.

16. Le Monde, 16 and 17 September 1982; Le Monde, 8 December 1982.

17. Les Echos, 11 October and 17 December 1982.

18. Jean-Pierre Dumont and Michel Noblecourt in Le Monde, 10 December 1982.

19. Le Monde, 16 December 1982; Les Echos, 17 December 1982.

20. OECD, Economic Outlook, published on 22 December 1982 and discussed by Pierre Bernard-Danay in Les Echos, 28 December 1982.

21. For a discussion of these ideas, see Bela Balassa, "The French Economy under the Fifth Republic," in William G. Andrews and Stanley Hoffmann, eds., The Fifth Republic at Twenty, pp. 213-19.

22. Ibid.

23. Paribas, bulletin of December 1982; Les Echos, 4 and 5 January 1983. For the trend since 1978, see Patrick Artus, Claude and Michele Debonneuil, "La pénétration étrangère sur le marché francais: vingt années plus une," Economie et statistique, July-August 1981, pp. 3-20.

24. Les Echos, 21 December 1982 (INSEE forecast) and 5 October 1982 (Ninth Plan).

25. At the end of 1982, the Commission of the European Community strongly urged a substantial and coordinated reduction of the work week. Adrien Popovici in Les Echos, 30 December 1982.

16
CONCLUSION

The time period extending from 1969, the year of Pompidou's assumption of the presidency, to the end of 1982 could be divided into economic cycles or else into political cycles; there is only a partial overlap. This book, in general, has followed the political criterion, and we shall do so again now in trying to distill the essence of the different periods that have been discussed. The three major periods, marked respectively by Pompidou, Giscard, and Mitterrand, are distinguished by different economic conditions, different political conditions in France, and different courses of policy adopted.

In retrospect, the Pompidou years may appear as the end of the golden age of the French economy. Growth rates were high, investment and wages increased regularly, and unemployment remained low. One major explanation for this lies, of course, in an international environment marked by a long phase of economic expansion, a phase which was coming to its close but which was for a last time fired up by a massive American boom. This coincided with the loosening of economic restraints (in particular wage restraints) in France following May 1968. Under the combined impact of these factors, the French economy was growing at rates that impressed and surprised many French and foreign observers alike. As usual under such circumstances, it was widely thought that the phenomenon could be made to last.

In electoral terms, Pompidou enjoyed comfortable majorities. His election in 1968 could almost be taken for granted. In a way, it was the certainty that he would be a candidate which had made de Gaulle expendable to many on the Right. There was no serious challenger; in particular, no united Left was backing a common candidate. (The Communists insisted on running their own candidate, and the Socialists were at one of the

245

lowest points of their postwar history.) In the National Assembly, Pompidou could count on the massive presence of Gaullists to support his policy, a majority that had been swept in by the elections after May 1968. And yet there was a curious fragility to the political power of Pompidou's governments. Even in the National Assembly, it was clear that the massive Gaullist majority was the result of unusual circumstances which were unlikely to be repeated. Previous elections had shown a slow but steady erosion of electoral support for Gaullism, a trend which resumed not unexpectedly with the elections of 1973.

If electoral and National Assembly support for Pompidou and his policy seemed hardly a problem, this was not considered sufficient to unequivocally establish his hold on the country. May 1968, which had come out of what seemed to be an almost blue sky, remained too vivid a memory throughout the Pompidou years. This memory also led to tangible results: not only to the presence of the riot police throughout the capital, but also to an economic policy that added to the boom, so that business might better be able to pay the higher wages which the workers had obtained in May 1968 with Pompidou's agreement, though contrary to de Gaulle's analysis. We do not know whether Pompidou could have imposed a policy of austerity to counteract the impulses of growth and inflation which resulted from the international environment. He did not attempt to do so. We do know that he practiced an expansionary policy partly for political reasons, since he believed that the Right could only remain in power if real incomes kept rising steadily. The men who conducted this policy during his first years in office, also saw in growth a means to reduce the tensions and blockages in French society; thus in particular Jacques Chaban-Delmas and Jacques Delors. Both were dropped when in 1972 Pompidou's "progressive" phase came to a close. Pierre Messmer, who followed Chaban-Delmas as prime minister, did not leave as important an impact on French political and economic life.

The high growth rates and favorable economic conditions which prevailed under Pompidou's presidency led to the development of new vistas and new appetites everywhere. For the political parties, this meant new goals to be set, and new improvements to be promised. The goals and the promises varied from one party to the other, but in common was the parties' ability to come up very rapidly with new uses for the anticipated economic surplus. The Gaullists wanted to realize their old aspirations of grandeur and national unity through economic growth and some form of corporatism that was to be organized around rising real incomes. The Socialists and the Communists produced a Common Program which was based on the assumption of growth rates higher yet than those achieved under Pompidou. That program promised higher wages, better welfare, expanded public services and investments, and many other desirable things as well. Economic growth, nationalizations and better taxation would make it all possible. Only some of the Centrists and the autogestion Socialists refused to join the general passion for growth, being skeptical about the claim that it brought only benefits. But the Centrist critique never went very deep; it focused not on the content of growth so much as on its rate, and proposed to bring about a slowdown. The autogestion Socialists went further in their analysis, but they lacked a political instrument. The ecologists, who soon took up similar complaints, remained a marginal group in French politics throughout the 1970s and into the 1980s, in an evolution quite different from that in West Germany.

The Pompidou years were marked by another important phenomenon. Many party programs and platforms were produced during this time period, and it was impressive how they were dominated by economic issues. But of course, the general thinking was marked by the assumption that economic growth would come easily. Those assumptions, now codified, became semi-permanent fixtures in French political-economic thinking. Paradoxically, they established themselves precisely at a time when the years of easy growth were about to run out. It is likely that these party platforms played their part in shaping the expectations of the French at least until the end of the 1970s, and probably beyond that date. The new reality that seemed to begin so suddenly in 1974 did not establish itself easily in the minds of either the political elites or the public; Barre was an exception to the rule.

Nineteen seventy-four was a year in which many changes co-incided. It was the year of the first oil crisis and thus of a much less favorable international environment for the French economy, heavily dependent on imported oil. It was also the year in which Pompidou died and was succeeded by Valéry Giscard d'Estaing, who put in place a new approach to economic policy. Finally, it was the year in which economic variables began to change. Growth became slower, investment was arrested in its previously regular growth, and unemployment began its upward path.

The political trend which had started earlier — the gradual weakening of the presidential coalition — was confirmed by the 1974 election. Gaullism did not die with de Gaulle, as many once expected, but for some time it seemed as though it might have died with Pompidou. The first round of the 1974 election saw the collapse of the Gaullist candidate Chaban-Delmas. The forces of the Left were united this time, and Giscard emerged with only a close victory over Mitterrand. After two years, Giscard's position was further weakened by the defection and growing opposition of Chirac, who had helped his election by bringing valuable Gaullist support. Now he led the Gaullists into a qualified opposition. A victory of the Left was widely anticipated for 1978, and was avoided only by the Left's own lack of unity.

Thus from 1974 to 1978, Giscard's political standing was not very impressive. Not surprisingly, this was reflected in his economic policies, which were quite sensitive to political conditions. The president was advocating economic liberalism, but his policy could not create the conditions that might have made it a success. When after 1978 Barre practiced such a policy with more energy and aggressiveness, the capital of confidence that the government might have enjoyed earlier was largely used up, and strong attacks now came from three of the four major parties.

The political landscape also underwent marked change under Giscard's presidency. In 1976, the two parties of the Right turned from allies into latent enemies, and a year later the Left split as well. Quite clearly these splits were caused by dissent over policy, not (or at least not primarily) by historical or personal quarrels. The resulting fourfold division of the French electorate, with only one quarter supporting the president without reservation, did not do much to strengthen Giscard's ability to impose his liberal policy. In fact, it was a tribute to the institutions of the Fifth Republic that the government could function as well as it did, given those conditions.

If Giscard and Barre managed to govern until 1981, they were thus frequently frustrated with regard to their policy intentions. For liberal capitalism to be a success, for a liberal economy to expand, invest and create employment, several conditions needed to be satisfied. First, entrepreneurs needed to be strengthened financially if they were to become more independent from state support. For this the redistribution of value added had to be shifted in their favor, and the shares of labor (wages and related costs) and government (taxes and social welfare contributions) reduced. Large amounts of capital had to be available to entrepreneurs in order to supplement internal financing. In addition, they needed sufficient confidence before risking large sums for new investments. Confidence that the venture would be profitable, and therefore confidence that the policy environment of the Giscard presidency would be both sufficiently advantageous and sufficiently stable to satisfy their requirements. Giscard and Barre tried their best to live up to these requirements, but only with partial success.

Barre attempted to reverse the trend regarding the distribution of value added. He tried in particular to halt the progression of real wages, a policy which began to show some effect as time went on. But this gradual evolution also undercut the political standing of the government, and more drastic actions he did not dare to undertake for fear of another May 1968. He could not halt the progression of social welfare contributions either, which resulted from the rise in unemployment and a generous legislation of social protection. Drastic cutbacks in the Social Security system might have permitted an earlier stabilization of these charges, but again the government seemed to hesitate for political reasons. While it placed much emphasis on austerity in its rhetoric, its actual practice was at times rather lax. For a real austerity Barre lacked the political means; even so his policy was harshly criticized by the Gaullists and condemned as reactionary by the Left who, at that time, was unwilling to admit that any part of Barre's policy might have some merit.

Thus entrepreneurs saw few results that could satisfy them regarding the distribution of income within the business enterprise. The declared intentions of the government were slow to be translated into tangible improvements. The distribution of value added did not change in favor of the entrepreneurs at all. As to the problem of facilitating access to outside capital, the government had taken some steps to facilitate investment. However, capital concentrated on real estate and not on industry. The financial conservatism of the French combined with the weak political standing of the government in paralyzing one of the main sources of vitality in a capitalist economy. The effective promotion of industry would probably have required certain penalties on real estate investment, but again this was too difficult a hurdle for a conservative government.

Under the circumstances, it is apparent that one basic ingredient of a successful liberal economy — confidence in a stable, favorable policy environment — could not be secured. President and prime minister meant to favor business, but the limits to their action were all too apparent. The government moderated its economic rigor in the hope that this would allow it to last for a longer time period. But until 1977–1978, the business community was skeptical about the political fortunes of the liberal Right. When this attitude finally changed, the change came too late to have much of an impact.

Under the Socialists, the problems of economic policy presented themselves in different terms. To begin with, the Socialists had based their policy on the assumption that private business in France would in any case not invest enough to provide sufficient employment at home and compete effectively for exports abroad; hence the nationalization program. However, this reasoning applied primarily to big business. As to small and medium-sized firms, the Socialists hoped that they could secure their cooperation. This they planned to do not by putting the emphasis on profitability at the expense of wages. Such a policy could only starve consumption and (indirectly) production and investment. They thought they could revitalize the economy in a different way — by stimulating consumption and by concentrating the investment effort on the public sector, where no entrepreneurial hesitations would hamper programs of expansion. Thus the policy of reflation (mostly by increasing low wages, pensions, and transfer payments) and the rush to nationalize. At the same time the country was saturated with appeals and encouragements, and the government tried very hard to build up the economic optimism of the nation, in the style of the Planning Commission's efforts decades earlier. The effect was disappointing; business investments kept on falling, and the increased demand benefitted primarily foreign producers. As to the massive investments in the nationalized sector, it would be years before they could have the desired impact.

It was then that the Socialists in turn discovered the importance of business finances. A financially stronger private sector was not just a condition for reconciling business, they now came to admit, but also necessary to secure the ability of private business to serve the governmental policy of expansion. This discovery was followed by a veritable conversion. Soon the Socialists set out to try what their predecessors had failed to achieve: reduce the share of labor, households, and the state in the gross domestic product, and increase the income of capital. It was not quite the same as under Barre, since the new policy was only applied after numerous social reforms had been adopted which had changed the distribution of incomes, rights, and duties. Socialist austerity was meant to be combined with social justice. This combination could also provide the policy with a more solid foundation in society. Whether it in fact did so is still doubtful; many of the Left must feel betrayed by the policy of rigor. Nor is the political will of the government entirely clear. However, it has already taken several steps that Giscard and Barre shied away from: cutting back on unemployment compensation and Social Security payments, or suspending the system of wage indexation, are quite clearly major steps.

It is logical enough that the Socialist government would concentrate as heavily on economic problems as it did, and plausible that its choices were so limited that its own policy in this area soon came to resemble in important aspects that of its predecessor. What is less evident is that the Socialists would exhaust so quickly their own store of ideas. In its days of rapid growth and high enthusiasm among its militants, the Socialist party drew much vitality from the links it entertained with the new social movements. Among Socialists, discussions took place not only on how production and welfare could be maximized, but also on what should be produced and how, and for what purposes. It is true that these discussions never became a top priority for the party (though they did lead at least to an alternative energy program).

Already in the late 1970s the role of these movements within the party seemed to be on the decline. By the time the Socialists came to power, this development had been consecrated by Rocard's yielding to Mitterrand's presidential candidacy, and by the subordinate role assigned to the C.F.D.T. If French socialism may seem a little grey today by comparison to what it was in the mid-1970s, this is not only the result of the difficult economic circumstances prevailing in the early 1980s. It may also be the fault of the Socialists' own constricted vision.

BIBLIOGRAPHY

BOOKS AND MONOGRAPHS

Adam, Gerard. <u>L'ouvrier francais en 1970</u>. Paris: Armand Colin, 1971.

Albert, Michel, and Ferniot, Jean. <u>Les vaches maigres</u>. Paris: Gallimard, 1975.

Andrews, William, G., and Hoffmann, Stanley, editors. <u>The Fifth Republic at Twenty</u>. Albany: State University of New York Press, 1981.

Andrieu, Rene. <u>Les communistes et la revolution</u>. Paris: Julliard, 1968.

Ardagh, John. <u>The New French Revolution</u>. New York: Harper & Row, 1969.

_____. <u>The New France</u>. Harmondsworth, England: Penguin, 1973.

Attali, Jacques, and Guillaume, Marc. <u>L'anti-economique</u>. Paris: Presses universitarires de France, 1975.

Barre, Raymond. <u>Le programme de Blois</u>. Paris: Fayard, 1978.

_____. <u>Une politique pour l'avenir</u>. Paris: Plon, 1981.

Baudrillard, Jean. <u>Pour une critique de l'economie politique du signe</u>. Paris: Gallimard, 1972.

_____. <u>Le miroir de la production</u>. Paris: Casterman, 1973.

<u>Bilan economique et social</u>. See Le Monde, <u>Bilan economique et social</u>.

Biolat, Guy. <u>Marxisme et environnement</u>. Paris: Editions sociales, 1973.

Bishop, Claire Huchet. <u>All Things Common</u>. New York: Harper, 1950.

Bizot, Jean-Francois. <u>Au parti des socialistes</u>. Paris: Grasset, 1975.

Blair, John M. <u>Economic Concentration</u>. New York: Harcourt, Brace, Jovanovitch, 1972.

Bonnal, Francoise. <u>L'evolution de l'opinion publique à l'egard de l'ecologie au travers des sondages</u>. Paper at symposium of the Fondation Nationale des Sciences Politiques, September 1980.

Bosquet, Michel. <u>Ecologie et politique</u>. Paris: Galilee, 1975.

Boublil, Alain. <u>Le socialisme industriel</u>. Paris: Presses universitaires de France, 1977.

Bourgeois, Christian; and Roux, Dominique de. <u>VIe Plan de developpement economique et social, 1971-1975</u>. Rapport general. Les objectifs generaux et prioritaires du VIe Plan. Paris: Editions 10/18, 1971.

Bredin, Jean-Denis. La République de Monsieur Pompidou. Paris: Fayard, 1974.

Calleo, David P.; and Rowland, Benjamin M. America and the World Political Economy. Bloomington: Indiana University Press, 1973.

Carre, Jean-Jacques; Dubois, Paul; and Malinvaud, Edmond. Abrégé de la croissance francaise. Paris: Editions du Seuil, 1973.

Centre d'étude des revenus et des coûts. Deuxième rapport sur les revenus des Francais. Paris: Albatros, 1979.

Cerny, Philip G., and Schain, Martin A. French Politics and Public Policy. New York: St. Martin's, 1980.

Chardonnet, Jean. L'économie francaise. Paris: Dalloz, 1974.

Charlot, Jean. Le phénomène gaulliste. Paris: Fayard, 1970.

Clapham, C. H. Economic Development in France and Germany, 1815-1914. 4th ed.; Cambridge: Cambridge University Press, 1936.

Codding, Jr.; George A.; and Safran, William. Ideology and Politics: The Socialist Party of France. Boulder: Westview Press, 1979.

Cohen, Stephen S. Modern Capitalist Planning: The French Model. Berkeley: University of California Press, 1977.

Cohen-Tanugi, Pierre; and Morrisson, Christian. Salaires intérêts profits dans l'industrie francaise, 1968-1976. Paris: Presses de la Fondation Nationale des Sciences Politiques, 1979.

Colson, Jean-Philippe. Le nucléaire sans les Francais? Paris: Maspero, 1977.

Commission of the European Communities. Eurostat Review, 1970-79. Brussels, 1980.

Conte, Arthur. L'homme Giscard. Paris: Plon, 1981.

Critiques écologiques sur le Programme commun de la gauche. Lyon: La vie nouvelle, January, 1975.

Crozier, Michel. La société bloquée. Paris: Le Seuil, 1970.

Dahrendorf, Ralf. Society and Democracy in Germany. Garden City: Doubleday, 1967.

Debbasch, Charles. La France de Pompidou. Paris Presses Universitaires de France, 1974.

Debré, Michel. Une certaine idée de la France. Paris: Fayard, 1972.

_____. Ami ou ennemi du peuple. Paris: Plon, 1975.

De Gaulle, Charles. Memoirs of Hope. New York: Simon and Schuster, 1971.

Delouvrier, Paul. 1985. La France face au choc du futur. Paris: A. Colin, 1972.

Dumont, Rene. L'utopie ou la mort! Paris: Le Seuil, 1973.

Economie et société humaine. Paris, Denoel, 1972.

Ehrmann, Henry. Organized Business in France. Princeton: Princeton University Press, 1957.

_____. Politics in France. 3rd edition; Boston: Little, Brown & Co., 1976.

Ellul, Jacques. The Technological Society. New York: Knopf, 1964.

Fournier, Pierre. Y'en a plus pour longtemps. Paris: Editions du square, 1975.

Garnier-Expert, Christian. L'environnement démystifié. Paris: Mercure de France, 1973.

George, Vic; and Lawson, George, eds. Poverty and Inequality in Common Market Countries. London: Routledge and Kegan Paul, 1980.

Giscard d'Estaing, Valéry. French Democracy. Garden City: Doubleday, 1977.

Held, Jean-Francis, ed. 78, si la gauche l'emportait. Paris: Ramsay, 1977.

Hirsch, Fred. Social Limits to Growth. Cambridge: Harvard University Press, 1976.

Hoffmann, Stanley, ed. In Search of France. New York: Harper & Row, 1963.

Hough, Jerry F.; and Fainsod, Merle. How the Soviet Union Is Governed. Cambridge: Harvard University Press, 1979.

Iribarne, Philippe d'. La politique du bonheur. Paris: Le Seuil, 1973.

Katzenstein, Peter J., ed. Between Power and Plenty. Madison: University of Wisconsin Press, 1978.

Kohl, Wilfrid L., and Basevi, Georgio, eds. West Germany: A European and Global Power. Lexington: Heath, 1980.

Kolm, Serge-Christophe. La transition socialiste. Paris: Editions du Cerf, 1977.

L'affaire de Marckolsheim. Montargis, France: Agence de presse rehabilitation écologique, April 1975, mimeo.

Landier, Hubert. Demain, quels syndicats. Paris: Livre de poche, 1981.

Laot, Laurent. La croissance économique en question. Paris: Editions ouvrieres, 1974.

Lattes, Robert. Pour une autre croissance. Paris: Le Seuil, 1972.

Laurens, André. D'une France à l'autre. Paris: Gallimard, 1974.

Le Monde. Bilan économique et social, 1979. Paris: Le Monde, 1980.

_____. Bilan économique et social, 1980. Paris: Le Monde, 1981.

_____. Bilan économique et social, 1981. Paris: Le Monde, 1982.

Lenoir, René. Les Exclus. Paris: Le Seuil, 1974.

La lettre Mansholt. Paris: Pauvert, 1972.

Lindblom, Charles E. Politics and Markets. New York: Basic Books, 1977.

Lyra, Rubens Pinto. Le parti communiste francais et l'inté-gration européenne. Nancy: Centre européen universitaire, 1974.

Macridis, Roy. French Politics in Transition. Cambridge: Winthrop, 1975.

Maire, Edmond; and Julliard, Jacques. La CFDT d'aujourd'hui. Paris: Le Seuil, 1975.

Manifeste du parti socialiste unifié. Paris: Tema, 1972.

Mansholt: See La lettre Mansholt.

Marchais, Georges. Le défi démocratique. Paris: Grasset, 1973.

Martinet, Gilles. Le système Pompidou. Paris: Le Seuil, 1973.

Masse, Pierre. La crise du développement. Paris: Gallimard, 1973.

Meadows, Donella H.; Meadows, Dennis L.; Randers, Jorgen; and Behrens, William W. The Limits of Growth. New York: New American Library, 1972.

Mendras, Henri. Sociologie de la campagne francaise. Paris: Presses universitaires de France, 1971.

Morazé, Charles. The French and the Republic. Ithaca, N.Y.: Cornell University Press, 1958.

Muraz, Roland. La parole aux Francais. Paris: Dunod, 1977.

OECD. Science, Growth and Society. Report of the Secretary-General's Ad Hoc Group on New Concepts of Science Policy (Brooks Report). Paris: OECD, 1971.

_____. Economic Surveys: France. Paris: OECD, January 1976.

_____. Main Economic Indicators. (Paris: OECD, August 1981).

_____. Economic Surveys: France. (Paris: OECD, 1982).

Olson, Gary L., ed. The Other Europe. Brunswick: King's Court, 1977.

Parodi, Maurice. L'économie et la société francaise depuis 1945. Paris: Armand Colin, 1981.

Parti communiste francais. Programme commun de gouvernement actualisé. Paris: Editions sociales, 1978.

Parti socialiste. Changer la vie. Programme de gouvernement du Parti Socialiste. Paris: Flammarion, 1972.

_____. Projet socialiste. Paris: Club socialiste du livre, 1980.

_____. Manifeste de Créteil. 110 propositions pour la France. Paris, 1981.

Pateman, Carole. Participation and Democratic Theory. Cambridge: Cambridge University Press, 1970.

Pautard, André. Valéry Giscard d'Estaing. Paris: EDIPA, 1974.

Peyrefitte, Alain. Le mal francais. Paris: Plon, 1976.

Plan intérimaire. Stratégie pour deux ans. Paris: La documentation francaise, 1981.

Pompidou, Georges. Le noeud gordien. Paris: Plon, 1974.

Poniatowski, Michel. Conduire le changement. Paris: Fayard, 1975.

Poujade, Robert. Le ministère de l'impossible. Paris: Fayard, 1974.

Pour le socialisme. Le livre des assises du socialisme. Paris: Stock, 1974.

Priouret, Roger. Les Francais mystifiés. Paris: Grasset, 1973.

Programme commun de gouvernement du parti communiste et du parti socialiste. Paris: Editions sociales, 1972.

Que faire aujourd'hui. October 1981. Special issue on energy and ecology.

Quin, Claude; and Herzog, Philippe. Ce que coûte le capitalisme à la France. Paris: Editions sociales, 1973.

Rapport de la commission des inégalites sociales. Paris: La documentation francaise, 1975.

Rapport sur l'orientation préliminaire du VIIe Plan. Paris: Imprimerie des journaux officiels, 1975.

Rassemblement pour la République. Propositions pour la France. Paris: Stock, 1977.

Rocard, Michel. Parler vrai. Paris: Le Seuil, 1979.

_____, and Gallus, Jacques. L'inflation au coeur de la crise. Paris: Gallimard, 1975.

Rocaute, Yves. Le P.C.F. et les sommets de l'Etat. Paris: Presses universitaires de France, 1981.

Rose, Richard, ed. Challenge to Governance. Beverly Hills: Sage, 1980.

Rothman, Stanley; Scarrow, Howard; and Schain, Martin. European Society and Politics: Britain, France and Germany. St. Paul: West Publishing Co., 1976.

Saint-Robert, Philippe de. Les septennats interrompus. Paris: Laffont, 1977.

Samuel, Pierre. Le nucléaire en questions. Paris: Entente, 1975.

Servan-Schreiber, Jean-Jacques. The American Challenge. Translated by R. Steel. New York: Avon, 1969.

_____, and Albert, Michel. Ciel et terre. Manifeste radical. Paris: Denoel, 1970.

_____, and Lecanuet, Jean. Le projet reformateur. Laffont, 1973.

Shirer, William L. The Collapse of the Third Republic. New York: Simon and Schuster, 1969.

Shonfield, Andrew. Modern Capitalism. Oxford: Oxford University Press, 1969.

Sixième Plan de développement économique et social, 1971-1975. Paris: Editions 10/18, 1971.

Stravrianos, L. S. The Promise of the Coming Dark Age. San Francisco: Freeman, 1976.

Stillman, Edmund O., et al. L'envol de la France dans les années 80. Paris: Hachette, 1973.

Stoffaës, Christian. La grande menace industrielle. Revised edition. Paris: Calmann-Lévy, 1979.

Stoléru, Lionel. L'impératif industriel. Paris: Le Seuil, 1969.

_____. Vaincre la pauvreté dans les pays riches. Paris: Flammarion, 1974.

Towards a European Model of Development. Brussels: The European Bookshop, no date (1972?).

Union des démocrates pour la République. L'Enjeu. Paris: Presses Pocket, 1975. Introduction by Jacques Chirac.

Viansson-Ponté, Pierre. Des jours entre les jours. Paris: Stock, 1974.

Williams, Phillip M.; and Harrison, Martin. Politics and Society in de Gaulle's Republic. Garden City: Doubleday, 1972.

Wylie, Laurence. Village in the Vaucluse. New York: Harper & Row, 1964.

_____, ed. Chanzeaux, a Village in Anjou. Cambridge: Harvard University Press, 1966.

ARTICLES

(Anonymous). "Le projet du parti socialiste." Citoyens, January-February 1980.

(Anonymous). "Les huit visages de Giscard d'Estaing." Economie et politique, January 1975.

Artus, Patrick, Sterdyniak, Henri, and Villa, Pierre. "Investissement, emploi et fiscalité." Economie et statistique, November 1980.

Barre, Raymond, interview. L'Expansion, September 1978.

Béaud, Michel. "Logique capitaliste et contenu de croissance." Nouvelle revue socialiste, May-June 1974.

Berger, Suzanne. "Politics and Antipolitics in Western Europe in the Seventies." Daedalus, vol. 108, no. 1 (1979), pp. 27-49.

Bertrand, Mireille. "Offensive antisociale et anti-nationale — une meme stratégie: celle du déclin." Cahiers du communisme, February 1979.

Boissonnat, Jean. "Le véritable objectif du plan Barre." L'Expansion, October 1976.

_____. "Raymond Barre m'a dit." L'Expansion, April 1977.

_____. "Les deux stratégies." L'Expansion, July-August 1977.

Bonis, Jean. "Nouveaux modes d'action managériales et syndicats." Economie et humanisme. May-June, 1981, pp. 31-39.

Bormann, Marc. "Le démantèlement du potentiel national." Cahiers du communisme, November 1976, pp. 23-30.

Boy, Daniel. "Le vote écologiste en 1978." Revue française de science politique, vol. 32, no. 2 (April 1981).

Bunel, Jean. "L'action syndicale: crise et recentrage." Economie et humanisme, January-February 1979, pp. 4-11.

Busséry, Henri. "La vérité est bonne à dire." Projet, September-October 1980, pp. 904-07.

Cahiers français. Issue of September-October 1973, devoted to the controversy surrounding economic growth.

Carmoy, Guy de. "Industrie francaise et industrie allemande: performances et stratégies." Politique internationale, no. 6, Winter 1979/80.

Chirac, Jacques. "Finalités de la croissance." Preuves, vol. 9 (1972), pp. 46-52.

_____, interview with. Paradoxes, February 1975.

_____. "La participation est la dernière chance de la liberté." Paradoxes, October-November 1977.

Clairvois, Marc. "Le frisson keynesien de Barre." L'Expansion, September 1979.

Dabeziès, Pierre. "Gaullisme et giscardisme." Pouvoirs, no. 9, 1979, pp. 27-36.

Debre, Michel. "Un grand dessein pour la France?" Bulletin ACADI, January-February 1978, pp. 34-58.

Delors, Jacques. "La nouvelle société." Preuves, 1970, volume 2.
_____, interview with. L'Expansion, 4 September 1981.

Dreyfus, Pierre, interview with. L'Expansion, 6 November 1981.

Dubois, Paul. "La rupture de 1974." Economie et statistique, August 1980, pp. 3-20.

Dufour, Claude, and Grevet, Patrice. "La politique sociale democratique." Economie et politique, September 1974.

Easterlin, Richard A. "Does Money Buy Happiness." The Public Interest. 30 (Winter, 1973), pp. 3-10.

Evin, Kathleen, and Cayrol, Roland. "Comment contrôler l'union? Les relations P.C.-P.S. depuis 1971." Projet, January 1978, pp. 64-74.

Favard, Emile. "Révisions déchirantes dans les syndicats." L'Expansion, December 1977.

Fayolle, Jacky. "Le comportement d'investissement depuis 1974." Economie et statistique, November 1980, pp. 21-37.

Ferry, Jacques. "Une nouvelle politique pour l'industrie." CNPF Patronat, February 1977, pp. 19-28.
_____. "Les impératifs de la croissance." CNPF Patronat, February 1978.

Gallie, Duncan. "Trade Union Ideology and Workers' Conception of Class Inequality in France." West European Politics, vol. 3, no. 1 (1980).

Gallus, Jacques. "A quoi sert le plan Barre." Faire, October 1976.

Gauche-Cazalis, Claude. "Une sidérurgie d'un type nouveau." Economie et politique, April 1979, pp. 60-66.

Gaudard, Jean-Pierre. "Quelle politique économique et sociale pour la France?" Cahiers du communisme, November 1977, pp. 14-23.

Giscard d'Estaing, Valéry. "Humaniser la croissance." Preuves, no. 10 (1972).

Harmel, Claude. "Ce que les communistes ont voulu." Est et Ouest, March 1978.

Juquin, Pierre. "Réflections sur crise et croissance." Cahiers du communisme, January 1975.

Kesselman, Mark J. "Changes in the French Party System." Comparative Politics, 4, no. 2 (January, 1972), pp. 281-301.

Laulan, Yves. "Une chance historique à ne pas manquer." Paradoxes, September-October 1978.
_____. "L'expérience Barre: une politique du possible." Revue politique et parlementaire, January-February 1981.

Lefournier, Philippe. "Plan Barre: un succès inavouable." L'Expansion, October 1977.

Levai, Ivan. "Michel Rocard fait le point." Paradoxes, February-March 1978.

McHale, Vincent, and Shaber, Sandra. "From Agressive to Defensive Gaullism: The Electoral Dynamics of a 'Catch-All' Party." Comparative Politics, vol. 8. no. 2 (January 1976), pp. 291-306.

"Manifeste d'agir pour la France." Arguments, March-April 1978.

Marchand, Olivier, and Revoil, Jean-Pierre. "Emploi et chômage: bilan fin 1980." Economie et statistique, February 1981, pp. 23-44.

Martinet, Gilles. "Pour une vraie politique de salut public." Faire, September 1979, pp. 3-6.

Marx, Bernard. "Sur la crise." Economie et Politique. January 1975.

_____. "Avec les communistes les moyens du changement." Economie et politique, February 1978, pp. 54-78.

Mauroy, Pierre. "Les deux faces du plan Barre." Revue politique et parlementaire, September-October 1976.

Meffredi, Yves. "Quelle strategie économique à moyen terme?" Projet, March 1978, pp. 327-36.

Mérigot, J. G. "Le plan Barre." Défense nationale, November 1976, pp. 99-109.

Meyer, Alain. "Requiem pour le socialisme." Nouvelle Revue socialiste, September-November 1980, pp. 87-95.

Muller, Pierre, and Tassi, Philippe. "1979: année favorable pour les entreprises industrielles." Economie et statistique, February 1981, pp. 3-16.

Nicolet, Claude. "A propos du manifeste radical." Revue francaise de science politique, XX, no. 5 (October, 1970), pp. 1011-20.

Parti communiste francais. "Manifeste de Champigny." Cahiers du communisme, January 1969.

Pelachaud, Guy. "'Zero Growth': Ideology and Politics." World Marxist Review, November 1975.

Perceval, Louis. "The Crisis of Capitalism and the Environment." World Marxist Review, November 1975.

Perrineau, Georges. "L'ampleur actuelle du champ des nationalisations." Revue politique et parlementaire, July 1981.

Perrot, Marguerite. "Le pouvoir d'achat des salaires." Economie et statistique, January 1980, pp. 41-52.

Petit, Juliette. "Siderurgie: Le P. S. contre la nationalisation." Economie et Politique, February 1978, pp. 49-51.

Phéline, C. "Répartition primaire des revenus et rentabilite du capital (1954-1973)." Statistiques et études financieres, no. 19, 1975.

Portelli, Hugues. "Que se passe-t-il au parti socialiste?" Projet, January 1978.

_____. "Guerre de succession au PS." Projet, June 1979, pp. 739-42.

Poulain, Jean-Claude. "Les questions sociales au centre de l'affrontement idéologique." Economie et politique, September 1974.

Rassemblement pour la République, "Déclaration politique du groupe parlementaire UDF, commentee par le RPR." Pouvoirs, 1979, no. 9, pp. 49-52.

Remond, René. "Les élections législatives." Paradoxes, April-May 1978, pp. 25-32.

Rocard, Michel. "La gauche et les pouvoirs." Bulletin ACADI, January-February 1978.

Rosanvallon, Pierre. "Le syndicalisme au tournant." Projet, November 1978, pp. 1033-59.

Simmons, J. C. "The French Communist Party in 1978: Conjugating the Future Imperfect." Parliamentary Affairs, vol. 32, no. 1 (Winter 1979), pp. 79-91.

Virieu, Francois Henri de. "Le patronat prépare 1978." Faire, November 1976, pp. 2-6.

Viveret, Patrick. "Débat avec Michel Rocard." Faire, September 1976.

Wubbels, Rolf E. "The French Economic Miracle: What a Difference Leadership Makes." Financial Analysts Journal, July-August 1978, pp. 23-27.

Ysmal, Colette. "Adhérents et dirigeants du Centre démocrate." Revue francaise de science politique, XXII, no. 1 (February 1972), pp. 77-88.

_____. "Parti communiste: les raisons d'un durcissement." Projet, January 1978, pp. 44-54.

_____. "Nature et réalité de l'affrontement Giscard-Chirac." Politique aujourd'hui, nos. 3-4, 1978.

OTHER PERIODICALS CONSULTED*

Après-demain
L'Aurore
La Croix
Démocratie moderne
Les Echos
Entreprise
European Economy
Eurostat Review
L'Expansion
L'Express
Le Figaro
Financial Times
Forum International
France Nouvelle
Industrial Short-Term Trends

Journal des Finances
Lettre de la Nation
Le Matin
Métra
Le Monde
La Nef
Le Nouvel Observateur
Paris-Match
Le Point
Revue C.N.P.F.
Sondages
La Vie Française
L'Unité
The Wall Street Journal

---

*Note: Most of the articles which appeared in monthly or quarterly publications are listed in the bibliography. The following list cites only those periodicals which were not mentioned earlier. It consists primarily of the dailies and weeklies that were consulted in the course of the research.

INDEX

advertising, 45, 58

aerospace, nationalization of, 37

affluence, 6-7, 9, 26, 56, 58

Afghanistan, 131, 145

Agence francaise de l'Energy, 200

Agence Nationale pour l'Emploi (A.N.P.E.), 195

agriculture, 38, 54, 132, 179

Albert, Michel, 26-27, 28

armament, nationalization of, 37

Attali, Jacques, 44-46, 121, 176

Aurox, Jean, 167, 192, 195, 197-198, 213, 220, 235

austerity, 5, 9, 25, 53, 56, 81, 103, 116, 122, 132, 140, 149, 173-79, 188, 212, 214, 233, 246, 249

autofinancement, 99-101

autogestion, 34, 41-47, 58, 75, 125, 127, 128, 142, 196, 198, 199, 247

Bank of France, 177

bankruptcy(ies), 84, 85, 99, 114, 126

banks, nationalization of, 35, 37, 38, 123, 164-68, 170, 236

Banque de Paris et des Pays-Bas, (Paribas), 165, 219

Barre, Raymond, 24, 25, 85, 89-106, 111-17, 132, 139-41, 149-51, 155, 161, 166, 171, 248-49

Blum, Leon, 215, 218, 219, 220

Boublil, Alain, 123-24, 164, 176, 202-03, 241

Boussac-Saint-Freres, 169

budget deficit, 95, 104, 113, 115, 169, 174-75, 177, 179, 189

buildings, high-rise, 22

business, 7-8, 9-11, 35, 36,

38, 84-85, 89-91, 92-103, 113-14, 132, 139-41; under Mitterand, 162, 170-73, 216-20, 236-37, 240, 249

business, small: 12, 13, 54-55, 115, 151, 171, 226, 249; survey of, 65, 72

capital gains tax, 24

capitalism: Communist critique of, 53-57, 128, 131, 143; labor unions on, 142, 143; Socialist critique of, 33, 40, 41-42, 43, 45, 128, 133, 166, 202-03

Cartel des Gauches, 210, 217

centralization, 44, 45, 103

Centre Democrate, 25, 27-28, 29

Centre des Democrates Sociaux (C.D.S.), 221

Centre d'etudes, de recherces et d'education socialistes (C.E.R.E.S.) 34, 121, 125, 127, 161

Centre national des independants et paysans, 20

centrists, 19-20, 28, 33, 63, 73, 227; Democratic, 25, 27-28, 29, 63

Chaban-Delmas, Prime Minister, 12, 91, 246, 247

Changer la vie, 34, 41, 202

Charbonnages de France, 163, 200

chemical industry, nationalization of, 37

Chevenement, Jean-Pierre, 34, 43, 121, 125, 127, 128, 226, 236

Chirac, Jacques, 13, 20, 103, 104, 106, 111-17, 122, 129, 132, 247-48; plan de relance, 25, 81, 85, 89, 99, 101, 112, 174, 176; public opinion under, 154; relance global, 112-13, 115

cities, 28, 44, 55, 174

civil service, 97, 127, 131,

265

ABOUT THE AUTHOR

Volkmar Lauber is Professor of Political Science at the University of Salzburg, Austria. Previously, he taught at West Virginia Wesleyan College; at the Johns Hopkins University Bologna Center in Italy; and at the University of South Florida in Tampa.

Dr. Lauber published in the areas of political economy, French politics, and on questions of energy and ecology. His publications have appeared in <u>Comparative Politics</u>, <u>Government and Opposition</u>, <u>The Washington Papers</u>, <u>Contemporary French Civilization</u>, <u>Alternative Futures</u>, and in multi-authored edited volumes.

He holds a Ph.D. in Political Science from the University of North Carolina at Chapel Hill, and law degrees from Harvard and the University of Vienna.